Praise for *Something*

"A pleasure to read . . . Alvarez speaks directly to her readers in these essays offering insight into the inspiration and craft that informs her work . . . A thoughtful self-analysis and a delightful primer on becoming a writer." —*The Denver Post*

"Spry, inviting pieces . . . Alvarez has clearly made her second language her own." —*Entertainment Weekly*

"An excellent accompaniment to her poetry and fiction. Once again, Alvarez breaks the boundaries to explore new literary frontiers." —Copley News Service

"With admirable candor and gentle touches of humor, she describes her struggles with cultural hybridism, historical and personal memory, the English language and the effects of all of these on her literary career." —*The New York Times*

"Julia Alvarez serves up exquisite, intimate portraits that chronicle her most significant journeys . . . and the road traveled to find her place as one of today's most celebrated writers." —*Latina*

"Evocative . . . Touching . . . Often amusing . . . A must read for anyone who loves and struggles with writing, and it is a witness to the ability of the human spirit to renew itself daily." —*Tampa Tribune and Times*

"Julia Alvarez is a breathtaking writer." —*St. Petersburg Times*

"Nonfiction as charming and open, personal and revealing, as Ms. Alvarez's fiction." —*Richmond Times-Dispatch*

"Julia Alvarez is a writer on a different kind of edge." —*The Nation*

"Vibrant . . . *Something to Declare* simultaneously reveals and masks what's upsetting with an abundance of humor and a measure of self-denigration." —*The Bloomsbury Review*

"Alvarez wields her legendary storyteller's power to hold an audience spellbound while enlarging its vision through the deft use of empathy." —*The Atlanta Journal-Constitution*

"To be read slowly and carefully, as a special gift from a writer whose skill and enthusiasm have enriched the country she now considers her home." —*The Anniston (AL) Star*

"Alvarez's keen observations of her interesting immigrant journey of self-discovery and self-invention prove that, indeed, she has much to declare." —*Austin American-Statesman*

"Poignant . . . Ironic . . . The writing transcends itself and becomes a new consciousness, a new place on the map."
—*The Virginian-Pilot*

"[Alvarez] paints with vibrant, earthy clarity . . . Open and lively." —*Publishers Weekly*

"A wonderful literary and biographical gift for both aspiring writers, teachers of literature, and the fans of Julia Alvarez."
—*Bookwatch*

"Touching and detailed descriptions of her immigrant family . . . Honest and enlightening." —*BookPage*

Something to Declare

Also by Julia Alvarez

Something to Declare

. . . .

Julia Alvarez

ALGONQUIN BOOKS OF CHAPEL HILL 2014

Published by
ALGONQUIN BOOKS OF CHAPEL HILL
Post Office Box 2225
Chapel Hill, North Carolina 27515–2225

a division of
Workman Publishing
225 Varick Street
New York, New York 10014

"The Red Wheelbarrow" by William Carlos Williams, from
Collected Poems: 1909–1939, Volume I. Copyright © 1938 by New
Directions Publishing Corp. Reprinted by permission of
New Directions Publishing Corp.

Library of Congress Cataloging-in-Publication Data
Alvarez, Julia
        Something to declare / by Julia Alvarez.
            p.   cm.
        ISBN 978-1-56512-193-5 (HC)
        1. Alvarez, Julia—Authorship.   2. Women and
    literature—United States—History—20th century.
    3. Dominican Americans—Intellectual life.
    4. Dominican Americans in literature.   5. Dominican
    Republic—In literature.   I. Title
    PS3551.L845Z47   1998
    814'.54—dc21   98-20994
                                                    CIP
        ISBN 978-1-61620-558-4 (PB)

10   9   8   7   6   5   4   3   2   1

Credits

· · · · · · · ·

"Chasing the Butterflies," *Martyrs: Contemporary Writers on Modern Lives of Faith* (San Francisco: HarperSanFrancisco, 1996).

"Doña Aída, with Your Permission," *Brújula/Compass 28*, winter 1998.

"El Doctor," *Outlooks and Insights: A Reader for Writers* (New York: St. Martin's Press, 1982).

"First Muse," published under the title, "One of a Thousand Scheherazades," *Mirror, Mirror, on the Wall: Women Writers Explore the Fairy Tales That Have Changed Their Lives* (New York: Anchor Books/Doubleday, 1998).

"Genetics of Justice," *Outside the Law* (Boston: Beacon Press, 1997).

"Imagining Motherhood," *Latina*, April/May 1997.

"I Want to Be Miss América," published under the title "Translating a Look," *Allure*, March 1995.

"My English," *Brújula/Compass*, fall 1992.

"My Second Opera," *The Lane Series*, 1992–1993.

"Our Papers," published under the title "Flight Plans," *Washington Post Magazine*, August 13, 1995.

"Picky Eater," *We Are What We Ate: What Contemporary American Writers Write about When We Write about Food* (A Share Our Strength Anthology, Harcourt Brace, 1998).

"So Much Depends," published under the title "On Finding a Latino Voice," *Washington Post Book World*, May 14, 1995.

"A Vermont Writer from the Dominican Republic," *Vermont*, February 1998.

Credits

A number of these essays have previously been published in magazines and anthologies. They would not have achieved their present state or even seen the light of day if it had not been for the help of numerous editors and muses. Special thanks to Mary Turner at *Allure;* to Marie Arana Ward at the *Washington Post;* to Susan Shreve and Deanne Urmy at Beacon Press; to Kate Bernheimer; to Susan Bergman; and to Paul Eschholz and Alfred Rosa, who gave me my first big chance in print. To Roberto Véguez, who helped me with mi español. To Shannon, who helped me put it all together in more ways than one. To Susanna, of the daily manna of friendship and encouragement. Finally, to my compañero Bill, who between his snow plowing and sweet-corn planting, his patients, and miracle working in the kitchen, finds time to read and comment on every one of these pages. And to you, Virgencita de la Altagracia, who put them all in my camino, ¡alta y ultima gracias!

Contents

· · · · · · · ·

Part Two: Declarations

Something to Declare
to My Readers

. . . .

The first time I received a letter from one of my readers, I was surprised. I had just published my first book of poems, *Homecoming,* which concludes with a sonnet sequence titled "33." My reader wanted to know why I had included forty-one sonnets when the title of the sequence was "33."

I considered not answering. Often, it is the little perplexities and curiosities and quandaries that remain after I have finished reading a book that send me to buy another book by that author. If I want to know more, the best way to find out is to read all the books that the author has written.

In the end, though, I couldn't resist. I wrote back, explaining how thirty-three represented my age at the time I wrote the sequence, how I had meant to include only thirty-three sonnets but I kept writing them and writing them, how the sonnets were not sonnets in the traditional sense. . . . Before I knew it, I had written my reader not just a note on my sonnet sequence but a short essay.

Many of the essays in this book began in just that way—as answers to such queries. Jessica Peet, a high-school student, read my first novel, *How the García Girls Lost Their Accents,* in her Vermont Authors class and wanted to know if I considered myself a Vermonter. The Lane Series, our local arts and entertainment series, wanted to know what I might have to say about opera. Share Our Strength was putting together a fund-raising anthology. Did I have anything at all to declare about food?

I could not really say to any of them, "Read my novels or my poems or my stories." These folks wanted what my boarding-school housemother used to call a straight answer. Which is where essays start. Not that they obey housemothers. Not that they list everything you are supposed to list on that Customs Declaration form. (How could the wild, multitudinous, daily things in anyone's head be inventoried in a form?) But that is the pretext of essays: *we have something to declare.*

And so this essay book is dedicated to you, my readers, who have asked me so many good questions and who want to know more than I have told you in my novels and poems. About my experience of immigration, about switching languages, about the writing life, the teaching life, the family life, about all of those combined.

Your many questions boil down finally to this one question: Do you have anything more to declare?

Yes, I do.

Something to Declare

Part One

. . . .

Customs

Grandfather's Blessing

. . . .

"What do you want to be when you grow up?" my grandfather asked, chuckling. It was a joke to think these little bits of Alvarez-Tavares, Tavares-Sánchez, Tavares-Kelner would grow up to drive jeepsters, run companies, nurse babies, and scold the maids.

Behind me the younger cousins were lined up, waiting for their moment of future at our grandfather's knee. This grandfather, my mother's Papi, was such a handsome gentleman, so slim, with such elegant long hands, such a fair complexion protected under his Panama hat, seersucker suit, and starched white shirt. He loved to recite bits of poetry, what he could remember. *Juventud, divino tesoro. How do I love thee? Let me count the ways. Out, out damned spot.* He also had excellent manners. He ate his fruit with a knife and fork—which was unheard of in the Dominican Republic. But then my grandfather had traveled. He had been to Spain, London, Mexico, Rome and had brought back native costumes for all his grandchildren. At parties, we assembled, a diminutive guard from Buckingham Palace, seven señoritas with beauty marks on their upper lips, several cowboys from the Old West, a Dutch girl in clogs. He took good care of his family. Of course, we wanted to impress him.

"A bullfighter," I announced when it was my turn. I had never seen a bullfight, but on the coffee table at my grandfather's house lay a book on bullfighting. I had fallen in love with the trim men in their tight black pants and ruffly shirts, frozen in beautiful dance poses. Those pictures set me dreaming of the future.

"Bullfighter?!" my grandfather lifted his eyebrows and chuckled again. "I don't think there are any *girl* bullfighters," he noted, not exactly discouraging me but letting me know the odds.

I walked away from our brief interview and headed for the coffee table. I paged through the bullfighting book much as I would later page through my anthologies looking for someone else with a Spanish-sounding name, someone else who had come to English when she was ten, someone else to prove that I could become what I dreamed of becoming. I learned early to turn to books, movies, music, paintings, rather than to the family to find out what was possible. The men in the bullfighting book all had little ponytails—they could have been girls. But when I looked at their chests, none of them had bosoms. Maybe my grandfather was right. You couldn't be female and fight the Furies, you couldn't be an Alvarez-Tavares girl and enter the ring and take on the dangerous future.

WHEN I HAD my next chance to proclaim my future, I told my grandfather I wanted to be a cowboy. I suppose this was an Americanization of my bullfighting dream. I had seen a poorly dubbed Western on a neighbor's new TV.

"You mean a cowgirl," my grandfather said, nodding as if this were much more reasonable than a bullfighter.

The next time he and Mamita came back from the United States of America, they brought me a cowgirl outfit. Somehow, the mock-leather skirt and vest and doodad tassels here and there didn't seem as serious as the cowboy outfits my boy cousins were wearing. Instead of a holster and gun, I got a little rawhide pocketbook with a mirror and a tiny brush and comb—nothing I could twirl, draw, aim, and shoot. All I could use my present for was to bribe the maids so they wouldn't tell on me when something broke or food was found floating in the water of the centerpiece orchids.

The cowboys, the wonderful, blond, and deeply tanned cowboys . . . They galloped across the screen, their horses' tails straight out behind them. My heart soared, my chest tightened. Could it be possible, really possible, to get that far away from my mother and the aunts trying to teach me to hold my skirt down when the wind was blowing?

"I want to be a cowboy," I repeated to my grandfather when he corrected me. "I don't want to ride sidesaddle" was the best reason I could give him.

"Well, well," he said, chuckling, the way grown-ups always did when what they meant to say was, "You are going to get over this."

MEANWHILE, THE COUNTRY was under tight rein. The dictatorship, twenty-five years old, was firmly in place. People were disappearing in the middle of the night. One evening the SIM, the military intelligence service, came for my grandfather and put him in jail for two days. He was not tortured but "persuaded" to sell a part of his land for the minimum price to the daughter of the dictator. It was property that my grandfather had been saving to give to his own children.

At parties, the handsome uncles were dancing flamenco on dining-room tables. My aunt Tití, who was not married at twenty-five because she knew Latin and read books and grew anthuriums in the garden instead of making herself pretty and positioning herself like a floral arrangement in the front parlor, designed an indoor pond in my grandparents' house. My grandfather stocked it with golden fish. When I thought no one was looking, I would lean over the tiled edge and try to catch them.

One day, I grabbed for one swirling bit of wonder and ended up falling into the pond. One of the maids found me.

After everyone had scolded me for almost getting myself killed, my grandfather took me aside. "Next time, call me. We'll catch the big gold one with the net. You'll be able to put your hand in and touch the scales."

MY GRANDFATHER OWNED a ranch out in the country where our milk, eggs, and most of our víveres or starch vegetables came from. The cows all had the names of his granddaughters. Every morning when the milk was delivered, my grandfather would announce who gave the most milk. For the rest of the day the human namesake preened herself on her cow's accomplishment. What is peculiar is how each of the grownup cousins now remembers that, on average, her cow gave the most milk.

On the way to the ranch, we sometimes stopped to visit the widow of one of my father's illegitimate brothers. My paternal grandfather, who was already dead by the time I was born, left twenty-five legitimate children and who knows how many illegitimate children behind. Many of the legitimates would have nothing to do with the illegitimates, which made it very difficult to draw up a guest list for a wedding or a noche buena party. Burials, like my dead uncle's burial, were easier because in the face of death everybody was supposed to know better than carry on grudges.

My father was the only legitimate who kept up with all the illegitimates and their families. So, whenever my grandfather and father took us to the ranch, we stopped to see my widowed aunt. She had three teenage sons whom I observed closely because I hoped that from them I might get a hint of things to come. One of the things I knew was coming to me was kissing.

My sisters and I had been practicing. We put a piece of paper between us because it wasn't really right for girls to kiss each other on the lips. We rubbed our mouths together until the paper between us was wet and shredded.

These young men were beginners as young men. Little bits of their younger selves still clung to them as if, like chicks, they had just crawled out of the cracked shells of their boyhood. Their voices did funny things, their hands and arms were too big for their bodies, their upper lips sported dark hairs and milk stains.

"They are good boys. They are studying hard," their widowed mother said in that weepy voice of mothers who secretly think their sons are depriving themselves if they aren't causing all the trouble their gender entitles them to enjoy.

One of the young men was going to be an engineer, like my grandfather. Another, a doctor. The third one wanted to be a poet. Actually, I met only the future engineer and the future doctor. The future poet will always be the sound of a shower running. Every time we stopped at their house, his mother said he was writing in the bathroom. He could only concentrate with the shower going to block out the noise of the rest of the world.

"But why?" I asked my grandfather when my father had taken his sister-in-law aside to give her some money. We had been left alone sipping our limonadas on the patio.

"¿Quién sabe?" my grandfather said, chuckling. "'Juventud divino tesoro. If music be the food of love, play on.'" He went through his repertoire of memorized poetry. His voice was hushed as if he were awed by the mysterious workings of talent. As if one of those beautiful, terrifying, uncontrollable bullfighting bulls were locked in that bathroom.

"I tell him he has to be careful," the widow explained to my grandfather a little later, "que no se enferme." That he doesn't get sick.

I had never in the world considered that books had that kind of power. They could make a person sick. They could make a young man lock himself in the bathroom with the shower going instead of coming out to say hello to visitors from the capital.

"He won't get sick," my grandfather reassured her. He himself had been one of three sons, raised by his two older brothers after their parents had died young. The older brothers had sent him to Cornell University where he studied engineering, though his passion for music and poetry might have tempted him in a different direction. But la familia

8

and what it mandated were the order of his day. Finally, he came home to set up a business and raise his own family. *Muy familial*, everyone said of my grandfather, a family man. It was the best thing you could say about a person after you said he was kind and handsome, which you could also say about my grandfather.

While the adults sat on the patio, visiting, I snuck back inside, drawn by the sound of water. I listened at the door, holding my breath, my heart beating so loud that I thought the young poet would think there was somebody knocking. But all I heard was the shower, and every once in a while, the turning of pages. I touched my cheek to the wood and felt the vibration of pounding water. After a few minutes, I turned and pressed my lips hard on a knot in the grain of the door.

"A MOVIE ACTRESS," I told my grandfather. "I want to wear all the costumes of the world and travel in airplanes and hot-air balloons." *Around the World in Eighty Days* had recently come to the Olympia movie theater.

My grandfather opened his eyes wide in a pantomime of surprise. "My, my," he said, "where does this little girl get such ideas?" My mother, who could never resist an opportunity to put in a plug for rules and regulations, noted, "If she wants to be an actress, she better learn to clean her plate."

That put a wrench in my dream. "Why?" I asked, disappointed. I had never heard that cleaning one's plate was one of the requirements of being an actress.

"You have to have legs and a *fundillo*," she said, slapping her bottom. "You have to put on some weight so you have something to show people."

9

"She could be a great dramatic actress," my grandfather intervened, "like Sarah Bernhardt. She could walk the boards of Covent Gardens. 'Out, out damned spot. The quality of mercy is not strained. To be or not to be.'" There was that far-off dreamy look in his eyes again, as if he could see the future, as if he had caught sight of me years and years from now, standing where I wanted to be, waving back at him.

But for the moment, I didn't know who Sarah Bernhardt was or what the difference was between a dramatic and movie actress. The only walking of the boards I knew about was what pirates made prisoners do on the high seas. But I did know that actresses got to be all kinds of different people, not just second daughters to strict mothers, not just third granddaughters to elegant grandfathers, not just another girl cousin in a line-up of cousins, one of dozens of nieces to a multitude of uncles and aunts, half-uncles and half-aunts, who didn't even talk to one another—in other words, an actress got to be more than just a family person.

"She better learn how to sing," one of the aunts noted. "You've got to sing as an actress, you know? And dance," she added pointedly. This was the same aunt who had laughed with my mother when they overheard me singing, "Yo soy el aventurero," with Gladys. The aunt had told Mami that I sounded like a cow with a stomachache. The maid sounded, she added, like a cow without a stomachache. The two women had burst out laughing. As for my having to learn to dance, this was a sore point. Recently, I had been thrown out of ballet class for giving Madame Corbett a general's salute when she tapped my butt with her dancing cane.

So I couldn't be an actress either? Well, at least there were still lots of other things to be in this world. "I want to drive a red pickup," I said, amending my future. "I want to go to the moon in a rocket ship and under water in a submarine and work in an ice cream shop and be a guard at Buckingham palace." I was stacking up all the exciting possibilities for the future, a big wall to keep everybody out. "And I want to be a pilot and go to Nueva York and shop for toys, and I want to be a poet and write lots and lots of poems."

"A poet?" my grandfather said, smiling dreamily. The room went silent, aunts and uncles bracing themselves for one of his recitations. But he did not recite. Instead, he took my face in his hand, tilting it this way and that, as if he had caught the big gold fish in his net and wanted to see it up close. "A poet, yes. Now you are talking."

Our Papers

. . . .

We never went on trips abroad when I was a child. In the Dominican Republic no one could travel without papers, and the dictatorship rarely granted anyone this special permission.

There were exceptions—my grandparents went to New York regularly because my grandfather had a post in the United Nations. My godmother, who was described as one of the most beautiful widows in the country, got permission to go on a trip because she was clever. At a state function, she told El Jefe that she knew he was gentleman, and a gentleman would not refuse a lady a favor. She wanted so much to travel. The next morning a black limousine from the National Palace rolled up to her door to deliver her papers, along with some flowers.

"Where did you want to go?" I asked her, years later.

"*Want* to go?" she looked at me blankly. "I didn't want to go anywhere. I just wanted to get away from the hell we were living in."

Those trips were not vacations—though they did share an aspect of vacations: they were escapes, not from the tedium of daily routines, but from the terror of a police state.

When I was a child, then, vacations meant a vacation from school. That was vacation enough for me! Summer vacations also meant a move. During the long, hot months of July and August, the whole extended family—uncles, aunts, sisters, cousins, grandparents—left the capital to get away from the heat and diseases that supposedly festered in the heat. My grandfather had bought an old house a short walk from the beach in the small fishing village of Boca Chica, close to where the new airport was being built. The house itself was nothing elegant: two stories, wood frame, a wraparound porch on the first floor, a large screened-in porch on the second, a big almond tree that dropped its fruit on the zinc roof. Ping! in the middle of the night. *What was that?*

We slept on cots, all the cousins, in that screened-in porch. Meals were eaten in two shifts on a big picnic table—first, the whole gang of children, our seating arrangement planned to avoid trouble, the rowdy ones next to the well-behaved ones, the babies with bibs in high chairs, looking like the little dignitaries of the gathering. The grown-ups ate after we were sent up to our cots to nap so we could "make our digestions" and be able to go swimming in the late afternoon. Our lives, which were communal during the rest of the year, since we all lived in neighboring houses, grew even more communal when we were all under the same roof. The men stayed on in the capital during the week, working hard, and appeared on Friday afternoons to a near-stampede of children running up from the beach to see what our papis had brought us from the city. During the rest of the week, it was just the cousins and our mothers and grandmother and aunts and nursemaids, and the great big sea that splashed in our dreams all night long.

It seemed then that we were not living in a dictatorship but in a fairyland of sand and sun and girlish mothers who shared in our fun. The perpetual worried look disappeared from my mother's face. She went barefoot on the beach, a sea breeze blew her skirt up in the air, she tried to hold it down. We chose the fish for our dinner right off the fishermen's boats. The women gossiped and told stories and painted their fingernails and toenails and then proceeded down the line to do the same for the girl children. They always had some little intrigue going. They especially loved to tease the husbands alone in the capital, making funny phone calls, pretending they were other women ("Don't you remember me, Edy querido?!") or pretending they were salesladies calling to say that their wives' order of a hundred dollars' worth of Revlon cosmetics had just arrived. Could payment be sent immediately?

Ha, ha, ha! The women held their sides and laughed wildly at the men's embarrassment. It was fun to see them having such a good time for a change.

And then, suddenly, in 1960, summers at the beach stopped altogether. We stayed home in the capital. The women were too worried to leave the men by themselves. Nightly, a black Volkswagen came up our driveway and sat there, blocking our way out. We were under virtual house arrest by the SIM.

The men talked in low, worried voices behind closed doors. The shadows under my mother's eyes grew darker. When we begged and pleaded to go to Boca Chica for the summer, she blurted out, "¡Absolutamente no!" before she was hushed by a more circumspect aunt.

That's when talk of a vacation began in my family—vacation as in the American understanding of vacation, a trip far away, for fun.

"Wouldn't you love to go to the United States and see the snow?" one aunt asked my sisters and me one day out of the blue.

"That would be so much fun!" another aunt chimed in.

We sisters looked from one to the other aunt, unsure. Something about the conversation seemed rehearsed. Some adult intrigue was afoot. This one would not involve giggles on the phone and howls of laughter over how gullible the men were. This one would be serious, but just how serious I did not understand until years later.

My father's activities in the underground were suspected, and it would be only a matter of time before he would be hauled away if we stayed. And who knew where else the ax might fall—on his wife and children? Friends in the States rigged up a fellowship for my father. The pretext was that he would study heart surgery there since there wasn't a heart surgeon in the Dominican Republic. What if our dictator should develop heart trouble? Papi was petitioning for a two-year visa for himself and his family. No, he told the authorities, he would not go without us. That would be a hardship.

"You bet," my mother tells me now. "We would have been held hostage!"

"Why didn't you tell us any of this back then?" I ask her. All we ever heard about was that we were taking a vacation to the United States. "Why didn't you just say, we're leaving forever?"

"Ay sí, and get ourselves killed! You had the biggest mouth back then—" She shakes her head, and I know what is coming, "and you still do, writing, writing, writing."

She is right, too—about the big mouth. I remember my three sisters and I were coached not to mention that we were going to the United States of America—at least not till our papers came, if they ever came.

Before the day was over, I had told our secret to the cousins, the maids, the dog, and the corner candy man, who was always willing to exchange candy for my schoolbooks and school supplies. I hadn't meant to disobey, but it was so tempting to brag and get a little extra respect and a free box of cinnamon Chiclets.

"I'm going to see the snow!" I singsang to my boy cousin Ique.

"So?" he shrugged and threw me a shadow punch. Needless to say, we were two of the rowdy ones.

Toys made a better argument. I was going to the land where our toys came from.

He raised his chin, struggling with the envy he did not want to admit to feeling. "Bring me back something?" he finally pleaded.

"Okay," I said, disarmed. No one had mentioned our return until this very moment. Surely, vacations were something you came back from?

When our papers finally arrived one morning in early August, Papi booked us on the next flight off the Island. The vacation was on. We could tell anybody we wanted. Now, I was the one who grew silent.

"Hello, very pleased to make your acquaintance?" one uncle joked in English, holding out his hand to me. He had come by to say good-bye, for we were leaving that very night. Meanwhile, we girls better practice our English! We would get so tall and pale and pretty in the United States, and smart! Maybe we would marry Americans and have little blue-eyed babies that didn't know how to speak Spanish!

That gripped my braggart's heart. We were going to be gone *that* long?

As the hours ticked by and more and more visitors and relatives snuck in the back way to say good-bye, my sisters and I grew pale with fear. We didn't really want to go to a place where buildings scraped the sky and everyone spoke English all the time, not just at school in English class. We didn't want to go someplace if all the cousins and aunts couldn't come along.

The uncles mocked us, lifting their eyebrows in shock. "How crazy! Do you know how many children would give their right arms to go to the United States of America?" Their argument, a variation on the starving Chinese children who would give their right arms to eat our vegetables, did not convince us. Our protests increased as the hour drew near.

I don't know which aunt it was, or perhaps it was our own distraught mother, who decided to trick us to calm us down. Never mind the United States, we were really going to Boca Chica! The story wasn't a total untruth. The new airport was on the way to the fishing village.

We were suspicious. Why were we dressed in party dresses

if we were going to the beach? Why did we have suitcases like foreign people, instead of the big hampers of clothes and provisions we took with us when we left for the summer for the beach house?

"That's enough, girls!" Mami snapped. "One more word from you and you can all stay here by yourselves!"

Now there was a threat worth its weight in silence. Abandonment was far worse than a long, maybe permanent vacation somewhere weird. By the time we boarded the plane, long past midnight, none of us had raised any further objections. Besides by now, it had been drummed into us— how lucky we were to have our papers, to be free to go on this long vacation.

Soon after the roar of takeoff, we fell asleep, so we did not see the little lights flickering in some of the houses as we flew over Boca Chica. Hours before dawn, the fishermen would already be casting their nets out in the ocean. By midmorning, when we would be gaping at the buildings in New York City, the fish would be laid out on a big board across the rowboats' length, their pink and silver scales iridescent with the water scooped over them to make them look fresher.

For weeks that soon became months and years, I would think in this way. What was going on right this moment back home? As the leaves fell and the air turned gray and the cold set in, I would remember the big house in Boca Chica, the waves telling me their secrets, the cousins sleeping side by side in their cots, and I would wonder if those papers had set us free from everything we loved.

My English

. . . .

Mami and Papi used to speak it when they had a secret they wanted to keep from us children. We lived then in the Dominican Republic, and the family as a whole spoke only Spanish at home, until my sisters and I started attending the Carol Morgan School, and we became a bilingual family. Spanish had its many tongues as well. There was the castellano of Padre Joaquín from Spain, whose lisp we all loved to imitate. Then the educated español my parents' families spoke, aunts and uncles who were always correcting us children, for we spent most of the day with the maids and so had picked up their "bad Spanish." Campesinas, they spoke a lilting, animated campuno, *ss* swallowed, endings chopped off, funny turns of phrases. This campuno was my true mother tongue, not the Spanish of Calderón de la Barca or Cervantes or even Neruda, but of Chucha and Iluminada and Gladys and Ursulina from Juncalito and Licey and Boca de Yuma and San Juan de la Maguana. Those women yakked as they cooked, they storytold, they gossiped, they sang—boleros, merengues, canciones, salves. Theirs were the voices that belonged to the rain and the wind and the teeny, teeny stars even a small child could blot out with her thumb.

BESIDES ALL THESE versions of Spanish, every once in a while another strange tongue emerged from my papi's mouth or my mami's lips. What I first recognized was not a language, but a tone of voice, serious, urgent, something important and top secret being said, some uncle in trouble, someone divorcing, someone dead. *Say it in English so the children won't understand.* I would listen, straining to understand, thinking that this was not a different language but just another and harder version of Spanish. *Say it in English so the children won't understand.* From the beginning, English was the sound of worry and secrets, the sound of being left out.

I could make no sense of this "harder Spanish," and so I tried by other means to find out what was going on. I knew my mother's face by heart. When the little lines on the corners of her eyes crinkled, she was amused. When her nostrils flared and she bit her lips, she was trying hard not to laugh. She held her head down, eyes glancing up, when she thought I was lying. Whenever she spoke that gibberish English, I translated the general content by watching the Spanish expressions on her face.

• • •

SOON, I BEGAN to learn more English, at the Carol Morgan School. That is, when I had stopped gawking. The teacher and some of the American children had the strangest coloration: light hair, light eyes, light skin, as if Ursulina had soaked them in bleach too long, to' deteñío. I did have some blond cousins, but they had deeply tanned skin, and as they grew older, their hair darkened, so their earlier paleness seemed a phase of their acquiring normal color. Just as strange was the little girl in my reader who had a *cat* and a *dog,* that looked just like un gatito y un perrito. Her mami was *Mother* and her papi *Father.* Why have a whole new language for school and for books with a teacher who could speak it teaching you double the amount of words you really needed?

Butter, butter, butter, butter. All day, one English word that had particularly struck me would go round and round in my mouth and weave through all the Spanish in my head until by the end of the day, the word did sound like just another Spanish word. And so I would say, "Mami, please pass la mantequilla." She would scowl and say in English, "I'm sorry, I don't understand. But would you be needing some butter on your bread?"

WHY MY PARENTS didn't first educate us in our native language by enrolling us in a Dominican school, I don't know. Part of it was that Mami's family had a tradition of sending the boys to the States to boarding school and college, and she had been one of the first girls to be allowed to join her brothers. At Abbot Academy, whose school song was our lullaby as babies ("Although Columbus and Cabot never heard of Abbot, it's quite the place for you and me"), she had become quite Americanized. It was very important, she kept saying, that we learn our English. She always used the possessive pronoun: *your* English, an inheritance we had come into and must wisely use. Unfortunately, my English became all mixed up with our Spanish.

Mix-up, or what's now called Spanglish, was the language we spoke for several years. There wasn't a sentence that wasn't colonized by an English word. At school, a Spanish word would suddenly slide into my English like someone butting into line. Teacher, whose face I was learning to read as minutely as my mother's, would scowl but no smile played on her lips. Her pale skin made her strange countenance hard to read, so that I often misjudged how much I could get away with. Whenever I made a mistake, Teacher would shake her head slowly, "In English, YU-LEE-AH, there's no such word as *columpio*. Do you mean a *swing*?"

I would bow my head, humiliated by the smiles and snickers of the American children around me. I grew insecure about Spanish. My native tongue was not quite as good as English, as if words like *columpio* were illegal immigrants trying to cross a border into another language. But Teacher's discerning grammar-and-vocabulary-patrol ears could tell and send them back.

SOON, I WAS talking up an English storm. "Did you eat English parrot?" my grandfather asked one Sunday. I had just enlisted yet one more patient servant to listen to my rendition of "Peter Piper picked a peck of pickled peppers" at breakneck pace. "Huh?" I asked impolitely in English, putting him in his place. *Cat got your tongue? No big deal! So there! Take that! Holy Toledo!* (Our teacher's favorite "curse word.") *Go jump in the lake! Really dumb. Golly. Gosh.* Slang, clichés, sayings, hot-shot language that our teacher called, ponderously, idiomatic expressions. Riddles, jokes, puns, conundrums. *What is yellow and goes click-click? Why did the chicken cross the road? See you later, alligator.* How wonderful to call someone an alligator and not be scolded for being disrespectful. In fact, they were supposed to say back, *In a while, crocodile.*

There was also a neat little trick I wanted to try on an English-speaking adult at home. I had learned it from Elizabeth, my smart-alecky friend in fourth grade, whom I alternately worshiped and resented. I'd ask her a question that required an explanation, and she'd answer, "Because . . ." "Elizabeth, how come you didn't go to Isabel's birthday party?" "Because . . ." "Why didn't you put your name in your reader?" "Because . . ." I thought that such a cool way to get around having to come up with answers. So, I practiced saying it under my breath, planning for the day I could use it on an unsuspecting English-speaking adult.

ONE SUNDAY AT our extended family dinner, my grandfather sat down at the children's table to chat with us. He was famous, in fact, for the way he could carry on adult conversations with his grandchildren. He often spoke to us in English so that we could practice speaking it outside the classroom. He was a Cornell man, a United Nations representative from our country. He gave speeches in English. Perfect English, my mother's phrase. That Sunday, he asked me a question. I can't even remember what it was because I wasn't really listening but lying in wait for my chance. "Because . . .," I answered him. Papito waited a second for the rest of my sentence and then gave me a thumbnail grammar lesson, "*Because* has to be followed by a clause."

"Why's that?" I asked, nonplussed.

"Because," he winked, "Just because."

A BEGINNING WORDSMITH, I had so much left to learn; sometimes it was disheartening. Once Tío Gus, the family intellectual, put a speck of salt on my grandparents' big dining table during Sunday dinner. He said, "Imagine this whole table is the human brain. Then this teensy grain is all we ever use of our intelligence!" He enumerated geniuses who had perhaps used two grains, maybe three: Einstein, Michelangelo, da Vinci, Beethoven. We children believed him. It was the kind of impossible fact we thrived on, proving as it did that the world out there was not drastically different from the one we were making up in our heads.

Later, at home, Mami said that you had to take what her younger brother said "with a grain of salt." I thought she was still referring to Tío Gus's demonstration, and I tried to puzzle out what she was saying. Finally, I asked what she meant. "Taking what someone says with a grain of salt is an idiomatic expression in English," she explained. It was pure voodoo is what it was—what later I learned poetry could also do: a grain of salt could symbolize both the human brain and a condiment for human nonsense. And it could be itself, too: a grain of salt to flavor a bland plate of American food.

WHEN WE ARRIVED in New York, I was shocked. A country where everyone spoke English! These people must be smarter,

I thought. Maids, waiters, taxi drivers, doormen, bums on the street, all spoke this difficult language. It took some time before I understood that Americans were not necessarily a smarter, superior race. It was as natural for them to learn their mother tongue as it was for a little Dominican baby to learn Spanish. It came with "mother's milk," my mother explained, and for a while I thought a mother tongue was a mother tongue because you got it from your mother's breast, along with proteins and vitamins.

Soon it wasn't so strange that everyone was speaking in English instead of Spanish. I learned not to hear it as English, but as sense. I no longer strained to understand, I understood. I relaxed in this second language. Only when someone with a heavy southern or British accent spoke in a movie, or at church when the priest droned his sermon—only then did I experience that little catch of anxiety. I worried that I would not be able to understand, that I wouldn't be able to "keep up" with the voice speaking in this acquired language. I would be like those people from the Bible we had studied in religion class, whom I imagined standing at the foot of an enormous tower that looked just like the skyscrapers around me. They had been punished for their pride by being made to speak different languages so that they didn't understand what anyone was saying.

But at the foot of those towering New York skyscrapers, I began to understand more and more—not less and less—English. In sixth grade, I had one of the first in a lucky line of great English teachers who began to nurture in me a love of language, a love that had been there since my childhood of listening closely to words. Sister Maria Generosa did not make our class interminably diagram sentences from a workbook or learn a catechism of grammar rules. Instead, she asked us to write little stories imagining we were snowflakes, birds, pianos, a stone in the pavement, a star in the sky. What would it feel like to be a flower with roots in the ground? If the clouds could talk, what would they say? She had an expressive, dreamy look that was accentuated by the wimple that framed her face.

Supposing, just supposing . . . My mind would take off, soaring into possibilities, a flower with roots, a star in the sky, a cloud full of sad, sad tears, a piano crying out each time its back was tapped, music only to our ears.

Sister Maria stood at the chalkboard. Her chalk was always snapping in two because she wrote with such energy, her whole habit shaking with the swing of her arm, her hand tap-tap-tapping on the board. "Here's a simple sentence: 'The snow fell.' " Sister pointed with her chalk, her eyebrows lifted, her wimple poked up. Sometimes I could see wisps of gray hair that strayed from under her headdress. "But watch what happens if we put an adverb at the beginning and a prepositional phrase at the end: 'Gently, the snow fell on the bare hills.' "

I thought about the snow. I saw how it might fall on the hills, tapping lightly on the bare branches of trees. Softly, it would fall on the cold, bare fields. On toys children had left out in the yard, and on cars and on little birds and on people out late walking on the streets. Sister Marie filled the chalkboard with snowy print, on and on, handling and shaping and moving the language, scribbling all over the board until English, those verbal gadgets, those tricks and turns of phrases, those little fixed units and counters, became a charged, fluid mass that carried me in its great fluent waves, rolling and moving onward, to deposit me on the shores of my new homeland. I was no longer a foreigner with no ground to stand on. I had landed in the English language.

My Second Opera

. . . .

A few months after we arrived in New York City, I was taken by my grandfather to see my first opera. He had gotten tickets to a matinee of *Aïda* at Lincoln Center, and he assured me that it would be great fun. My grandmother, whose ticket I would be using, rolled her eyes.

She had promised me an outing to the downtown Macy's to see the bewitched doors and the magic staircase if I took her place.

"You know what my favorite part of the opera is?" she asked me with a twinkle in her eye *after* I had agreed to our deal. I, not sure at age ten what an opera was, shook my head.

"When everybody starts to die because then I know the end is in sight." She held her sides, trying to contain her laughter.

"Let's keep an open mind, shall we?" my grandfather reminded her. "An opera *is* great fun," he assured me. We heard him hum a little tune that sounded rather triumphant.

"Great fun," my grandmother mimicked, lifting her hand, the pinky out.

I didn't think an opera could be all that bad if I got to see a bunch of people die right before my eyes. In addition, there would be the Macy's payoff. The month before, my grandfather had taken me to a ballet at Lincoln Center, and I still daydreamed of being a pretty ballerina in a fluffy petticoat walking on my tiptoes.

My grandfather went to many of these events because he considered them part of his job. He was the cultural attaché to the United Nations, an honorary post that required nothing of him, but he took the assignment seriously. When he was sent free tickets to an event, he went, honored that he had been, well, honored. He had no idea how he had been given the job since he had not applied for it. He had merely put in a request for a visa to the United States in order to visit doctors for his and my grandmother's health troubles and—he had not stated this, of course—for respite from the stress of living under a dictatorship. The post had been offered to him, and all he could figure out was that the "government" was functioning in the usual mad, surreal way of police states where a man who asks for a license to drive a taxi has his right hand chopped off for stealing radishes.

My grandmother knew better why my grandfather had gotten to leave the country, and so did I. Superstitious, and determined to get her family out safely before anyone was disappeared for some imagined offense, she asked our Haitian maid for help. So Misiá attended a voodoo ceremony and took me with her, because a minor petition, along with the big one that we all escape the country, was that I learn to be a fine young lady instead of the loudmouthed tomboy I was bent on becoming.

The "job" had been done by a hougan whose entranced, rhythmic chant was answered by a chorus of attendants. There was much drumming and dancing to appease or please one spirit or another. Gourds of nuts and spices were carried out by women wearing colorful kerchiefs and deposited on an altar of burning candles and images. One woman sprinkled me with something fragrant, then touched my throat with her wet fingers. At one point, a goat was brought forth, bleating in terror, but after he'd been garlanded with a necklace of white jasmine, he was hauled away unharmed.

A week later, my grandfather was offered his post, my father's papers arrived, permitting the whole family to accompany him on his fellowship to New York, and I was decidedly better behaved. In part, this was because I had been told that unless my behavior improved I would not be allowed in the United States.

FROM THE MOMENT the red velvet curtains lifted at Lincoln Center, I was transported. I leaned forward in my seat so I could see better in the gap between two adult heads. What magic on the stage! An Egyptian palace appeared before my very eyes. During the Triumphant March, a stallion jingling with gold harness, a small monkey with a collar, numerous splendid parrots, and even a camel, who dropped turds cleaned up by a slave with a collar, too, were marched on stage. Large, fleshy bodies sang with the voices of angels, and all around me, in hushed silence, the audience watched like believers in a church.

I had never seen anything like this—or had I? The pageantry reminded me of the high masses at la catedral, which I had attended every Sunday in a crowd of cousins back on the Island. And something else . . . Then, of course, I realized that the magic and pageantry I was seeing and the awe and wonder I was feeling reminded me of the voodoo ceremony I had attended with Misiá.

Is it sacrilegious to say so? To compare grand art from Europe to a voodoo ceremony in a little Caribbean island? Maybe I was just a little jibarita hick who thought electric-eye doors and escalators were operated by trickster spirits? Maybe so, but in another great work of Western tradition, the grand and mighty are reminded to pay attention to what comes *out of the mouths of babes.* The child at the opera in Lincoln Center knew she was experiencing an event similar in spirit to the voodoo ceremony in the Dominican Republic.

"I have immortal longings in me," says Shakespeare's Cleopatra, and each culture responds to these longings with one or another sacred or art form evolved through tradition, taught through craft, depended upon, vitally, by its members in order to survive and triumph. These days, even the Keepers of High Art would be reluctant to deny the indigenous ceremonies and art forms of the New World some place under the cultural sun. My own grandfather, biased towards the European, would have said Island practices were more savage than *real* Art. But then, that same grandfather used the best litmus test for an art form, the most difficult test it has to pass: It better be great fun.

And *Aïda* was great fun. I became an opera fan, and also a

wily intriguer. See, if I played my cards right, I could have it both ways: I could attend every opera in my grandmother's place *and* go on shopping trips as a reward for rescuing her from the dying divas. I suppose opera turned out to be like the voodoo ceremony in that way as well—a way for me to get other things.

That evening, when we returned from *Aïda,* my grandmother greeted us at the door. "How was it?" she asked my grandfather and me, a smile lurking on her lips.

"Great fun!" my grandfather said, taking off his coat, and humming that little triumphant tune again. "Wouldn't you say so?" he asked me.

I nodded. My grandmother winked at me, as if we knew better. But I had not yet figured out the advantage of keeping my mouth shut and pretending to suffer through opera. "It *was* fun," I agreed with my grandfather. "It was just like that other opera with the goat and the singing and dancing."

"What other opera was that?" my grandfather turned to my grandmother.

Hands on her hips, my grandmother challenged my grandfather, "Now would I send anyone to an opera?! The child has some imagination!" She gave me the look that meant, keep your mouth shut, and maybe we will go to Macy's twice in one week.

I Want to Be Miss América

· · · · · · · ·

As young teenagers in our new country, my three sisters and I searched for clues on how to look as if we belonged here. We collected magazines, studied our classmates and our new TV, which was where we discovered the Miss America contest.

Watching the pageant became an annual event in our family. Once a year, we all plopped down in our parents' bedroom, with Mami and Papi presiding from their bed. In our nightgowns, we watched the fifty young women who had the American look we longed for.

The beginning was always the best part—all fifty contestants came on for one and only one appearance. In alphabetical order, they stepped forward and enthusiastically introduced themselves by name and state. "Hi! I'm! Susie!

Martin! Miss! Alaska!" Their voices rang with false cheer. You could hear, not far off, years of high-school cheerleading, pom-poms, bleachers full of moon-eyed boys, and moms on phones, signing them up for all manner of lessons and making dentist appointments.

There they stood, fifty puzzle pieces forming the pretty face of America, so we thought, though most of the color had been left out, except for one, or possibly two, light-skinned black girls. If there was a "Hispanic," she usually looked all-American, and only the last name, López or Rodríguez, often mispronounced, showed a trace of a great-great-grandfather with a dark, curled mustache and a sombrero charging the Alamo. During the initial roll-call, what most amazed us was that some contestants were ever picked in the first place. There were homely girls with cross-eyed smiles or chipmunk cheeks. My mother would inevitably shake her head and say, "The truth is, these Americans believe in democracy—even in looks."

We were beginning to feel at home. Our acute homesickness had passed, and now we were like people recovered from a shipwreck, looking around at our new country, glad to be here. "I want to be in America," my mother hummed after we'd gone to see *West Side Story,* and her four daughters chorused, "OK by me in America." We bought a house in Queens, New York, in a neighborhood that was mostly German and Irish, where we were the only "Hispanics." Actually, no one ever called us that. Our teachers and classmates at the local Catholic schools referred to us as "Porto Ricans" or "Spanish." No one knew where the Dominican Republic was on the map. "South of Florida," I explained, "in the same general vicinity as Bermuda and Jamaica." I could just as well have said west of Puerto Rico or east of Cuba or right next to Haiti, but I wanted us to sound like a vacation spot, not a Third World country, a place they would look down on.

Although we wanted to look like we belonged here, the four sisters, our looks didn't seem to fit in. We complained about how short we were, about how our hair frizzed, how our figures didn't curve like those of the bathing beauties we'd seen on TV.

"The grass always grows on the other side of the fence," my mother scolded. Her daughters looked fine just the way they were.

But how could we trust her opinion about what looked good when she couldn't even get the sayings of our new country right? No, we knew better. We would have to translate our looks into English, iron and tweeze them out, straighten them, mold them into Made-in-the-U.S.A. beauty.

So we painstakingly rolled our long, curly hair round and round, using our heads as giant rollers, ironing it until we had long, shining shanks, like our classmates and the contestants, only darker. Our skin was diagnosed by beauty consultants in department stores as sallow; we definitely needed a strong foundation to tone down that olive. We wore tights even in the summer to hide the legs Mami would not let us shave. We begged for permission, dreaming of the contestants' long, silky limbs. We were ten, fourteen, fifteen, and sixteen—merely children, Mami explained. We had long lives ahead of us in which to shave.

We defied her. Giggly and red-faced, we all pitched in to buy a big tube of Nair at the local drugstore. We acted as if we were purchasing contraceptives. That night we crowded into the bathroom, and I, the most courageous along these lines, offered one of my legs as a guinea pig. When it didn't become gangrenous or fall off as Mami had predicted, we creamed the other seven legs. We beamed at each other; we were one step closer to that runway, those flashing cameras, those oohs and ahhs from the audience.

Mami didn't even notice our Naired legs; she was too busy disapproving of the other changes. Our clothes, for one. "You're going to wear *that* in public!" She'd gawk, as if to say, What will the Americans think of us?

"This *is* what the Americans wear," we would argue back.

But the dresses we had picked out made us look cheap, she said, like bad, fast girls—gringas without vergüenza, without shame. She preferred her choices: fuchsia skirts with matching vests, flowered dresses with bows at the neck or gathers where you wanted to look slim, everything bright and busy, like something someone might wear in a foreign country.

Our father didn't really notice our new look at all but, if called upon to comment, would say absently that we looked beautiful. "Like Marilina Monroe." Still, during the pageant, he would offer insights into what he thought made a winner. "Personality, Mami," my father would say from his post at the head of the bed, "Personality is the key," though his favorite contestants, whom he always championed in the name of personality, tended to be the fuller girls with big breasts who gushed shamelessly at Bert Parks. "Ay, Papi," we would groan, rolling our eyes at each other. Sometimes, as the girl sashayed back down the aisle, Papi would break out in a little Dominican song that he sang whenever a girl had a lot of swing in her walk:

I Want to Be Miss América

Yo no tumbo caña,
Que la tumba el viento,
Que la tumba Dora
Con su movimiento!

("I don't have to cut the cane,
The wind knocks it down,
The wind of Dora's movement
As she walks downtown.")

My father would stop on a New York City street when a young woman swung by and sing this song out loud to the great embarrassment of his daughters. We were sure that one day when we weren't around to make him look like the respectable father of four girls, he would be arrested.

My mother never seemed to have a favorite contestant. She was an ex-beauty herself, and no one seemed to measure up to her high standards. She liked the good girls who had common sense and talked about their education and about how they owed everything to their mothers. "Tell that to my daughters," my mother would address the screen, as if none of us were there to hear her. If we challenged her— how exactly did we *not* appreciate her?—she'd maintain a wounded silence for the rest of the evening. Until the very end of the show, that is, when all our disagreements were forgotten and we waited anxiously to see which of the two finalists holding hands on that near-empty stage would be the next reigning queen of beauty. How can they hold hands? I always wondered. Don't they secretly wish the other person would, well, die?

My sisters and I always had plenty of commentary on all

the contestants. We were hardly strangers to this ritual of picking the beauty. In our own family, we had a running competition as to who was the prettiest of the four girls. We coveted one another's best feature: the oldest's dark, almond-shaped eyes, the youngest's great mane of hair, the third oldest's height and figure. I didn't have a preferred feature, but I was often voted the cutest, though my oldest sister liked to remind me that I had the kind of looks that wouldn't age well. Although she was only eleven months older than I was, she seemed years older, ages wiser. She bragged about the new kind of math she was learning in high school, called algebra, which she said I would never be able to figure out. I believed her. Dumb and ex-cute, that's what I would grow up to be.

As for the prettiest Miss America, we sisters kept our choices secret until the very end. The range was limited—pretty white women who all *really* wanted to be wives and mothers. But even the small and inane set of options these girls represented seemed boundless compared with what we were used to. We were being groomed to go from being dutiful daughters to being dutiful wives with hymens intact. No stops along the way that might endanger the latter; no careers, no colleges, no shared apartments with girlfriends, no boyfriends, no social lives. But the young women on-screen, who were being held up as models in this new country, were in college, or at least headed there. They wanted to do this, they were going to do that with their lives. Everything in our native culture had instructed us otherwise: girls were to have no aspirations beyond being good wives and mothers.

Sometimes there would even be a contestant headed for

law school or medical school. "I wouldn't mind having an office visit with her," my father would say, smirking. The women who caught my attention were the prodigies who bounded onstage and danced to tapes of themselves playing original compositions on the piano, always dressed in costumes they had sewn, with a backdrop of easels holding paintings they'd painted. "Overkill," my older sister insisted. But if one good thing came out of our watching this yearly parade of American beauties, it was that subtle permission we all felt as a family: a girl could excel outside the home and still be a winner.

Every year, the queen came down the runway in her long gown with a sash like an old-world general's belt of ammunition. Down the walkway she paraded, smiling and waving while Bert sang his sappy song that made our eyes fill with tears. When she stopped at the very end of the stage and the camera zoomed in on her misty-eyed beauty and the credits began to appear on the screen, I always felt let down. I knew I would never be one of those girls, ever. It wasn't just the blond, blue-eyed looks or the beautiful, leggy figure. It was who she was—an American—and we were not. We were foreigners, dark-haired and dark-eyed with olive skin that could never, no matter the sun blocks or foundation makeup, be made into peaches and cream.

Had we been able to see into the future, beyond our noses, which we thought weren't the right shape; beyond our curly hair, which we wanted to be straight; and beyond the screen, which inspired us with a limited vision of what was considered beautiful in America, we would have been able to see the late sixties coming. Soon, ethnic looks would be in. Even Barbie, that quintessential white girl, would suddenly be available in different shades of skin color with bright, colorful outfits that looked like the ones Mami had picked out for us. Our classmates in college wore long braids like Native Americans and embroidered shawls and peasant blouses from South America, and long, diaphanous skirts and dangly earrings from India. They wanted to look exotic —they wanted to look like us.

We felt then a gratifying sense of inclusion, but it had unfortunately come too late. We had already acquired the habit of doubting ourselves as well as the place we came from. To this day, after three decades of living in America, I feel like a stranger in what I now consider my own country. I am still that young teenager sitting in front of the black-and-white TV in my parents' bedroom, knowing in my bones I will never be the beauty queen. There she is, Miss America, but even in my up-to-date, enlightened dreams, she never wears my face.

El Doctor

· · · · · · · ·

"Lights! At this hour?" my father asks, looking up from his empty dinner plate at the glowing lamp my mother has just turned on above the table. "Are we in Plato's cave, Mami?" He winks at me; as the two readers in the family we show off by making allusions my mother and sisters don't understand. He leans his chair back and picks up the hem of the curtain. A dim gray light falls into the room. "See, Mami. It's still light out there!"

"Ya, ya!" she snaps, and flips the switch off.

"Your mother is a wonder," he announces, then he adds, "El Doctor is ready for bed." Dinner is over; every night my father brings the meal to a close with a third-person good-night before he leaves the room.

Tonight he lingers, watching her. She says nothing, head

bent, intent on her mashed plantains with oil and onions. "Yessir," he elaborates, "El Doctor—" The rest is garbled, for he's balled up his napkin and rubbed his lips violently as if he meant to erase them from his face. Perhaps he shouldn't have spoken up? She is jabbing at the few bites of beefsteak on her plate. Perhaps he should have just let the issue drop like water down his chest or whatever it is the Americans say. He scrapes his chair back.

Her scowl deepens. "Eduardo, please." And then, because he already knows better, she adds only, "The wax finish."

"Por supuesto," he says, his voice full of false concern as he examines her spotless kitchen floor for damages. Then, carefully, he lifts his chair up and tucks it back in its place. "This old man is ready for bed." He leans over and kisses the scowl off her face. "Mami, this country agrees with you. You look more beautiful every day. Doesn't she, girls?" And with a wink of encouragement to each of us, he leaves us in the dark.

I remember my mother at all times of the day: slapping around in her comfortable slippers, polishing her windows into blinding panes of light. But I remember him mostly at night, moving down the dark halls, undressing as he climbed the dark stairs to bed.

I want to say there were as many buttons on his vest as stairs up to the bedroom: it seemed he unbuttoned a button on each step so that by the time he reached the landing, his vest was off. His armor, I thought, secretly pleased with all I believed I understood about him. But his vest couldn't have had more than six buttons, and the stairs were long and narrow. Then again, I couldn't see that well in the dark he insisted on.

"I'm going to take this dollar," he showed me, holding a bill in one hand, a flickering lighter in the other, "and I'm going to set fire to it." He never actually did. He spoke in parables, he complained in metaphors, because he had never learned to say things directly. I already knew what he meant, but I had my part to play.

"Why would you want to do something like that?" I asked.

"Exactly! Why burn up money with all these lights in the house?"

As we grew up, confirmed in our pyromania, he did not bother to teach us to economize, but went through the house, turning off lights in every room, not noticing many times that we were there, reading or writing a letter, and leaving us in the dark, hurt that he had overlooked us.

At the bedroom door he loosened his tie and, craning his neck, undid the top button of his shirt. Then he sat at the edge of the bed and turned on his bedside lamp. Not always; if a little reflected sun dappled the room with shadowy light, if it was late spring or early fall or summertime, he waited until the last moment to turn on the lamp, sometimes reading in the dark until we came in and turned it on for him. "Papi, you're going to ruin your eyes," we scolded.

Once I worked it out for him with the pamphlet the electric company had sent me. Were he to leave his bedside light, say, burning for the rest of his evenings—and I allowed him a generous four decades ("I won't need it for that long," he protested; I insisted)—the cost (side by side we multiplied, added, carried over to the next column) would be far less than if he lost his eyesight, was forced to give up his practice, and had to spend the next four decades—

"Like your friend Milton," he said, pleased with the inspired possibilities of blindness. Now that I was turning out to be the family poet, all the greats were my personal friends. " 'When I consider how my light is spent,' " he began. Just like my mother's father, my own father loved to recite, racing me through poems to see who would be the first one to finish.

" 'How my light is spent,' " I echoed and took the lead. " ' 'Ere half my days, in this dark world and wide . . .' "

Just as I was rounding the line break to the last line, he interjected it, " 'They also serve who only stand and wait.' "

I scowled. How dare he clap the last line on after I had gone through all the trouble of reciting the poem! "Not every blind man is a Milton," I said, and I gave him the smirk I wore all through adolescence.

"Nutrition," he said mysteriously.

"What about nutrition?"

"Good nutrition. We're starting to see the effects: children grow taller; they have better teeth, better bones, better minds than their elders." And he reached for his book on the bedside table.

Actually, the reading came later. First there is the scene that labels him immigrant and shows why I could never call him, sweetly, playfully, "Daddy." He took from his back pocket a wad of bills so big his hand could not close over it. And he began to count. If at this point we disturbed him, he waved us away. If we called from downstairs, he did not answer. All over the bed he shared with my mother were piles of bills. I do not know the system; no one ever did. Perhaps all the fives were together, all the tens? Perhaps each pile was a specific amount? But this was the one private moment he insisted on. Not even catching him undressing, which I never did, seems as intimate a glimpse of him.

After the counting came the binding and marking: each pile was held together with rubber bands he saved up from the rolled-up *New York Times,* and the top bill was scribbled on. He marked them as a reminder of how much was in each pile, I'm sure, but I can't help thinking it was also his way of owning what he had earned, much as ranchers brand their cattle. The secretary of the treasury had signed this twenty; there was Andrew Jackson's picture; he had to add his hand to it to make it his—to try to convince himself that it was his, for he never totally believed it was. Even after he was a successful doctor in New York with a house in the suburbs and lands at "home," his daughters in boarding schools and summer camps, a second car with enough gadgets to keep him busy in bad traffic, he was turning off lights, frequenting thrift shops for finds in ties, taking the 59th Street bridge even if it was out of his way to avoid paying a toll to cross the river.

He could not afford the good life; he could only pass it on. And he did. Beneath the surface penny-pinching, his extravagance might have led him to bankruptcy several times had my mother not been there to remind him that the weather was apt to change. "Save for a snowy day," she advised him.

"Isn't it 'rainy day'?" he enlisted me. He was always happy to catch his wife in an error since she spoke English so much better than he did. "Save it for a rainy day?"

Eager to be an authority on anything, I considered my role as Arbiter of Clichés a compliment to my literary talent. "Save it for a rainy day," I agreed.

"See, Mami."

She defended herself. "Snow is much worse than rain.

For one thing, you need to own more clothes in the winter. You get more colds in the winter."

Out from his pocket came a ten when we needed small change for the subway. Away at college I opened the envelope, empty but for the money order for fifty, a hundred; typed out in the blank beside *memo* was his note: "Get yourself a little something in my name." It was the sixties, and parental money was under heavy suspicion; my friends needed me as a Third World person to be a good example of poverty and oppression by the capitalist, military-industrial complex. I put my little somethings quietly in the bank. By the time I graduated from college, I had a small, corrupt fortune.

But my rich father lived in the dark, saving string, going the long way. I've analyzed it with my economist friends. Perhaps since his fortune came from the same work which in his country had never earned him enough, he could not believe that his being well-to-do wasn't an I.R.S. oversight. My psychologist friends claim that it is significant that he was the youngest of twenty-five children. Coming after so many, he would always fear that the good things would run out. And indeed he had a taste for leftovers, which made his compliments come a day or two after a special meal. Whenever we had chicken, he insisted on the wings and the neck bone because those had been the portions left by the time the platter got to him, the baby. He liked the pale, bitter center of the lettuce. ("The leaves were gone when I got the salad bowl.") And when we had soup, he was surprised to find a bit of meat bobbing at the surface. "Someone missed this one."

Unlike my mother, he saved for a sunny day. Extravaganza! On his birthday, at Christmas, on his saint's day (which was never celebrated for anyone else), his presents multiplied before us. Beside the ones we had bought for him, there were always other glossy packages, ribboned boxes, which dwarfed ours. The cards were forged: "To my dearest Papi from his loving daughter." "Which of you gave me this?" he asked with mock surprise and real delight. Cordelias all, we shook our heads as he unwrapped a silk lounging jacket or a genuine leather passport case. I wish he had allowed us to give him something of value.

Perhaps we did, on those evenings after the money was counted and put away, and he was ready for company. With an instinct for his rituals, we knew when it was time to come into the bedroom. We heard the bathroom door click shut; he was undressing, putting on his pajamas. The hamper lid clapped on its felt lip. We heard steps. The bed creaked. We found him in the darkening room with a book. "Papi, you're ruining your eyes!"

"Oh my God, it's gotten dark already," he would say, almost thanking us.

He wanted company, not conversation. He had us turn on the television so we could learn our English. This after years here, after his money had paid for the private schools that unrolled our rs and softened our accents; after American boyfriends had whispered sweet colloquialisms in our ears. As the television cowboys and beauty queens and ladies with disappointing stains in their wash droned on in their native English, he read the usual: a history book in Spanish. We sat at the edge of the king-size bed and wondered what he wanted from us. He wanted presences: his children, his wife, Walter Cronkite, the great men of the past, Napoleon, Caesar,

Maximilian. If one of us, bored with his idea of company, got up to leave, he lowered his book. "Did you know that in the campaign of 1808, Napoleon left his general behind to cut off the enemy from the rear, and the two divisions totally missed each other?" That was the only way he knew to ask us to stay, appealing to history and defeat, to wintry campaigns, bloody frost-bitten feet, a field strewn with war dead.

I taste the mints that he gave us, one each. He kept a stash of them in a drawer next to his bed like a schoolboy and ate exactly one each night and gave away four. That was the other way he kept us there if we got up to go after Napoleon's troops had been annihilated. "Don't you want a mint?" He didn't mean right then and there. It was a promise we had to wait for, perhaps until the chapter ended or the Roman empire fell or he was sure we had given up on the evening and decided to stay, talking in code with each other about school, our friends, our wild (for that room) adventures.

We were not fooled into rash confessions there, for at the merest hint of misadventure, the book came down like a coffin lid on Caesar or Claudius. Oh, we confessed, we were just exaggerating! Of course we didn't raid the dorm kitchen at midnight; our friends did. "Tell me who your friends are," he said in Spanish, "and I'll tell you who you are." No, we hadn't gotten help on our math. "The man who reaches the summit following another's trail will not find his way back to his own valley." If he caught us, hurrying, scurrying, here, there, he stopped us midflight to tell us what Napoleon had said to his valet, "Dress me slowly—I'm in a hurry."

But why look beyond one's own blood for good examples? "You come from good stock," he bragged when I came home from boarding school, my pride wounded. I'd been called names by some great-great-granddaughters of the American Revolution. "You tell them your great-grandfather was the son of a count." He had paid a lot of money on a trip to Barcelona to find that out from a man who claimed he was licensed to do family trees. The elaborate chart, magnificently framed in curlicued wood, hung in the waiting room of his office in Spanish Brooklyn, along with his medical degrees. His patients, I suppose, were meant to be reassured that their ailments would be treated, not only by the valedictorian of the faculty of medicine of La Universidad de Santo Domingo, but also by the descendant of a count. "We were in this hemisphere before they were. In fact, the first Americans—"

"You don't understand, you don't understand," I wailed, hot tears welling in my eyes. And I closed the door of my room, forbidding anyone to enter.

"What's she doing in there, Mami?" I heard him ask her.

"I don't know. Writing poetry or something."

"Are you sure? You think she's all right?"

I had been reading Sylvia Plath, and my talk was spiked with suicide.

"These girls are going to drive me crazy!" my mother said. "That's what I'm sure of. One of them has to have straight hair. Straight hair, at this stage of the show! Another wants to spend the weekend at a boy's school. All the other girls get to! This one wants to die young and miserable!" She glared at my father as if it were all his fault. "I'm going to end up in Bellevue!" she yelled. "And then you'll all be safe and sorry!" I heard her rushed steps down the stairs, the bang of the screen door, finally the patter of water as she hosed down the obedient grass in the growing darkness.

He knocked first. "Hello?" he asked tentatively, the door ajar. "Hello, hello, Edgar Allan Poe," he teased, entering. He sat at the foot of my bed and told me the story of his life.

"The point is," he concluded, " 'La vida es sueño y los sueños, sueños son.' " He stood by the window and watched Mami watering her fussy bushes as if she could flush roses out of them. "My father," he turned to me, "used to say that to my mother: 'Life is a dream, Maurán, and dreams are dreams.' "

He came across the shadowy room as if he did not want anyone to overhear. It was getting late. In the darkening garden she would be winding the hose into drooping coils. "Always, always," he said. "I always wanted to be a poet. 'La vida es sueño. They also serve who only stand and wait. To be or not to be.' Can you imagine? To say things that can fill the mind of another human being!" I nodded, too stunned at his flood of words to ask him what he meant. "Everyone gets a little something," he cupped his hands towards me, "and some make a great building." He made a building with a wave of his hand. "Some," he rubbed his thumb and index finger together, "make money. Some make friends, connections, you know. But some, some make something that can change the thinking of mankind!" He smacked his forehead with his palm in amazement. "Think of the Bible. Think of your friend Edgar Allan Poe. But then," he mused, "then you grow older, you discover . . ." He looked down at me. I don't know what he saw in my eyes, perhaps how young I still was, perhaps his eyes duplicated in my face. He stopped himself.

"You discover?" I said.

But he was already halfway across the room. "Papi?" I tried to call him back.

"Your mother," he explained, letting himself out of the room and the revelation. "I think she is calling for me."

A few days later as I sat in his bedroom after supper, waiting for him to fall asleep, I tried to get him to finish his sentence. He couldn't remember what he was about to say, he said, but speaking of discoveries, "We're descended from the conquistadores, you know? Your grandfather traveled the whole north coast on horseback! Now there was a great man!" The supporting evidence was slim. "He looked like an Irishman, big and pink-tinted—what is that word? Rowdy?"

"You mean *ruddy*?" I said, knowing Don José de Jesús was probably ruddy with drink and rowdy with women. He had sired twenty-five children, was widowed once, and kept a couple of mistresses who raised the figure to thirty-plus children. Of course, my father never told us that; Mami did when she explained how one of our uncles could have been born within two months of my father's birthday. She cautioned us never ever to mention to Papi what she had told us.

The youngest did, pretending ignorance, practicing addition. If Teolinda, the first wife, had ten children, and Maurán, the second one, had fifteen, and ten of the kids had already died, then how come there were still thirty uncles and aunts left? "They were not hijos de padre y madre," he explained. "You know where that term came from? *Hijos de padre y madre?* When the Spaniards—"

"Where did the extra uncles and aunts come from?" My youngest sister was not one to be diverted by a red herring

55

twitching in the sun when a skeleton was rattling in the closet.

So, so, he said. The time had come. The uncles and aunts were half-brothers and -sisters. The mothers were wives, yes, in the eyes of God, where it really mattered.

When we raised our eyebrows and pressed the smile out of our lips, he would have none of it. Customs changed. Our grandfather was a patriotic man. There had been a terrible epidemic, the island was underpopulated, the birthrate was low, the best men did what they had to do. "So," he looked pointedly at each of us. "There's a good ejemplo for you. Always put in that extra little bit in whatever you do," he said, lifting up the history of Constantinople or Machu Picchu or Rome.

His mother? He sighed. His mother was a saint. Sweet, very religious, patience personified, always smiling. They didn't make them like that anymore, with a few exceptions. He winked at me.

But since Maurán knew about the half-children, and was very religious, she must have believed that she and her husband would spend eternity separated. I imagined her as a dour and dowdy woman, alternately saying her rosary when her husband transgressed and having his children when he didn't.

"Does Mami remind you of her?" I asked, thinking that leading questions might help him remember what he had been about to say in my room a few nights before.

"Your mother is a wonder," he said. A good woman, so devoted, so thorough, a little nervous, so giving, a little forceful, a good companion, a little too used to her own way, so generous. "Every garland has a few thorns," he added.

"I heard that," she said, coming into the room. "What was that about too used to my own way?"

"Did I say that, girls?" My father turned to us. "No, Mami, you misheard."

"Then what did you say?"

"What did I say, girls?"

We shrugged, leaving him wide open.

"I said, Mami," he said, unwrapping a rare second mint and putting it into his mouth to buy time, "I said: so used to giving to others. Your mother has a heart full of gold," he addressed his daughters.

"Ay, put gravy on the chicken." She waved him off, obviously pleased as my father winked at our knowing looks.

A few nights later, still on the track of his secret self, I asked him, "Papi, how do you see yourself?" Only I, who had achieved a mild reputation as a deep thinker, could get away with such questions.

"You ask important questions," he mused, interrupting Napoleon's advance across the Russian steppes. "I like that."

He offered me my mint and unwrapped his. "I am the rock," he said, nodding.

"Ay, Papi, that's so impersonal. How do you perceive yourself? What kind of man are you?" I was young and thought such definitions could be given and trusted. I was young and ready to tear loose, but making it harder for myself by trying to understand those I was about to wound.

"I am a rock," he repeated, liking his analogy. "Your mother, you girls, my sisters, everyone needs my support. I am the strong one!"

That admission put a mermaid on the rock, luring me back with a touching song about loss and youth's folly and the loneliness of the father. "But, Papi," I whispered as I moved from the armchair to the foot of his bed, "you don't always have to be strong."

That was my mistake. The conversation was over. He hated touching scenes; they confused him. Perhaps as the last child of an older, disappointed woman, he was used to diffuse attention, not intimacy. To take hold of a hand, to graze a cheek and whisper an endearment were beyond him. Tenderness had to be mothered by necessity: he was a good doctor. Under the cover of Hippocrates' oath, with the stethoscope around his neck and the bright examination light flushing out the personal and making any interchange completely professional, he was amazingly delicate: tapping a bone as if it were the fontenelle of a baby, easing a patient back on a pillow like a lover his sleeping beloved, stroking hair away from a feverish forehead. But now he turned away.

He fell asleep secretly in that room full of presences, my mother beside him. We looked at him during a commercial or when a slip of the tongue had implicated us in some forbidden adventure. The book had collapsed like a card house on his chest and his glasses rode down the bridge of his nose like a schoolmarm's. But if we got up to leave and one of us reached for his glasses, he woke with a start. "I'm not asleep!" he lied. "Don't go yet, it's early."

He fell asleep in the middle of the Hundred Days while Napoleon marched towards Waterloo or, defeated, was shipped off to St. Helena. We stifled our giggles at his comic-book snores, the covers pulled up to his ears, his nose poking out like a periscope. Very quietly, widening our eyes at each other as if that might stop any noise, we rose. One turned off the set and threw a kiss at Mami, who put her finger to her lips from her far side of the bed. Another and another kiss traveled across the hushed room. A scolding wave from my mother hurried my sisters out.

I liked to be the one who stayed, bending over the bedside table strewn with candy wrappers, slipping a hand under the tasseled shade. I turned the switch on, once. The room burst with brighter light, the tassels swung madly, my mother signaled to me, crossly, Out! Out at once! I shrugged apologies. Her scowl deepened. My father groaned. I bent closer. I turned the switch again. The room went back into economical darkness.

La Gringuita:
On Losing a Native Language

· · · · · · · ·

The inevitable, of course, has happened. I now speak my native language "with an accent." What I mean by this is that I speak perfect childhood Spanish, but if I stray into a heated discussion or complex explanation, I have to ask, "Por favor ¿puedo decirlo en inglés?" Can I please say it in English?

How and why did this happen?

When we emigrated to the United States in the early sixties, the climate was not favorable for retaining our Spanish. I remember one scene in a grocery store soon after we arrived. An elderly shopper, overhearing my mother speaking Spanish to her daughters, muttered that if we wanted to be in this country, we should learn the language. "I do know the language," my mother said in her boarding-school English, putting the woman in her place. She knew the value of speaking perfect English. She had studied for several years at Abbot Academy, flying up from the Island to New York City, and then taking the train up to Boston. It was during the war, and the train would sometimes fill with servicemen, every seat taken.

One time, a young sailor asked my mother if he could sit in the empty seat beside her and chew on her ear. My mother gave him an indignant look, stood up, and went in search of the conductor to report this fresh man. Decades later, hearing the story, my father, ever vigilant and jealous of his wife and daughters, was convinced—no matter what my mother said about idiomatic expressions—that the sailor had made an advance. He, himself, was never comfortable in English. In fact, if there were phone calls to be made to billing offices, medical supply stores, Workman's Compensation, my father would put my mother on the phone. She would get better results than he would with his heavy, almost incomprehensible accent.

At school, there were several incidents of name-calling and stone-throwing, which our teachers claimed would stop if my sisters and I joined in with the other kids and quit congregating together at recess and jabbering away in Spanish. Those were the days before bilingual education or multicultural studies, when kids like us were thrown in the deep end of the public school pool and left to fend for ourselves. Not everyone came up for air.

Mami managed to get us scholarships to her old boarding school where Good Manners and Tolerance and English Skills were required. We were also all required to study a foreign language, but my teachers talked me into taking

French. In fact, they felt my studying Spanish was equivalent to my taking a "gut course." Spanish was my native tongue, after all, a language I already had in the bag and would always be able to speak whenever I wanted. Meanwhile, with Saturday drills and daily writing assignments, our English skills soon met school requirements. By the time my sisters and I came home for vacations, we were rolling our eyes in exasperation at our old-world Mami and Papi, using expressions like *far out,* and *what a riot!* and *outta sight,* and *believe you me* as if we had been born to them.

As rebellious adolescents, we soon figured out that conducting our filial business in English gave us an edge over our strict, Spanish-speaking parents. We could spin circles around my mother's *absolutamente no* by pointing out the flaws in her arguments, in English. My father was a pushover for pithy quotes from Shakespeare, and a recitation of "The quality of mercy is not strained" could usually get me what I wanted. Usually. There were areas we couldn't touch even with a Shakespearean ten-foot pole: the area of boys and permission to go places where there might be boys, American boys, with their mouths full of bubblegum and their minds full of the devil.

Our growing distance from Spanish was a way in which we were setting ourselves free from that old world where, as girls, we didn't have much say about what we could do with our lives. In English, we didn't have to use the formal *usted* that immediately put us in our place with our elders. We were responsible for ourselves and that made us feel grown-up. We couldn't just skirt culpability by using the reflexive: the bag of cookies did not finish itself, nor did the money disappear itself from Mami's purse. We had no one to bail us out of American trouble once we went our own way in English. No family connections, no tío whose name might open doors for us. If the world was suddenly less friendly, it was also more exciting. We found out we could do things we had never done before. We could go places in English we never could in Spanish, if we put our minds to it. And we put our combined four minds to it, believe you me.

My parents, anxious that we not lose our tie to our native land, and no doubt thinking of future husbands for their four daughters, began sending us "home" every summer to Mami's family in the capital. And just as we had once huddled in the school playground, speaking Spanish for the comfort of it, my sisters and I now hung out together in "the D.R.," as we referred to it, kibitzing in English on the crazy world around us: the silly rules for girls, the obnoxious behavior of macho guys, the deplorable situation of the poor. My aunts and uncles tried unsuccessfully to stem this tide of our Americanization, whose main expression was, of course, our use of the English language. "Tienen que hablar en español," they commanded. "Ay, come on," we would say as if we had been asked to go back to baby talk as grown-ups.

By now, we couldn't go back as easily as that. Our Spanish was full of English. Countless times during a conversation, we were corrected, until what we had to say was lost in our saying it wrong. More and more we chose to answer in English even when the question was posed in Spanish. It was a measure of the growing distance between ourselves and our native culture—a distance we all felt we could easily retrace with just a little practice. It wasn't until I failed at first love, in Spanish, that I realized how unbridgeable that gap had become.

That summer, I went down to the Island by myself. My sisters had chosen to stay in the States at a summer camp where the oldest was a counselor. But I was talked into going "home" by my father, whose nephew—an older (by twenty years) cousin of mine—had been elected the president of El Centro de Recreo, the social club of his native town of Santiago. Every year at El Centro, young girls of fifteen were "presented" in public, a little like a debutante ball. I was two years past the deadline, but I had a baby face and could easily pass for five years younger than I was—something I did not like to hear. And my father very much wanted for one of his daughters to represent la familia among the crème de la crème of his hometown society.

I arrived with my DO-YOUR-OWN-THING!!! T-shirt and bell-bottom pants and several novels by Herman Hesse, ready to spread the seeds of the sixties revolution raging in the States. Unlike other visits with my bilingual cousins in the capital, this time I was staying in a sleepy, old-fashioned town in the interior with Papi's side of the family, none of whom spoke English.

Actually I wasn't even staying in town. Cousin Utcho, whom I called *tío* because he was so much older than I was, and his wife, Betty—who, despite her name, didn't speak a word of English either—lived far out in the countryside on a large chicken farm where he was the foreman. They treated me like a ten-year-old, or so I thought, monitoring phone calls, not allowing male visitors, explaining their carefulness by reminding me that my parents had entrusted them with my person and they wanted to return me in the same condition in which I had arrived. Out there in the boonies, the old-world traditions had been preserved full strength. But I can't help thinking that in part, Utcho and Betty treated me like a ten-year-old because I talked like a ten-year-old in my halting, childhood Spanish. I couldn't explain about women's liberation and the quality of mercy not being strained, in Spanish. I grew bored and lonely, and was ready to go back to New York and call it quits on being "presented," when I met Dilita.

Like me, Dilita was a hybrid. Her parents had moved to Puerto Rico when she was three, and she had lived for some time with a relative in New York. But her revolutionary zeal had taken the turn of glamour girl rather than my New-England-hippy variety. In fact, Dilita looked just like the other Dominican girls. She had a teased hairdo; I let my long hair hang loose in a style I can only describe as "blowing in the wind." Dilita wore makeup; I did a little lipstick and maybe eyeliner if she would put it on for me. She wore outfits; I had peasant blouses, T-shirts, and blue jeans.

But in one key way, Dilita was more of a rebel than I was: she did exactly what she wanted without guilt or apology. She was in charge of her own destino, as she liked to say, and no one was going to talk her into giving that up. I was in awe of Dilita. She was the first "hyphenated" person I had ever met whom I considered successful, not tortured as a hybrid the way my sisters and I were.

Dilita managed to talk Utcho into letting me move into town with her and her young, married aunt, Carmen. Mamacán, as we called her, was liberal and light-hearted and gave us free rein to do what we wanted. "Just as long as you girls don't get in trouble!" Trouble came in one denomination, we knew, and neither of us were fools. When the matrons in town complained about our miniskirts or about our driving around with boys and no chaperons, Mamacán threw up her hands and said, "¡Pero si son americanas!" They're American girls!

We hit it off with the boys. All the other girls came with their mamis or tías in tow; Dilita and I were free and clear. Inside of a week we both had boyfriends. Dilita, who was prettier than I, landed the handsome tipo, tall Eladio with raven-black hair and arched eyebrows and the arrogant stance of a flamenco dancer, whereas I ended up with his chubby sidekick, a honey-skinned young man with wonderful dimples and a pot belly that made him look like a Dominican version of the Pillsbury doughboy. His name was Manuel Gustavo, but I affectionately nicknamed him Mangú, after a mashed plantain dish that is a staple of Dominican diet. A few days after meeting him, Mangú's mother sent over an elaborate dessert with lots of white frosting that looked suggestively like a wedding cake. "Hint-hint," Dilita joked, an expression everyone was using at her school, too.

Every night the four of us went out together: Dilita sat up front with Eladio, who had his own car, and I in the backseat with Mangú—a very cozy boy-girl arrangement. But actually, if anyone had been listening in on these dates, they would have thought two American girlfriends were out for a whirl around the town. Dilita and I yakked, back and forth, starting first in Spanish out of consideration for our boyfriends, but switching over into English as we got more involved in whatever we were talking about. Every once in a while, one of the guys would ask us, "¿Y qué lo que ustedes tanto hablan?" For some reason, this request to know what we were talking about would give us both an attack of giggles.

Some times, Eladio, with Mangú joining in, sang the lyrics of a popular song to let us know we were being obnoxious:

> Las hijas de Juan Mejía
> son bonitas y bailan bien
> pero tienen un defecto
> que se rien de to' el que ven.
>
> (The daughters of Juan Mejía
> dance well and are so pretty
> but they've got one bad quality,
> they make fun of everybody.)

Las gringuitas, they nicknamed us. Delita didn't mind the teasing, but Mangú could always get a rise out of me when he called me a gringa. Perhaps, just a few years away from the name-calling my sisters and I had experienced on the school playground, I felt instantly defensive whenever anyone tried to pin me down with a label.

But though he teased me with that nickname, Mangú made it clear that he would find a real gringa unappealing. "You're Dominican," he declared. The litmus test was dancing merengue, our national, fast-moving, lots-of-hip-action dance. As we moved across the dance floor, Mangú would whisper the lyrics in my ear, complimenting my natural rhythm that showed, so he said, that my body knew where it came from. I was pleased with the praise. The truth is I wanted it both ways: I wanted to be good at the best things in each culture. Maybe I was picking up from Dilita how to be a successful hybrid.

Still, when I tried to talk to Mangú about something of substance, the conversation foundered. I couldn't carry on in Spanish about complicated subjects, and Mangú didn't know a word of English. Our silences troubled me. Maybe my tías were right. Too much education in English could spoil a girl's chances in Spanish.

But at least I had Dilita to talk to about how confusing it all was. "You and I," she often told me as we lay under the mosquito net in the big double bed Mamacán had fixed for us, "we have the best of both worlds. We can have a good time here, and we can have a good time there."

"Yeah," I'd say, not totally convinced.

Down on the street, every Saturday night, the little conjunto that Eladio and Mangú had hired would serenade us with romantic canciones. We were not supposed to show our faces, but Dilita and I always snuck out on the balcony in our baby dolls to talk to the guys. Looking down at Mangú from above, I could see the the stiffness of the white dress shirt his mother had starched and ironed for him. I felt a pang of tenderness and regret. What was wrong with me, I wondered, that I wasn't falling in love with him?

After the presentation ball, Dilita left for Puerto Rico to attend a cousin's wedding. It was then, when I was left alone with Manuel Gustavo, that I realized that the problem was not me, but me *and* Manuel Gustavo.

Rather than move back to the lonely boonies, I stayed on in town with Dilita's aunt for the two weeks remaining of my visit. But without Dilita, town life was as lonely as life on a chicken farm. Evenings, Mangú would come over, and we'd sit on the patio and try to make conversation or drive out to the country club a borrowed car to dance merengue and see what everyone else was doing. What *we* were doing was looking for people to fill up our silence with their talk.

One night, Mangú drove out towards Utcho's chicken farm and pulled over at a spot where often the four of us had stopped to look at the stars. We got out of the car and leaned against the side, enjoying the breeze. In the dark, periodically broken by the lights of passing cars, Mangú began to talk about our future.

I didn't know what to say to him. Or actually, in English, I could have said half a dozen ambivalent, soothing things. But not having a complicated vocabulary in Spanish, I didn't know the fancy, smooth-talking ways of delaying and deterring. Like a child, I could just blurt out what I was thinking. "Somos diferente, Mangú." We are so different. The comment came out sounding inane.

"No, we're not," he argued back. "We're both Dominicans. Our families come from the same hometown."

"But we left," I said, looking up at the stars. From this tropical perspective, the stars seemed to form different constellations in the night sky. Even the Big Dipper, which was so easy to spot in New England, seemed to be misplaced here. Tonight, it lay on its side, right above us. I was going to point it out to Mangú—in part to distract him, but I could not remember the word for *dipper*—la cuchara grande, the big spoon?

But Mangú would not have been interested in the stars anyway. Once it was clear that we did not share the same feelings, there was nothing much left to say. We drove back to Mamacán's house in silence.

I don't know if that experience made Mangú forever wary with half-breed Dominican-York girls, *gringuitas,* who seemed to be talking out of both sides of their mouths, and in two different languages, to boot. I myself never had a Spanish-only boyfriend again. Maybe the opportunity never presented itself, or maybe it was that as English became my dominant tongue, too many parts of me were left out in Spanish for me to be able to be intimate with a potential life partner in only that language.

Still, the yearning remained. How wonderful to love someone whose skin was the same honey-dipped, sallow-based color; who said *concho* when he was mad and *cielito lindo* when he wanted to butter you up! "¡Ay! to make love in Spanish . . .," the Latina narrator of Sandra Cisneros's story, "Bien Pretty," exclaims. "To have a lover . . . whisper things in that language crooned to babies, that language murmured by grandmothers, those words that smelled like your house. . . ." But I wonder if after the Latina protagonist makes love with her novio, she doesn't sit up in bed and tell him the story of her life in English with a few palabritas thrown in to capture the rhythm of her Latin heartbeat?

As for Manuel Gustavo, I met up with him a few years ago on a visit to the Island. My husband, a gringo from Nebraska, and I were driving down the two-lane autopista on our way up to the mountains on a land search. A pickup roared past us. Suddenly, it slowed and pulled onto the shoulder. As we drove by, the driver started honking. "What does he want me to do?" my husband shouted at me. I looked over and saw that the driver was still on the shoulder, trying to catch up with us. I gestured, what do you want?

"Soy yo," the man called out, "Manuel Gustavo."

Almost thirty years had passed. He had gotten heavier; his hairline had receded; there was gray in his hair. But the dimples were still there. Beside him sat a boy about seven or eight, a young duplicate of the boy I had known. "Mangú!" I called out. "Is that really you?"

By this time my husband was angry about the insanity of this pickup trying to keep up with us on the narrow shoulder while Mack trucks roared by on the other lane. "Tell him we'll stop ahead, and you guys can talk."

But the truth was that I didn't want to stop and talk to Manuel Gustavo. What would I have said to him now, when I hadn't been able to talk to him thirty years ago? "It's good to see you again, Mangú," I shouted. I waved good-bye as my husband pulled ahead. In my side mirror, I watched as he signaled, then disappeared into the long line of traffic behind us.

"Who was that?" my husband wanted to know.

I went on to tell my husband the story of that summer: the presentation; Utcho and Betty; my worldly-wise friend Dilita; Eladio, who looked like a flamenco dancer; the serenades; the big double bed Dilita and I slept in with a mosquito net tied to the four posts. And of course, I told him the story of my romance with Manuel Gustavo.

And, as I spoke, that old yearning came back. What would my life have been like if I had stayed in my native country?

The truth was I couldn't even imagine myself as someone other than the person I had become in English, a woman who writes books in the language of Emily Dickinson and Walt Whitman, and also of the rude shopper in the grocery store and of the boys throwing stones in the schoolyard, their language, which is now my language. A woman who has joined her life with the life of a man who grew up on a farm in Nebraska, whose great-grandparents came over from Germany and discouraged their own children from speaking German because of the antipathy that erupted in their new country towards anything German with the outbreak of World War I. A woman who is now looking for land in the Dominican Republic with her husband, so that they can begin to spend some time in the land she came from.

When we took the turnoff into the mountains, we rolled up our windows so we could easily hear the cassette player. My husband had ordered Spanish-language tapes a while back from the Foreign Service Institute so that he could keep up with my family in the capital. Recently, he had dusted them off and started listening to them to prepare himself for our land hunt. I had decided to join him in these lessons, in part to encourage him, but also because I wanted to regain the language that would allow me to feel at home again in my native country.

Picky Eater

· · · · · · · ·

I met my husband in my late thirties, and when we were beginning to date, I was surprised by his preoccupation with food. "Can we go out to dinner?" was, I believe, the second or third sentence out of his mouth. That first date, we ate at a local restaurant, or I should say, he ate and talked, and I talked and picked at my food. "Didn't you like your stir-fry?" he asked me when the waitress removed my half-eaten plate.

"Sure, it was okay," I said, surprised at this non sequitur. We had been talking about India, where he had recently done volunteer surgery. I hadn't given the food a thought—except in ordering it. Being a picky eater, my one criterion for food was, is it something I might eat? Once it met that standard, then it was okay, nothing to think or talk too much about.

Mostly, if I was eating out, I didn't expect food to taste all that good. This was a carryover from my childhood in a big Dominican family in which the women prided themselves on the fact that nobody could put a meal on the table like they could put a meal on a table. You went out for the social purpose of seeing and being seen by your friends and neighbors, but you never went out to have a good meal. For that, you stayed home or went over to a relative's house, where you could be sure that the food was going to be prepared correctly—that is, hygienically—and taste delicious.

Perhaps this bias had to do with the fact that I grew up in the 1950s in a small underdeveloped country where there were very few tourists and, therefore, few eating establishments that catered to pleasure dining. The common comedores were no-nonsense, one-room eating places for workers, mostly male, who all ate the same "plate of the day," on long tables with small sinks and towels in a corner for washing their hands and toothpicks for cleaning out their teeth when they were done. Little stands on the street sold fried pastelitos or frío-frío in paper cones or chunks of raspadura wrapped in palm leaves, treats I was never allowed to taste.

Eating en la calle was strictly forbidden in my family. We came home from school at noon for the big dinner meal. On long trips into the interior to visit Papi's family, we carried everything we might need on the way, including water. It was dangerous to eat out: you could get very sick and die from eating foods that had gone bad or been fixed by people who had diseases you could catch. In fact, the minute any of us children complained we didn't feel right, the first question asked of our nursemaids was "Did they eat anything on the street?"

My mother and aunts were extremely careful about food preparation. Had the vegetables been properly peeled and boiled so that no microbios were left lodged in the skins? Was the lettuce washed in filtered water? Since electricity, and therefore refrigeration, were not dependable, was the meat fresh or had it been left to lie around? During certain seasons in the tropics, some kinds of fish carry toxins—so that had to be taken into account as well. Had the milk been pasteurized? Had tarantulas gotten into the sugar or red ants into the cocoa powder? To get a healthy meal on the table seemed to be an enterprise laden with mythic dangers—no wonder a street vendor couldn't be trusted.

In short, I cannot remember ever eating out at a restaurant before coming to live in this country. The one exception was La Cremita, an ice cream shop that had recently opened up near the hospital. On Sundays, after we'd accompanied him on his rounds, my father took my sisters and me to La Cremita, where we picked out one small scoop apiece of our favorite helado. "Don't tell your mother," my father would say. I don't know if he was worried that my mother would accuse him of ruining our appetites before the big Sunday afternoon meal at my grandparents' house or if he was afraid she would fuss at him for exposing us to who knows what microbios the owners might have put into those big vats of pistachio or coconut or mango ice cream.

But even when we ate perfectly good, perfectly healthy food at home, my sisters and I were picky eaters. I remember long postmeal scenes, sitting in front of a plate of cold food, which I had to finish. One "solution" my mother came up with was a disgusting milk drink, which she called engrudo. Whatever my sisters and I left on our plates was ground up and put in a mixer with milk. This tall glass of greenish brown liquid was then placed before us at the table. We were given a deadline, five minutes, ten minutes. (It seemed hours.) At the end of that time if we had not drunk up our engrudos, we were marched off to our rooms to do time until my father came home.

In defense of engrudos, I have to say that my sisters and I were very skinny and not always healthy. One sister had a heart ailment. Another had polio as a young child. I myself lost most of my hair at age three from a mysterious malady. The doctors finally diagnosed it as "stress." (Probably from having to drink engrudos!) My mother worried herself sick (literally, with bad migraines) that her children would not make it through childhood. In a country where the infant mortality rate was shockingly high, this was not an irrational worry. Of course, most of these young deaths tended to be among the poor who lacked proper nutrition and medical care. Still, in my father's own family, only one of his first ten siblings survived into adulthood.

And so childhood meals at home were battlegrounds. And even if you won the dinner battle, refusing to clean your plate or drink your engrudo, you inevitably lost the war. Weekly, my sister and I got "vitamin shots," B12 and liver, which really were for "our own good." But to this day, every time I go to the doctor and have to have blood drawn, I feel a vague sense that I am being punished for not taking better care of myself.

Once we came to this country, the tradition of family meals stopped altogether. We were suddenly too busy to eat together as a family. Breakfasts were catch-as-catch-can before running down the six or seven blocks to school. We kept forgetting our lunches, so Mami finally gave up and doled out lunch money to buy what we wanted. What we wanted was the "junk food" we had never before been allowed to eat. My sisters and I started putting on weight. I think we all gained five or ten pounds that first year. Suddenly I had leg and thigh and arm muscles I could flex! But what good were they when there were no cousins to show them off to? As for dinner—now that Papi was working so hard and got home late at night, we couldn't have this meal together, either. My sisters and I ate earlier whenever the food was done. When Papi got home, he ate alone in the kitchen, my mother standing by the stove warming up a pot of this or that for him.

In a few years, when my father's practice was doing better, he started coming home in time to join us for dinner. Actually, he had shifted his hours around so that, instead of staying at the office late at night, he opened at five-thirty in the morning. This way, his patients, many of them Latinos with jobs in *factorías,* could see the doctor before going to work on the first shift. Since Papi had to get up at four-thirty, so he could dress, have breakfast, and drive the half hour or so to Brooklyn, we ate dinner the minute he got home. As soon as he finished eating, my father would go upstairs and get ready for bed.

My mother and my sisters and I stayed behind at the table, Mami eating her Hershey bars—she'd pack in two or three a night, but then put Sweet'n Low in her cafecito! Now that her daughters were in the full, feisty bloom of adolescent health, she no longer worried over our eating habits or got insulted if we didn't eat her cooking. She had hired a Dominican maid to do the housework, so she could spend the day helping Papi out at his oficina. Lunch was take-out from a little bodega down the street. It was safe to eat out now. This was America. People could be put in jail for fixing your food without a hair net or serving you something rotten that made you sick to your stomach.

The family plan had always been to go back home once the dictatorship had been toppled. But after Trujillo's assassination in 1961, politics on the Island remained so unstable that my parents decided to stay "for now." My sisters and I were shipped off to boarding school, where meals again became fraught with performance pressures. We ate at assigned tables, with a teacher, a senior hostess, and six other girls. The point was to practice "conversational skills" while also learning to politely eat the worst food in the world. Everything seemed boiled to bland overdoneness. And the worst part of it was that, as in childhood, we had to eat a little serving of everything, unless we had a medical excuse. My father, who was still as much of a spoiler as back in his La Cremita days, agreed to let me fill in the infirmary form that asked if we had any special allergies or needs. I put down that I was allergic to mayonnaise, brussels sprouts, and most meats. No one, thank God, challenged me.

In college, at the height of the sixties, I finally achieved liberation from monitored eating. Students had to be on the meal plan, unless they had special dietary needs. A group of my friends applied to cook their own macrobiotic meals in a college house kitchen, and I joined them. I soon discovered vegetarianism was a picky eater's godsend. You could be fussy *and* high-minded. Most meats were on my inedible list already, and mayonnaise was out for macrobiotics who couldn't eat eggs. As for brussels sprouts, they were an establishment vegetable like parsnips or cauliflower, something our parents might eat as an accompaniment to their meat.

All through my twenties and thirties as a mostly single woman, my idea of a meal was cheese and crackers or a salad with anything else I had lying around thrown in. I don't think I ever used the oven in my many rentals, except when the heat wasn't working. As for cooking, I could "fix" a meal, that is, wash lettuce, open a can, or melt cheese on something in a frying pan, but that was about the extent of it. The transformations and alchemy recorded in cookbooks were as mysterious to me as a chemistry lab assignment. Besides, once I got a soufflé or a lasagna out of the oven, what was I supposed to do with it? Eat it all by myself? No, I'd rather take a package of crackers and a hunk of cheese with me in my knapsack to work. For an appetizer, why not a cigarette, and for dessert, some gum?

When I had friends over, a meal was never the context. Some other pretext was—listening to music, reading a new poetry book together, drinking a cup of coffee or a bottle of wine, munching on some more cheese and crackers. I'd clear off the dining table, which I had been using as my desk, to hold this feast of bottles and boxes and packages and ash trays.

Had I had a family, I would no doubt have learned how to cook persuasive, tasty meals my children would eat. I would have worried about nutrition. I would have learned to knit the family together with food and talk. But just for myself, I couldn't be bothered. Cooking took time. Food cost money. I was too busy running around, earning a living, moving from job to low-paying job. Sometimes I lived in boarding-houses where I didn't even have access to a kitchen. I grew as thin in my twenties and thirties as I had been as a child. My mother began to worry again about my eating. Maybe I had a touch of that anorexia disease American girls were increasingly getting?

"No," I protested, shades of engrudos lurking in my head. I preferred to think of myself as a picky eater. But probably all these bad eating habits and attitudes are "kissing cousins." Eating is dislodged from its nurturing purpose and becomes a metaphor for some struggle or other. My own experience with food had always been fraught with performance or punishment pressures. No wonder I didn't enjoy it, didn't want to deal with it, didn't want to cook it, or even serve it. (My one waitressing job lasted less than a week. I kept forgetting what people had ordered and bringing them the wrong things.)

Of course, there was a way in which my whole apprehensive approach to food fell right in with the American obsession with diets and fear of food additives and weight gain. As a child, I had never heard of diets, except as something that people who were ill were put on. It was true that women sometimes said they were watching their figure, but it was vain and rude to stick to a diet when someone had gone to the trouble of putting some tasty dish on the table before you. The story is still told of my coquettish great-grandmother who was always watching her "little waist." She would resolve to keep a strict diet—only one meal per day, but then, approaching the table, she would invariably be tempted by an appetizing dish. "Well," she'd say, "I'm going to have lunch but I'll skip supper." At supper, she again couldn't resist what was on the table. "Well," she'd say, "I'm

Picky Eater

going to have a little supper, but I'll skip breakfast." By the time she died in her nineties, she owed hundreds upon hundreds of skipped meals.

And so, when at thirty-nine I married a doctor who was very involved with food and food preparation, I seemed to be returning to the scene of earlier emotional traumas to settle some score or exorcise some demon. A divorced father with two teenage daughters, my new husband had learned to cook out of necessity. Since his boyhood on a farm in Nebraska, he had always been involved in growing food, but the responsibility of nurturing his two girls as a single parent had turned him into a chef. Enter: one picky eater.

"What would you like to eat tonight?" my husband would ask me over the phone when he called me at lunch from his office. "I don't know," I'd say. Did I really have to make up my mind now about what I was going to eat in seven or eight hours?

With all this food planning and preparation going on around me, I started to worry that I was not pulling my share. One night, I announced that I thought we should each make dinner every other night. My husband looked worried. The one time I had invited him over to my house for dinner before we were married, I had served him a salad with bottled dressing and a side plate of fried onions and tofu squirted with chili sauce. This is a story my husband likes to tell a lot. I am always aggrieved that he forgets the dinner rolls, which I bought at the Grand Union bakery, something I would normally not do, since I much preferred crackers as "the bread" to have with my dinner.

But he liked doing the nightly cooking, he explained. It was his way to relax after a day at the office. Why not just

83

help him out? I could do the shopping, which he didn't like to do. It turned out that he had to be very specific about what he put on the list or I would get "the wrong thing": baking powder instead of baking soda, margarine instead of butter. "You're so picky!" I would say, not always immediately aware of the irony. One stick of yellow grease was very much like another.

I also helped with making dinner, though he gave me so little to do, beyond washing the lettuce and keeping him company while he did the rest, that I began to suspect he didn't trust me even to help. Finally, we settled that I would be in charge of making the desserts. For months we had brownies, which were really quite good when I remembered to put the sugar in.

Meals, which had been something I did while doing something else, now took up big blocks of time, especially on Sundays, when Bill's parents came over for dinner. First, we had soup, and then when we were done with the soup, several platters made the rounds, and then there was dessert. Then, coffee. During all these courses there was much talk about what we were eating and other memorable variations of what was on the table. If you were to take one of those pies statisticians use to show percentages and were to cut out a serving that would represent how much of the time we talked about food, I would say you'd have to cut yourself at least half the pie, and probably a second serving before the night was over. It took so long to eat!

True, when I was a young girl, the weekly dinners in my grandparents' house were long, lingering family affairs, but that was true only for the adults. Once we children got through the chore of finishing what was on our plates, we would be excused to go play in the garden while the grown-ups droned on over their everlasting courses and cafecitos. (No engrudos when we ate at somebody else's house!)

But now, I was one of those adults at the table of a family that was obviously bound together, not at the hip, but the belly. Traditionally, my husband's people have been farmers, intimately connected with food—growing it, serving it, preserving it, preparing it. As we lingered at the table, I listened, not understanding at first what the fuss was about. What was the difference between a Sun Gold tomato and a Big Boy? Why was sweet corn better than regular corn? What was the difference between a Yukon Gold and a baking potato? What did it mean when they said raspberries were setting on? And how come the second crop was always bigger, juicier?

Eventually, I realized that if I ate slowly and kept my ears opened, I could learn a lot. I also started to taste the food, instead of swallowing it, and slowly I developed new criteria—not just, would I eat it or not? Did the flavors work together? Was the polenta bland or the bread chewy enough? As my own cooking repertoire expanded beyond brownies, I discovered the wonderful pleasure of transforming a pile of ingredients into a recipe that nurtured and sometimes delighted the people I love. It was akin to writing a poem, after all.

Now, eight years into sharing our table, my husband and I have developed a fair and equitable cooking arrangement. I am in charge of certain recipes—and not just desserts. I've even learned to cook certain meats for him and his parents, though I still don't eat them. For holidays, when the house is humming with beaters, hissing with steamers, beeping with oven timers, I feel the pulse of happiness whose center is the kitchen.

But I admit that years of picky eating don't vanish over-night. I still worry when we go out if there will be anything in the category of things-I-eat. There are still times when I walk back from the kitchen and spy my husband and his family gathered at the table, talking away about the differ-ence between this week's crust and last week's crust or how you can get the peak in those whipped potatoes or individual grains in the rice, and I wonder if I belong here. Will I ever stop feeling as if I've wandered into one of those Norman Rockwell scenes of a family sitting around a table laden with platters and pies? But each time I've put down what I had in my hands — my contribution to the feast — and looked around, I've found a place set for me at the table.

Briefly, a Gardener

· · · · · · · ·

From my study window I watch my husband out on his tractor plowing under the row of sweet corn that has done so well for him this summer. Despite his medical training, farming is his first love. May through September he comes home from the office with a gleam in his eye, kisses me a quick hello, races upstairs to change into his work clothes, and goes to catch the last few hours of light, to plow or harvest or carry water in the bucket loader from tree to tree when there's a drought.

I've tried to share his passion with him, just as he has tried to share mine. Many a weekend morning, he has sat before a new manuscript with strict instructions to be "critical," to tell me exactly what he doesn't like. Often the manuscript comes back to me with a few spelling errors corrected or a note in the margin saying that I can't have sheep lambing in July because that's too late to have sheep lambing if I've set the story in Vermont. "So what else?" I ask him.

"What else what?" he wants to know. I see his eyes drifting over my shoulder. The window behind me gives him a great view of his latest farming project—a strip of wildflowers sown between the sweet corn and the sunflowers. The sun has already dried the dew on the grass. He should be out there pulling the buckwheat that is invading those wildflowers. "I think it's perfect," he says.

I sigh, torn between pleasure at his unconditional praise and a desire to have one of those George Eliot/George Henry Lewes liaisons, Leonard Woolf/Virginia Woolf marriages, Gertrude Stein/Alice B. Toklas partnerships, where the couple sits by a fire talking about the life of the imagination. And yet how can I hide my admiration for who he is? He knows about real life, real things, real tomatoes and cucumbers that we can really eat. All I know can be put between the covers of a book, and it won't feed the hungry or fill the kitchens of the poor. His surplus feeds a clutch of grateful, elderly women in the condo complex where his own ex-farming parents now live, women on fixed incomes who prize a basket of Roma tomatoes or Yukon Gold potatoes or yellow peppers, delicacies that only the rich can buy in gourmet groceries.

And so in admiration, in shame, in a desire to understand how sitting on a tractor, haying, can be as much fun as reading and writing—I announce that I, too, will share in the gardening this year. "Give me a little tiny thing I can do," I ask him. "Something manageable. Something I won't destroy with my ignorance."

He has to think about it, which surprises me. I admit I share in the arrogance of the bookish who believe farmers don't have to be very smart. Nature tells them what to do. We thinkers have to come up with solutions on our very own.

"I've got it," he says a day or two later, coming into my study where I am working on a story that has been giving me trouble. "We'll make you a little raised bed—"

(Eight years ago when we met in the grocery store—he remembers I was buying a big plastic bottle of Sprite; he was buying buttermilk—I would have guessed a raised bed is what ex-hippies started to sleep on once they decided to get their mattresses up off the floor.)

"—a small raised bed and you can have an herb garden, how's that?"

"Terrific," I say. I like the sound of it, an herb garden. But I should guess where my heart is when the next words out of my mouth—had I not checked them—would have been, "Call me when it's ready."

"I'll get it ready for you, okay?" he offers as if he has read my thoughts. "But you'll have to tell me what herbs you want in it."

"Herbs," I muse. I'm in the thick of a passage of dialogue that doesn't sound right. Would the daughter really say that to her father? Given this preoccupation, it's hard to come up with the names of some herbs. Then I recall how my mother used to buy tidy little satchets of herbs, called bouquets garnis. What was in those things?

"I don't know, honey," I finally give up. His bright face falls. He has been so excited about my new project, my wanting to share in his passion. Surely, I can come up with the name of one or two herbs, and then, knowing him, he'll take over the herb garden; he'll plant a whole load of herbs, buckets that the elderly population in our town can use to spice up their bland New England boiled suppers. He just wants to see that I am involved. That I really want this herb garden.

"I know," I say, thinking about our shelf of herbs and spices downstairs. Musical names roll off my tongue. "How about some rosemary and cardamom and cloves. . . . ?" I'm on a roll, I'm thinking, but he is shaking his head, and then, suddenly, he's laughing.

"Honey," my husband finally says, when he has stopped laughing, "I'm afraid cloves and rosemary and cardamom wouldn't do very well in Vermont."

For the umpteenth time I wonder what I am doing in my husband's Nebraskan farm family. I recall that at Sunday supper his mother had registered surprise that a middle-aged woman neighbor of hers was not married. "She can cook up such a good peach pie!" I sat there thinking, O my God, *not* cooking a good peach pie is probably grounds for divorce in Nebraska.

WE PLOT AND we plan, and finally, the herbs are settled in, oregano and thyme, some chives, a little parsley. I feel so proud of myself that I can identify the specifics of this clutter of green. I walk around the garden proudly in my boots with my garden gloves and shiny garden spade he has bought me in anticipation of our gardening partnership. He has praised how pretty my bed looks. He has helped me pick some flowers and ground cover to put into the bare spots, some dusty miller and three kinds of thyme as well as lavender and bee balm, valerian, sage, and something called veronica which I picked out at Agway because I liked the name. Everything is noted in my journal. I get ambitious, and I go out on my own and buy a columbine, a lovely anemone, a lupine, and something else that when it starts to bloom I search fruitlessly for in my flower book and journal. I must have forgotten to write its name down or stick its tag in the ground. It bothers me that I can't point to my mystery flower and announce, "And that's a lady's mantle," or whatever.

I drive over to Agway to see if I can't find this flower and copy down its name in my journal. But the sales guy has sold out on many of his specimens during last week's sale. He can't find another duplicate of what I'm describing: the drizzly little leaves, the pretty whitish flowers, the kind of purply buds that hang this-a-way from the stem. "I really don't have any more, lady," he concludes after we've examined every one of his slats of perennials. "Whadda ya hafta know the name for anyways?"

I keep my mouth from dropping. After all, I have to live with the people in this small town long after whatever it is has withered in the frosts of October. "I wouldn't want anything in my garden I can't name," I feel like saying in a snooty voice. Instead I say, apologetically—because people in gardening stores, in car parts stores, in garages do make me feel uneasy and ignorant—"I just like to know the names of things in my garden, that's all."

I drive home defeated. The map of my garden in my journal has a blank spot, the list of my plantings is incomplete. I find my husband busy in my herb garden. He seems disappointed in me.

"I thought you said you were going to weed this," he points to the small plot whose perfection has decreased with each passing day. Everything is running into everything else. But my journal is a jewel of thorough record-keeping and naming. Except for my one omission. "Why didn't you tell me you were going out?" he wants to know.

"You were on your tractor," I say accusingly. We both know what that means. How many times haven't I tried to catch his attention when an emergency call has come in, running behind the tractor throwing little stones in the air and hollering at him? We have had fights about this. I want him to carry a beeper. He insists that real farmers don't carry beepers. Yeah, I fight back. They marry wives who turn their ankles running after their tractors, calling them in for a snack of fresh milk and warm peach pie.

"Anyhow, I went to Agway," I say self-righteously. Agway is where serious, nonshopping men like him go of a Saturday afternoon to buy something they need for their fields and gardens.

"Agway?!" he repeats, alarmed. He has already told me to stop buying things. The herb garden is small. It cannot accommodate every plant whose name I like.

"Yeah, Agway. You know how I bought all those plants last week? Well, I lost the tag to that flower—" I point.

But my beauty is gone! The drizzly little leaves, the pretty whitish flowers, the kind of purply buds that hang this-a-way on the stem! Now the blank spot is not just in my journal but in my garden as well.

"Where did you put it?" I ask accusingly.

"You mean this here," he holds up a wilted, green stem. It looks like the plant world's equivalent of a plucked chicken. "It's a weed, my dear."

"It is not!" I shoot back. I see through this trick. In a fit of annoyance at my leaving the weeding in my herb garden to him, he plucks my mystery flower and then, when I catch him at it, he tells me it's a weed. "I bought it at Agway."

He is shaking his head and laughing the same laugh as when I told him I wanted to grow cardamom in Vermont. "If you did buy it at Agway, you can sue them for false product-labeling."

"Okay, okay," I stand up, eyes narrowed. "If it's a weed, then name it."

Of course, he doesn't know. And he's got a perfect excuse. "It's a weed. Weeds don't have names."

That is the silliest thing I ever heard! "That's like saying people you dislike don't have inner lives or something. If weeds don't have names, they should," I proclaim. And with that fine point made, I make an exit indoors to put on my gear and shoo him out of my herb garden. I'll do the weeding myself, thank you. He raises his hands, palms out. "It's all yours," he says. "And believe me, it needs a good weeding." Off he goes to his alfalfa strip, his pumpkin patch, his raspberry canes, his thriving fields that manifest his good husbanding.

I squat amid the plenty I've ignored for weeks, turning the soil, and savoring the names of the herbs and flowers before me: woolly thyme, mother of thyme, veronica, sage, chives, oregano, valerian, and then, there it is, my mystery flower, again and again and again.

Imagining Motherhood

· · · · · · · ·

Finally, in late fall 1995, my last childless sister became a mother. Forty, single, unlucky in finding a lifelong match, she decided to have a baby on her own. In anticipation of the phone call from the Dominican Republic that would let her know a baby had been found, my sister painted her spare bedroom a soft lavender; she went shopping for baby clothes; she considered a dozen names and heard feedback on possible awful nicknames that might come of them; she baby-proofed her house. And she talked and talked and talked about the upcoming baby.

Every time she'd start in, I'd feel my chest tightening. Pushing its thorny head through the veneer of cheeriness and encouragement was that old monster all sisters are well acquainted with: jealousy. It was like being back in childhood, in the full of summer, with my sister anticipating her big birthday party in July while mine had already gone by way back in March.

My other two sisters had raised their babies in a flurry of diapers and photo albums full of the cute little critters. That was back in my early thirties. I loved my niece and nephews to bits. I uncurled their tiny infant hands, smelled their baby-powder skin, wrote them poems on every occasion, but I was glad to hand them over at the end of the visit and get back to my writing.

You mean they didn't stop howling like that when you wanted to finish a chapter? They had to be driven to what? Suzuki recorder lessons, just when your editor called with a request you had to mail out that night? No, thanks. I'd gladly be the godmother, sending birthday checks and little gifts, but as for being the good mother, well, I just didn't have the time.

Then suddenly mid-forty, I realized what most of my women friends must have realized in high school. We *are* mortal. We don't have an endless supply of time. By now, I'd already used up half of mine or more, and I had only a couple of years left if I truly wanted a child. I could always adopt, but I had to make up my mind soon or I'd be following that poor kid to school on my walker, for heaven's sake.

But it was more than a biological clock that was ticking away; it was a familial one as well. In my family of four sisters, two and two is a fine balance, but if three sisters go a certain route, the fourth sister can't bear the loneliness and caves in to the majority choice. It's the old story of women living together in a house; their menstrual periods will eventually synchronize.

With us, it went further—we all got married within the space of a few years, at least the first time around. Overnight, we all had the same sensible short haircut because our sixties manes were just too hard to keep up (and made us look passé). Then, we all seemed to find silk one Christmas, shimmering loose outfits that freed us to move without constraints (no funny bras safety-pinned to things we had to be careful not to tear, no tight waistlines reminding us that we were eating too much of Mami's flan de guayaba). Only two stayed in long-term marriages, leaving the other two to commiserate over the dearth of good middle-aged men.

Then last November, my compañera in childlessness, my baby sister and fellow maverick, became a mami. When she called from the Dominican Republic with the news, I burst into tears. "I'm so . . . happy," I sobbed, "so, so happy."

And I was. Who wouldn't be? To have my beautiful niece suddenly bringing up the rear of the next generation of our family! Had any child ever been so cute! I mean, Benetton babies, beware! I went through my town, showing off photos. On the way home, it struck me that I was acting as if I were the proud mother. But it was my sister's birthday party. Again, I burst into tears.

"Nothing in the world compares to this, nothing," my sister kept saying. I finally asked her to please stop saying so, please.

Because the yearning hit strong. Suddenly, I noticed there were babies everywhere. Every junior colleague had a babe in her arms, and these moms were getting their writing done as well. How did younger women learn to do that? As for my women friends—those old-world fems, as these younger women now refer to us—my "old" friends were suddenly busy with babies, too. Most of them, having reared their children, had joined me in our knockabout middle years, their empty nests looking a whole lot like my one-person one. But now they were becoming grandmothers of beautiful grandbabies they couldn't stop talking about.

By this time, I had remarried, but alas, my husband's two daughters were grown girls I couldn't sit on my knee and cuddle. So, of course, the question came up: Why not have or adopt our very own child?

"What do you think?" I kept asking Bill.

His face would get a stricken look. He had already raised his babies, and though it was worth (almost) every minute of it, he didn't want to start all over again at fifty. He was at the stage I was in during my late twenties and thirties when I wanted to give those pooping, wailing babies back to their mothers.

But hearing my tearful plaints month after month, he finally caved in. "If it's something you really think you have to have, I'll do it for you."

With the choice presented in terms of what *only* I wanted, the same indecisiveness struck again. Oh, I knew Bill would rally one hundred percent to become a father. Still, hadn't I been inside marriages where my life's direction was dictated by a partner's passion, not my own? How long and dreary that road can become! And at our age—a phrase I find myself saying more and more—there just isn't time to be taking too many tangents away from where we have left to go.

But my decision was not ultimately a submission to Bill's preference. I had to face the fact that it had been my own choice not to become a mother. The thought of putting aside—even for just a few years—what I had always considered my real calling, the writing, putting it aside now in my mid-forties when I was finally hitting my full stride, gave me cold feet. I came to realize with that straight, clear-eyed vision of a writer analyzing her fictional characters that I didn't really want to be a mother solely for the sake of being a mother.

Yet I still felt the pressure to at least say I wanted to be a mother. For all our talk of feminism and pro-choice, willful childlessness continues to have a bad reputation. That Victorian view of childless women as not fully realized lingers. A woman who doesn't care to have a child is considered foolish at best. At worst, as I heard one lecturer proclaim, she is "committing genetic suicide."

Among my friends and acquaintances in rural Vermont, the rearing, educating, and taking care of children has been a major focus of their lives. "You're lucky," they tell me, but beyond a momentary weariness, what I hear in their voices is a secret pride at the fecundity of their lives.

And if being childless is unusual in rural Vermont, it is mucho más odd in my own Latin culture, where being a woman and a mother are practically synonymous. Being childless—by choice—is tantamount to being wicked and selfish. Marriage is a sacrament for the procreation of children, how many times have my old tías told me that? Even the one family holdout, my maiden aunt who grew orchids and read books and knew Latin, finally married in her thirties and had her one child. "I won't deny," she has told me, "that this has been the most significant event of my life."

Ever since I married Bill, the pressure has mounted. On my annual visit to the Island, the inevitable question pops up, Don't I want a child? More tactful aunts approach the topic through my eating habits. Don't I know I have to put aside that vegetarian foolishness in order to strengthen my body for a child? "But you have to have your niño," my aunt's maid told me. It's mandatory, she might as well have said. Last year, when my sister adopted, I almost canceled my trip.

"That'll make you feel even worse," my husband wisely counseled. He was right.

The only way to come to terms with the yearning was to accept that it was a loss. Just as never having learned a musical instrument or never having become a bullfighter or a ballerina is a loss. As is never having grown up in the Dominican Republic amid my own people; never having learned the languages to read Dante, Tolstoy, Rilke in the original. All these are losses now—instead of possibilities to be left open—because I know that given my age, there isn't time enough for all that I once meant to do with my life. You can't have everything, our mothers used to tell us. So why *is* it that our me generation tends to feel cheated if we can't have everything? Maybe part of accepting childlessness is accepting this rude fact.

But in accepting my chosen loss, I've come to realize that, ironically, I was grieving over the loss to my writing more than anything else. A good part of my sudden, last-minute reconsideration of motherhood has sprung from a writer's approach to life: I do not want to miss out on a valuable experience that might help me to understand people better, that might inform my spirit and intelligence, make me a better human being, and (dare I say it?) a better writer.

As my best woman friend, thrice a mother, and recently a new grandmother reminds me: What is the imagination for if everything requires life experience? She's right. I can imagine motherhood. I don't need to subject a child to my writerly personal growth experience, if that's what I'm after. Spare the poor kid a grandmother-mother who wears dentures. (I can just imagine a whole new category of your-mama-wears-army-boots jokes!) Now, when I travel to my native Dominican Republic, and my tías inquire after my sister and her new baby, and winking at Bill, ask us if we don't feel inspired, I will have to say, "Yes, I feel inspired."

Inspired, that is, to come home and write about it.

A Genetics of Justice

. . . .

Perhaps because I was spared, at ten, from the dictatorship my parents endured most of their lives, I often imagine what it must have been like for them growing up under the absolute rule of Generalísimo Rafael Leonidas Trujillo.

Especially, I imagine my mother's life. Respectable families such as hers kept their daughters out of the public eye, for Trujillo was known to have an appetite for pretty girls, and once his eye was caught, there was no refusing him.

My mother must have been intrigued. She knew nothing of the horrid crimes of the dictatorship, for her parents were afraid to say anything—even to their own children— against the regime. So, as a young girl, my mother must have thought of El Jefe as a kind of movie star. She must have wanted to meet the great man.

Images of the dictator hung in every house next to the crucifix and la Virgencita with the declaration beneath: *In this house Trujillo is Chief.* The pale face of a young military man wearing a plumed bicorne hat and a gold-braided uniform looked down beneficently at my mother as she read her romantic novelas and dreamed of meeting the great love of her life. Sometimes in her daydreams, her great love wore the handsome young dictator's face. Never having seen him, my mother could not know the portrait was heavily retouched.

By the time my mother married my father, however, she knew all about the true nature of the dictatorship. Thousands had lost their lives in failed attempts to return the country to democracy. Family friends, whom she had assumed had dropped away of their own accord, turned out to have been disappeared. My father had been lucky. As a young man, he had narrowly escaped to Canada after the plot he had participated in as a student failed. This was to be the first of two escapes. That same year, 1937, El Generalísimo ordered the overnight slaughter of some eighteen thousand Haitians, who had come across the border to work on sugarcane plantations for slave wages. It was from my father that my mother learned why Trujillo hated blacks with such a vengeance, how he disguised his own Haitian ancestry, how he lightened his skin with makeup.

Perhaps because she had innocently revered him, my mother was now doubly revolted by this cold-blooded monster. He became something of an obsession with her—living as she was by then in exile with my father, isolated from her family who were still living on the Island. As my sisters and I were growing up, Trujillo and his excesses figured in many of my mother's cautionary tales.

Whenever we misbehaved, she would use his example as proof that character shows from the very beginning. One such story showed the seeds of Trujillo's megalomania. As a child, Trujillo had insisted his mother sew coke bottle tops or chapitas to his shirt front so that he could have a chest of medals. Later, the underground's code name for him would be Chapita because of his attachment to his hundreds of medals.

When my sisters and I cared too much about our appearance, my mother would tell us how Trujillo's vanity knew no bounds. How in order to appear taller, his shoes were specially made abroad with built-in heels that added inches to his height. How plumes for his Napoleonic hats were purchased in Paris and shipped in vacuum-packed boxes to the Island. How his uniforms were trimmed with tassels and gold epaulettes and red sashes, pinned with his medals, crisscrossing his chest. How he costumed himself in dress uniforms and ceremonial hats and white gloves—all of this in a tropical country where men wore guayaberas in lieu of suit jackets, short-sleeved shirts worn untucked so the body could be ventilated. My mother could go on and on.

At this point I would always ask her why she and my father had returned to live in the country if they knew the dictatorship was so bad. And that's when my mother would tell me how, under pressure from his friends up north, Trujillo pretended to be liberalizing his regime. How he invited all exiles back to form political parties. How he announced that he would not be running in the next elections. My father had returned only to discover that the liberalization was a hoax staged so that the regime could keep the goodwill and dollars of the United States.

My father and mother were once again trapped in a police state. They laid low as best they could. Now that they had four young daughters, they could not take any chances. For a while, that spark which had almost cost my father his life and which he had lighted in my mother seemed to have burnt out. Periodically, Trujillo would demand a tribute, and they would acquiesce. A tax, a dummy vote, a portrait on the wall. To my father and other men in the country, the most humiliating of these tributes was the occasional parade in which women were made to march and turn their heads and acknowledge the great man as they passed the review stand.

If you did not march, your cédula would not be stamped, and without a stamped identification card, you could do nothing; in particular, you could not obtain your passport to leave the country under the pretext of wanting to study heart surgery. This was the second escape—this time with his whole family—that my father was planning.

The day came when my mother had to march. The parade went on for hours in the hot sun until my mother was sure she was going to faint. Her feet were swollen and hurting. The back of her white dress was damp with sweat. Finally when she thought she could not go one more step, the grandstand came into sight, a clutter of dress uniforms, a vague figure on the podium.

When I run through my mother's memory of this parade, there is a scene I imagine that she has not told me about. My mother walks into El Jefe's line of vision, the parade stops. Somebody ahead of Mami has fainted, and orderlies are rushing forward with their stretcher to resuscitate the woman in question. Under her breath, my mother is cursing this monster who drags thousands of women out on the hot streets to venerate him. She looks up at him, and what she sees makes it all worthwhile, somehow.

For there, no more than ten steps away, he stands, a short, plump man sweating profusely in his heavy dress uniform. The medals on his chest flash brightly in the hot sun so that he looks as if he has caught on fire. She can see the rivulets of sweat under his Napoleonic hat, making his pancake makeup run down his face, revealing the dark skin beneath. I invent this scene because I want my mother to see what she cannot yet imagine: El Jefe coming undone.

Eventually, the parade moved on, and my mother marched out of sight. It was the one and only time that my mother saw, up close, the man who had ruled her imagination most of her life.

ON MAY 30, 1961, nine months after our escape from our homeland, the group of plotters with whom my father had been associated assassinated the dictator. Actually, Dominicans do not refer to the death as an assassination but as an *ajusticiamiento,* a bringing to justice. Finally, after thirty-one years, Trujillo was brought to justice, found guilty, and executed.

But the execution was an external event, not necessarily an internal exorcism. All their lives my parents, along with a nation of Dominicans, had learned the habits of repression, censorship, terror. Those habits would not disappear with a few bullets and a national liberation proclamation. They would not disappear on a plane ride north that put hundreds of miles distance between the Island and our apartment in New York.

And so, long after we had left, my parents were still living in the dictatorship inside their own heads. Even on American soil, they were afraid of awful consequences if they spoke out or disagreed with authorities. The First Amendment right to free speech meant nothing to them. Silence about anything "political" was the rule in our house.

In fact, my parents rarely spoke about the circumstances of our leaving the Island. To us, their daughters, they offered the official story: my father wanted to study heart surgery. We were not told that every night our house had been surrounded by black Volkswagens; that the SIM had been on the verge of arresting my father; that we had, in fact, *escaped* to the United States. But this great country that had offered my parents a refuge had also created the circumstances that made them have to seek refuge in the first place. It was this same United States that had helped put our dictator in place during their occupation of the country from 1916 to 1924. As Secretary of State Cordell Hull had said, Trujillo is an SOB, but at least he's our SOB. About all these matters, my parents were silent, afraid that ungratefulness would result in our being sent back to where we had come from.

My mother, especially, lived in terror of the consequences of living as free citizens. In New York City, before Trujillo was killed, Dominican exiles gathered around the young revolutionary Juan Bosch planning an invasion of the Island. Every time my father attended these meetings, my mother would get hysterical. If the SIM found out about my father's activities, family members remaining behind were likely to be danger. Even our own family in New York could suffer consequences. Five years earlier, in 1955, Galíndez, an exile anti-Trujillo teaching at Columbia University, had disappeared from a New York subway. The same thing could happen to us.

I don't know if my father complied or just got too busy trying to make a living in this country. But after a few months of hotheaded attendance, he dropped out of these political activities and his silence deepened. During my early teen years in this country, I knew very little about what was actually going on in the Dominican Republic. Whenever la situación on the island came up, my parents spoke in hushed voices. In December 1960, four months after our arrival, *Time* magazine reported the murder of the three Mirabal sisters, who along with their husbands had started the national underground in the Dominican Republic. My parents confiscated the magazine. To our many questions about what was going on, my mother always had the ready answer, "En boca cerrada no entran moscas." No flies fly into a closed mouth. Later, I found out that this very saying had been scratched on the lintel of the entrance of the SIM's torture center at La Cuarenta.

Given this mandate of silence, I was a real thorn in my mother's side.

SHE HAD NAMED me, her second of four daughters, after herself—so we shared the same name. Of all her babies, she reports, I was the best behaved, until I learned to talk. Then, I would not shut up. I always had to answer her back when I disagreed with her. Childhood was rocky, but adolescence was a full-fledged war.

Still, my mother found ways of controlling me. The Trujillo cautionary tales worked momentarily, in that I loved to hear those outlandish stories. Her threats to disown me for being disrespectful were more effective. The definition of disrespect—as she had learned in the dictatorship—was anything short of worship. When Eleanor Roosevelt's grandson published a biography of his famous grandmother, my mother said he should be ashamed of himself for calling his grandmother "a plain woman."

"But she was a plain woman," I argued. "That's just saying the truth."

"Truth! What about honoring his grandmother?" My mother's eyes had that look she saw in my eyes when she said, "If looks could kill . . ."

Unfortunately for my mother, I grew up to be a writer publishing under my maiden name. At first, my mother flushed with personal pride when friends mistook her for the writer. "The poem in your Chrismas card was so beautiful! You're quite the poet, Julia!" But after I became a published writer, friends who had read a story or an essay of mine in some magazine would call up and say, "Why, Julia, I didn't know you felt that way. . . ." My mother had no idea what ideas she was being held responsible for. When I published a first novel with a strong autobiographical base, she did not talk to me for months.

Then I started to work on my second novel. My mother heard from one of my sisters that I was writing about the dictatorship. The novel would be a fictional retelling of the story of three Mirabal sisters, contemporaries of my mother, whose murder had been reported in that confiscated *Time* magazine. This time, my mother warned, I was not just going to anger family members, but I would be directly reponsible for their lives. There were still old cronies of the dictator around who would love an excuse to go after my family, after my father, after her.

This was one of the hardest challenges I had ever had to face as a writer. If my mother were indeed speaking the truth, could I really put my work above the lives of human beings? But if I shut up, wouldn't I still be fanning the embers of the dictatorship with its continuing power of censorship and control over the imagination of many Dominicans? I talked to my cousins in the Dominican Republic and asked them if my mother's dire predictions had any foundation. "The old people still see a SIM agent under every bush!" they said, shaking their heads.

When the novel came out, I decided to go ahead and risk her anger. I inscribed a copy to both Mami and Papi with a note: "Thank you for having instilled in me through your sufferings a desire for freedom and justice." I mailed the package and—what I seldom do except in those moments when I need all the help I can get—I made the sign of the cross as I exited the post office. Days later, my mother called me up to tell me she had just finished the novel. "You put me back in those days. It was like I was reliving it all," she said sobbing. "I don't care what happens to us! I'm so proud of you for writing this book."

I stood in my kitchen in Vermont, stunned, relishing her praise and listening to her cry. It was one of the few times since I had learned to talk that I did not try to answer my mother back. If there is such a thing as genetic justice that courses through the generations and finally manifests itself full-blown in a family moment, there it was.

Family Matters

. . . .

E ver since I became a published writer, my family has been trying to figure out where the writing talent came from. The Espaillats have always been poets, one uncle (on the Espaillat side) noted. Another uncle believed that I probably got the writing genes from my father's side of the family.

I can't help thinking that maybe my writing genes, in fact, come directly from my father. When we emigrated to this country and my father had to start over as a doctor, he gave up his other life's ambition of writing books. Instead, he wrote weekly letters to my sisters and me in boarding school in which he detailed the adventures of a young boy, Babinchi, an autobiographical version of himself. At the end of each letter was the little moral we should learn from this recent scrape Babinchi had gotten himself into.

My sisters and I would roll our eyes, but in fact, we cared very much for those letters, "the favorite" bragging that she had gotten the original as opposed to one of three carbon copies. (Papi finally figured out how to sidestep our jealousy by regularly rotating the carbons.) Obviously, I have gotten a touch of the poet from him.

It's nice to have the family finally arguing over who can lay claim to me. In fact, it's the fulfillment of the childhood desire in the playground to be picked for one of the teams instead of left over to be taken on as a handicap: "Okay, we'll take Alvarez, but we get to have four outs instead of three."

For so many years, I was an embarrassment that my parents had to explain to the rest of the Dominican family. Those were knockabout years of sporadic employment, failed marriages, eccentric lifestyles. ("What is a group home?" an old tía once asked me.) The thing that had gone wrong with my sisters and myself, according to the extended family back home, was that we had settled in the United States of America where people got lost because they didn't have their family around to tell them who they were. Instead, they spent their lives, wandering around, doing crazy things trying "to find themselves."

The family was partly right, of course. My sisters and I entered this country *and* our turbulent teens at the height of the sixties, in the company of friends who were, many of them, dropping out of their families, joining communes, demonstrating against the war, spending the night in jail or in someone-they-weren't-married-to's bed. Meanwhile, back home, our female cousins were having their quinceañera parties in which they waltzed with their papis in sight of any relative still able to sit upright and sip a rum-coke.

By twenty-five, many were leading settled lives with children, households, a battalion of maids to do their bidding. They knew who they were, Alvarez or Tavares, Bermúdez or Espaillat. But in America, you didn't go by what your family had been in the past, you created yourself anew. This was part of the excitement as well as the confusing challenge of America.

Well, at long last, after almost thirty years of self-creation, I began publishing novels, which were well received. Now my family saw those endless years of struggle in a whole new light. I had shown this poetic talent from the beginning, and they had always known it. I had never let mishaps or misfortunes and unemployment get in my way.

The change in their attitude proves, if nothing else, how even our memories favor the classic Aristotelian structure of narrative—with a beginning, middle, and end. If the ending is "happy," then the events that precede it suddenly light up with meaningful significance.

But where *did* it come from, this writing talent? It is a family habit, after all, to trace the features of its present members back to the faces of the ancestors. Every time a new grandchild or grand niece arrives, the old tías stand around the crib, trying to decide whose nose little Gaby is wearing. Those hands are pure Rochet. The ears are González. As for the dark skin, that comes from the Gómez side.

It gratifies me that whatever talent I do have might have come from somewhere else. For one thing, it clears me of blame for upsetting those same members of my family when they actually sit down and read what I've written. But also it reminds me that I am just one more embodiment of that force for expression and clarity and comprehension which has nothing specifically to do with me, or just with me. As Jean Rhys, another writer with a strong connection to the Caribbean, once said to a young writer wanting some advice, "Feed the sea, feed the sea. The little rivers dry up, but the sea continues." All that we write and achieve as individuals means finally very little compared to the great body of work—books, music, dance, art, inventions, ideas—that forms the culture and context of our human family.

But as we droplets head for the sea, the tributary that forms the channel in which we travel, the current that thrusts us forward, the very composition of the water that makes up our droplets are our history, our families and neighborhoods and countries of origin, all of the forces that have shaped us and continue to shape us as persons and, therefore, as writers. For me, with my childhood history set in the Dominican Republic, family was the only neighborhood and country of origin I knew, and so it matters in a way that nothing else has since, except the writing.

I am talking now primarily about my extended familia in the Dominican Republic, complete with uncles and aunts and cousins and great-aunts and godmothers and political uncles and aunts of affection and nannies who wiped my bottom when I was a baby and so can tell me what to do even if I am a married woman with graying hair and six books.

Part of the reason I've always felt at home in rural American settings, especially in the South, is that in these places, family—in the extended and historical sense—still operates as the basic social unit. Not office staffs, health clubs, therapy groups, women's groups, play groups, or even nuclear family groups; not AA or Masonic clubs or where you went to college or even the United States of America, but

FAMILY in the big, everlastingly messy and complicated way of my Dominican family.

I see myself primarily in the context of this childhood family, rather than in the family I joined a few years ago with my husband and his two daughters and his siblings and "Mom and Dad" from Nebraska. Perhaps if my husband and I had married earlier in our lives, I would think of *our* family as the family I talk about when I talk about family. I would have looked in the faces of our children trying to find this next generation's borrowing of parts. Instead, I see myself as coming into *his* family, which has allowed me to perch on one of the branches of its family tree, even though it is clear that I am a bird of a different feather altogether, a tropical parrot, say, who has flown in from her jungle to this northern forest of pine and fir trees.

Or perhaps my even thinking so shows how powerful that first allegiance to la familia continues to be. When the wiring in my head was being spliced together; when, as I read recently about infants, my newborn brain was a big plate of spaghetti piled high with all the genes I was born with, which now it was environment's turn to sort out; in other words, when I was a little girl growing up in the Dominican Republic in the company of my mother's sister and brothers and their families and my grandparents, all living in close proximity in nearby houses, la familia was the only world I knew. Even the school I went to had its beginnings as a family school. The story goes that Carol Morgan, an American missionary and a friend of my grandmother, Mamita, was giving lessons to her children at home. When Mamita found out, she asked her friend to take on the family children. Thus was born "the Carol Morgan School."

And so the only other world I knew outside the family—my school world—was also filled with family.

At home, we were raised by the extended family, the cousins all hanging out in a pack in the large communal garden that connected several pieces of property. If one cousin got the chicken pox, we were all thrown together, so the whole brood could go through that childhood illness at once. Birthdays were celebrated in big parties for the crop of births of that season. Once a year, Papi brought home his doctor's bag, and everyone got their vaccinations. I remember the stampede of little girl cousins into one of the bedrooms where they locked themselves up, howling that they didn't need shots. The boys lined up bravely, and I, who wanted so much to be one of them, was the first on the line since the doctor was *my* father.

"Did it hurt?" one of the girl cousins would ask, sniffling as she was led forward from the bedroom. The gardener had thrust a broom handle in the window, lifted the latch, and the aunts dashed in to fling open the door. "Not at all," I would boast, then clutch my side and fall down dead on the floor. I was a little hellion all right. The hellion gene had come from the big hellion in the family, my grandmother, who winked at me whenever I misbehaved.

But one thing that was not tolerated was acting up *against* the family. I still remember being in a fistfight with my cousin, and my aunt separating us and saying, in effect, "You can't do that, you're primos hermanos," literally, brother-cousins.

"Come meet an uncle," was the way I was introduced to a stranger who had been allowed entry into our family circle. If someone was not related by blood or marriage, he or she probably had some connection to someone related to us, "This is your tío Manuel's classmate from Yale." The ultimate compliment, of course, was, this is someone who is "just like family. Call him *tío!*" In my father's more old-fashioned family, the added command was, "He's your tío. Bésale la mano." Kiss his hand.

La familia were the only people I was taught to trust. We were living in a dictatorship with a network of spies operating everywhere. Even in private homes, the maid or gardener could be informing on the owners. Organizations toed the party line just as individuals did. The Catholic Church and its hierarchy offered weekly Te Deums in honor of the dictator and homilies praising his regime. Your co-worker could spread lies about you. Even your parish priest might turn you in. But no matter what, la familia would stand by you.

The fate of an individual was tied to his family, and vice versa. The first thing Trujillo would do when someone's anti-regime activities were discovered was to go after the whole family. He knew that if someone was disaffected, la familia was probably not far behind. In fact, one of the "signs" that you were a true Trujillista was if you hung the dictator's picture up on your wall of family portraits. Another Trujillo strategy was to become the padrino, or godfather, for hundreds of young babies in mass baptisms. The padrino relationship is sacrosanct: the godfather, in effect, joins the family as a cofather, com-padre. By aligning himself to hundreds of families, Trujillo was ensuring the loyalty of his compadre-countrymen.

When my parents and sisters and I came to this country, we left behind the protection and patronage of the larger familia. We were on our own. In this country, we had only ourselves to count on. "You tell those kids that you come from a good family," my mother would counsel me when I came home from school with bruises on my legs. A gang of boys had chased after me, telling me to go back to where I came from, pelting me with little stones. This was a bitter and more wounding variation of not being chosen to be a member of either team for a game in the school playground.

Our parents, who had always been our protectors, could no longer help us. What good were their epistles and reminders to "comport yourselves" like "gente," like people from nice families? Though they could still try to parent us in the smaller—and it seemed smaller and smaller—family circle, they could not really prepare us for the world they had brought us into. In fact, they were trying hard to survive in it themselves.

Still, they insisted on the old standards, and my sisters and I tried to please them. But how could we keep our mouths shut out of respeto for our parents when, in the very boarding schools they paid for, we were being taught to speak up and debate, if need be, with our teachers? How could we insist that our hippy boyfriends have "marriage as their intention" when no one in our age group was getting married but "living together" instead? And would our parents really have wanted us to marry these hippy types who came from who knows what kind of families? How could we live at home with Mami and Papi when we had to go out and earn a living in jobs that might be halfway across the country? My sisters and I were caught between worlds, value systems, languages, customs. The big question, of course, was, how could we stay in la familia *and* also survive as individuals in our new country.

"Why put up with it?" our American friends counseled. "Be your own person!" But how could we survive outside our family? We had been raised as members of a family, not just individuals. It's as if our faces, hands, feet would disappear if we cut ourselves off from their originals. In fact, the ultimate threat my parents could hurl at us was that they would "disown" us.

"How do you disown your child?" a therapist once asked me, and she didn't mean the question rhetorically, in a plaintive way; she was truly curious. In English, in the United States of America, such a threat sounded implausible; in fact, it sounded operatic and old-world and un-American. There was also the tinkle of money in the phrase, disowning as in disinheriting, as if we were still connected to old money whose flow would stop coming to us now that we had done the unthinkable.

But my sisters and I knew exactly what was meant. It meant if we went off with male friends for a weekend, we didn't have a mother and father, or by extension, la familia, to come back to. It meant if we moved in with boyfriends, we were no longer "part of the family"; we were "dead to the clan"; we couldn't come and ask our father's blessing on his deathbed. . . .

"Huh?" is as close a verbal approximation to the expression on the therapist's face, even while her training led her to nod and say, "I understand."

She didn't understand. One doesn't do that to a child. In America, especially the America of the eighties, treating a child that way was grounds for therapy. In America, also, such dependency on family was considered a form of pathology on our part. Suddenly I would find myself defending my parents even though I, too, was troubled and hurt by their responses. They had been raised in a culture where this was what parents did to a child who broke their hearts. They clipped off that branch from the family tree in order to protect the honor of the larger familia. Or at least they threatened to do so—the branch would soon discover that it could not survive detached from its progenitors

But in this country, the job and social world didn't operate by family alliances, so my sisters and I couldn't be controlled by these old pressures. But still, these threats tugged at our hearts. What else could they tug? It was this mixture of our parents' powerlessness and their power over us that made the whole situation so confusing and painful.

Perhaps if we had been sons, it would have been easier for our parents to allow us the independence we needed in order to survive in this new country. After all, many of their ultimatums and threats had to do with customs, which in the old country could only be broken at a female's peril. Underlying these customs was a basic assumption that as a female you gave yourself to your familia. All other allegiances were secondary to that central one.

We all struggled, but as a writer, I especially found my vocation at odds with my training as a female and as a member of la familia. It was a woman's place to be the guardian of the home and the family secrets, to keep things entre familia, to uphold the family honor (I'm still not sure what this means). A woman did not have a public voice. She did not have a public life, except through her husband, her brothers, her sons, and her endless stream of male cousins.

I remember that same therapist who asked about family disowning remarking to me about a prolonged writer's block, "You probably know all hell will break loose if you write."

"What do you mean?" I asked, baffled. I was known as la poetisa in the family. Wouldn't it be natural and expected for la poetisa to write a book?

"Try it," she said quietly.

I did, and she was right. All hell broke loose. But the worse hell came from the internal familia, that pile of speaking spaghetti in my head. *Your sisters are going to be so mad. Your godfather won't let you kiss his hand. Your cousin will get in more than a fistfight with you. You will be no one without your familia to stand by you.*

I told myself what all writers tell themselves when these voices speak up in their heads, that I was making them up. My fears were getting the better of me. But when my first novel was published—before it received some attention and I was ultimately welcomed back as a kind of minor celebrity in the family—I was surprised at how many of these voices in my head *did* have real counterparts out there in the world of la familia.

"My mother told me never ever to repeat this story," Maxine Hong Kingston begins her memoir, *The Woman Warrior.* And those same words could have been spoken to me by any number of women and men in my family. I had transgressed an unspoken rule of la familia. By opening my mouth, I had disobeyed. By opening my mouth on paper, I had done even worse. I had broadcast my disobedience.

No amount of explaining about the workings of the imagination, about what Flannery O'Connor or Faulkner or Conrad had said about the writer's commitment to the truth of the human heart eased the tide of family disapproval. I was quoting the wrong sources for my family and culture. In a country that is still basically oral, storytelling is the way to tell the facts. The writer Alastair Reid, who has spent many years living in a small vecindad on the north coast of the Dominican Republic, recounts that for most of his neighbors who cannot read or write "their mode, their natural wavelength is to put themselves in story form. They have saved their personal history in the form of a set of stories. . . . Travelling from teller to teller, quite ordinary happenings often turn into wonders."

And so, I grew up hearing that my grandmother was the most beautiful woman on the Island, that my grandfather was so good he peed holy water, that my mother and uncle had a British nanny who turned out to have a police record with the Scotland Yard, and so on. In my familia, fiction *is* a form of fact.

This fictive cast of mind extends, of course, beyond families and small communities to politics and government and to the wider culture. Who more than my Dominican family should understand this? We had undergone thirty-one years of a dictatorship in which the wildest myths had to be accepted as facts on pain of death. The dictator, for instance, decreed the country officially a "white nation" even though we are ninety percent mulatto and proof of that fact is all around us. There was also the fiction presented to the world and acted out by Dominicans that we had a democratic form of government. Every four years the populace went out and voted for the one candidate allowed on the ballot, handpicked by Trujillo. Sometimes this candidate was Trujillo himself!

This is not just a south-of-the-border habit of mind, by

any means. Many North American writers run into similar problems with their families. But I think this is particularly true for writers with complicated, tribal families like my own; writers from areas of the country (like the South) or ethnic groups (like the Italians or Jews) where the basic unit of self-understanding is primarily the family.

One of the family surprises that helped me survive publication fallout was the discovery that la familia, which had always seemed so monolithic to me, was really quite diverse in its opinions. There were camps among my people. It was one of the advantages of coming from a large, tribal family. A couple of cousins were not talking to me—well, there were at least two dozen who were. My uncle was miffed at something on page forty-four? An aunt who had never gotten along with him told me to just put him out of my mind. "He's always been like that, but what are we going to do? He's family."

Being thrown back so fully into the attention of la familia, I also discovered where the writing talent *had* come from. It was not an individual gene, but a family skill, and indeed, as Alastair Reid had noted, a cultural habit. I heard dozens of stories correcting the "fiction" I had written, and then dozens more stories correcting the corrections. "That's not true," an uncle would begin, hearing what another uncle had told me. "What really happened was . . ." The storyteller had brought out the storytelling in the family.

Indeed like any small tribe my familia has its national literature: the family stories. And, of course, so much of my material has been inspired by these stories. I don't mean that my fiction slavishly recounts "what really happened," but that my sense of the world, and therefore of the world I re-create in language, comes from that first encompassing experience of familia with its large cast of colorful characters, its elaborate branchings hither and yon to connect everyone together, its Babel of voices, since everyone has to put his or her spoon in the sancocho. But it isn't only my material—even my manner of telling a story is muy familial, a bittersweet approach, the heart in turmoil but a twinkle in the eye, much like my grandmother winking at my "corpse," or a drunk uncle dancing flamenco on the dining-room table with the secret police knocking at the door.

But what most surprises me—especially since I am now working in another language—is to discover how much of my verbal rhythm, my word choices, my attention to the sound of my prose comes from my native language as spoken by la familia.

"When are you going to write shorter sentences?" one reader asked during the question-and-answer period after one of my book tour readings. I went back to my hotel room and counted words. The next day I bought a paperback of Raymond Carver's stories at the airport bookstore, and when I did the numbers, I saw what my questioner meant: Carver's sentences stayed at a ten-word average; mine were at least twice that. Carver favored simple sentences; I tended towards complex sentences with their subordinate clauses, their appositives, their balanced opposites. (I think you can count all the semicolons in a book by Carver on your two hands.) My sentences were lush, tropical, elaborate, like those of that other southerner, Faulkner, adding a phrase here, and then returning to the main point there, subordinating one clause to another, training the wild, luxuriant language on the trellis of syntax until a dozen bright blooms of meaning burst open for the reader.

In another instance, an editor who was working with me on a magazine story noted that I overused the word "little." A little coffee, a little dessert, a little cough. And sure enough with the computer word-finder I discovered a dozen more examples of my overuse. Then I realized, I was translating from the Spanish diminutive, so common in family usage, where nicknames and small versions of large versions are always being distinguished and derived from each other: Mamayaya, my great-grandmother, as opposed to Mamayoya, my great-aunt, as opposed to Mamita, my grandmother, as opposed to Mami, my mother. There was Julia, called Juyi, my prima hermana (sister-cousin), to distinguish her from Julia, my mother, to distinguish her from Juliminga, that's me, who wrote that terrible book about the family.

It still hurts, of course, not to be accepted by my own. Ironically, I have been given the goods, the style, the genes, the full plate of spaghetti (some would question this assertion) by la familia, only to be cast off—by some members—because they are not pleased with the results. But they are right—these older members that hold to that "old high way" of family honor and ancestor worship. My writing does proceed from a new attitude towards familia, not unquestioning worship, but a desire to see and celebrate human beings in their full complexity rather than as icons.

But it goes further than that—and la familia with its fine nose inherited from any number of shrewd ancestors caught scent of this: as a writer I *have* switched my primary allegiance from *them* to *my* work. My first loyalty is to present as honestly as I can with as much skill as I have my vision of the world according to my lights. Of course, this is a pliant vow, as every writer finds herself making compromises to spare feelings and protect intimacies. We are people in the world, after all, members of families we deeply care for, fragile beings connected to other fragile beings. But beyond this respect for privacy, this care not to damage another's self-respect, there are lots of gray areas that self-interested relations might want to censor out of vanity or fear or a desire to control the family's reputation.

One night on tour in San Francisco or Portland or Seattle I woke up at three in the morning in that cold metaphysical sweat of absolute terror. The spaghetti in my head was talking again. *What's going to happen when your husband deserts you and you don't have your familia to come back to? What's going to happen when you're old and dying and you don't have your familia to comb your white hair and change your diapers? What's going to happen when the tropical parrot flies back to her jungle only to find her feathered butt isn't welcomed anywhere?*

It was too early to bother my agent in New York or my editor in North Carolina, neither of them family that I could treat with such confianza. Instead, I dialed my aunt who has been like a mother to my sisters and myself in the Dominican Republic. "Tía," I asked, my voice shaky, as if I were still a child with bruises on my legs, "you're not going to throw me off if you don't like my book, are you?"

"Ay, Juliminga, of course, I'm not," she promised. "I know how much your writing matters to you," she added when I tried explaining my intentions as a writer.

"La bendición, mi 'ja," she said as we hung up. It was always our custom that she gave me her blessing before we parted.

Bless you, my daughter. I know how much your writing matters. The sweetness of both those statements, so rarely put together! Daughter and writer. Part of la familia and also my own person, that full and impossible combination! Isn't that what we all want — to put it all together and become that bigger version of our selves *and* still be loved by those who have only partially known us?

The work of all of us, not just writers, is to feed that sea, as Jean Rhys put it. What can we offer it, but our very own drop of talent and personal truth, not a special doctored version that will make a certain group feel good or make our lives easier, keep our mothers happy, and promote family honor. And as for my own case, it is my family's fault anyway. Not only did they pass on to me the storytelling gene, but in bringing me up to belong not just to myself but to la familia, they also taught me to give myself to something bigger than myself.

And that is precisely what I find myself doing through the act of writing. In fact, it is through writing that I give myself to a much larger *familia* than my own blood. As Robert Stone told a group of writers one summer at the Bread Loaf Writers' Conference, writing is how we take care of the human family. This is what happens when the little rivers flow down the mountain and lose themselves in the sea.

Part Two

· · · · · · · ·

Declarations

First Muse

· · · · · · · ·

Once upon a time, I lived in another country and in another language under a cruel dictatorship, which my father was plotting to overthrow. But what I remember is not the cruel dictator, not the disappearances, not my parents' nervous voices behind closed doors, but the storybook that helped me get through the long, dull school days that were my understanding of what dictatorships made children do.

I lay on my stomach under my bed, a six-, seven-, eight-, nine-, ten-year-old girl—this went on for a long time, as long times do during childhood. With the bedskirt providing a perfect cover, I felt as if I had actually been transported to a silken tent in a faraway country with nothing but my wits to keep me alive. The storybook I was reading was one that my maiden aunt Tití, the only reader I knew, had given me. *The Thousand and One Nights,* it was called, and on its cover sat a young girl with a veil over her long, dark hair and beside her, reclining on one elbow and listening to what she was saying, was a young man with a turban on his head. What I liked about this young girl was that unlike the fair princesses in the other storybooks, Scheherazade could have been a Dominican girl: dark-haired, almond-eyed, with color in her skin.

This book was the only voluntary reading I did, for I was a poor student and poorly behaved. In fact, if you want to know the truth, the reason I was hiding under the bed early in the morning instead of reading my book openly on top of my bed was to avoid having to go to school that day.

Every morning after breakfast my mother and aunts rounded up my sisters and cousins for the drive to school. There was a crowd of us—three cars were needed—and by the time one car was filled up and on its way, the aunts weren't quite sure who had already gone and who was left to transport. So, if I slipped away from my sisters and cousins, and hightailed it to my bedroom, and threw myself under the bed, and stayed there, quietly reading my book of stories, it would not be until midday, when the school crowd returned for la comida del mediodía, that my mother realized that I had played hooky again right under her very nose.

Why did I do this? School was deadly. I thought I would surely die of boredom sitting on that hard chair listening to Mrs. Brown talk about the pilgrims or *i* before *e* or George Washington cutting down a cherry tree. We were attending the Carol Morgan School because my parents had decided that we should learn English and get "an American education" rather than a Dominican one. To this day, they claim this choice made our transition to the United States so much easier. But how could they have known back then that we would be going into exile in a few years?

So what I was learning in school had nothing to do with the lush, tropical, and dangerous world around me. We were living in a dictatorship, complete with spies, late-night disappearences, torture, and death. What, indeed, did this world have to do with the capital of Alabama and Dick and Jane and a big red bouncing ball? And what on earth was apple pie? Was it anything at all like a pastel de tamarindo? No wonder I shut the doors to my attention and refused to do my homework. My education was a colonialist one: not imposed from the outside but from within my own family. I was to learn the culture, tongue, manners of the powerful country to our north that had set our dictator in place and kept him there for thirty-one years. Maybe my parents did know what they were doing.

And maybe, I, sensing the unspoken world of intrigue and danger around me, where El Jefe ruled supreme, found kinship with the girl on the cover of my storybook.

Certainly she had more to say to me than Dick and Jane.

I AM SCHEHERAZADE, she would always begin. *I am a girl stuck in a kingdom that doesn't think females are very important.*

Why, that's just like me, I'd pipe up. It's always the boy cousins who are asked what they want to do with their lives. Girls are told we are going to be wives and mothers. If we're asked at all, it's usually how many children we want and whom we might want to marry.

But even though I am a girl, Scheherazade went on, *I am ambi-*

tious and clever and I've found ways of getting around the restraints put upon me.

Why, that's just like me, I put in. Here I am, hiding under this bed in the middle of a school day, doing what I please. And I've found other ways of getting around things as well. I can learn any poem by heart if I hear it read out loud a few times. When company comes, Mami dresses me up in my first communion dress and takes me out to recite in front of everyone. They reward me with pesetas and sometimes a whole peso. I've already told Mami that when I grow up, I'll go ahead and have those half-dozen babies I'm supposed to have, but I'm also going to become a famous actress who gets to travel around the world and do whatever she wants—

Very recently, I had a shock, Scheherazade interrupted. (Pobrecita, she could hardly get a word in edgewise!) *I found out that I am living in a country where our cruel sultan is killing all my girlfriends. First he marries them, then the next day he kills them. I've been racking my brains, trying to figure out a way to stop all this killing, and I think I've finally got a plan.*

Far off in the direction of the palacio nacional, a siren sounded. I wasn't sure what it meant. Sometimes the siren meant a "resignation," with the retiree appearing in the papers a few days later in a black-outlined box with a crucifix and "Que descanse en paz" above a blurry photo of his face. Sometimes the siren meant our jefe, Rafael Leonidas Trujillo, was going out, and so the streets had to be cleared. I am sure that siren also meant other things my parents were afraid to tell me.

What I am going to do, Scheherazade confided, *is marry the sultan, and then, before he can kill me the next morning, I'm going to tell him a story.*

That's worked for me, I said, nodding at her bright-eyed

face on the cover. Many, many times I had escaped punishment with a story. Just last week, Mami came rushing to find
out who had broken my grandmother's blue crystal ball that
sat on a pedestal under the tamarind tree. Of course, it
seemed pretty obvious to her when she found my cousin Ique
and me holding rakes, but I set her straight. I told Mami that
the reason we were holding rakes was that we had just chased
off the man who had broken the ball.

"And what man would that be?" my mother asked, eyes
narrowed.

Hmm, I thought. What man would that be? I knew my
parents were afraid of the guardia who periodically came on
the property searching for an acquaintance or just asking
for un regalito to buy their cigarillos. So, I explained that the
man we had chased off was a guardia whom we had caught
snooping around the property.

That sent a volley of terrified looks among the adults who
had followed my mother outside at the sound of breaking
glass. How was I supposed to know that my father and uncles
had joined the underground and were plotting the overthrow of the dictator? That my parents' seeming compli-
ance was all show. That guardia on the grounds meant my
family's participation had been uncovered. The adults went
off in a cold sweat to a private conference behind locked
doors while Ique and I were left to enjoy the tamarinds we
had knocked down with our rakes.

I finally talk my father into going along with my plan, Scheherazade
continued, *and so after my first night with the sultan, just as the sun is
coming up, I say to the sultan, Oh, sultan, would you like to hear one of my
wonderful stories? And the sultan shrugs, sure, go ahead—*

Just then, the bedskirt was lifted up. My mother's face

peered angrily at me. "So, this is where you are. Come out this instant!" I crept out slowly, hunching my shoulders as if to take up less space on this earth. My mother shook me by the arm. "You better have a good explanation as to what you're doing under that bed instead of at school with your sisters."

Her yanking shook the book out of my hands. It fell, face up, on the floor. Scheherazade gazed up at me with an eager look in her eye, as if to say, "Go ahead, girl. Think up something!"

SO, EARLY ON, I learned that stories could save you. That stories could weave a spell even over powerful adults and get them off your case and on to other things like talking politics behind closed doors or making a tamarind pastel in the kitchen.

The power of stories was all around me, for the tradition of storytelling is deeply rooted in my Dominican culture. With over eighty percent illiteracy when I was growing up, the culture was still an oral culture. Rarely did I see anyone reading a book, except for my aunt Tití—and that was the reason, everyone knew, why she wasn't yet married. (She also wore pajamas and knew Latin, and read the dictionary, which didn't help.) Mostly people listened to radio programs and to each other. Streets were known, not by street signs, but by the stories or characters or events associated with them. The street where Chucho lives. You know, Chucho, the man born with a sixth finger on each hand because when his mother was pregnant, she stole a piece of pudín de pan from a neighbor, and so God punished her by putting an extra, shoplifting finger on her son's hands.

Ah yes, *that* Chucho, *that* street!

So it is no surprise, given my island oral tradition, that I became a storyteller. But it is still a surprise to me—given my nonliterary childhood, my aversion to writing and to anything that smacked of a classroom—that I grew up to write books and be a teacher.

Of course, what clinched it was an even bigger surprise, the surprise of my life, you could call it: escaping to the United States in August 1960, with the SIM on my father's tail. Overnight, we lost everything: a homeland, an extended family, a culture, and yes, as I've already said, the language I felt at home in. The classroom English I had learned at Carol Morgan had very little to do with the English being spoken on the streets and in the playgrounds of New York City. I could not understand most things the Americans were saying to me with their marbles-in-their-mouths, fast-talking, elided American English, which Walt Whitman rightly termed "that barbaric yawp."

One thing I did understand: boys at school chased me across the playground, pelting me with stones, yelling, "Spic! Spic! Go back to where you came from!"

"No speak eengleesh," I lied, taking the easy way out, instead of being brave and speaking up like Scheherazade.

But my silence was also strategy. Inside my head a rich conversation had started, inspired by the world of books. Not just *The Thousand and One Nights,* but Nancy Drew mysteries, *Little Women, Winnie the Pooh.* I was encouraged by teachers who asked me to write down what I remembered about that world I was so homesick for. I found that if I wrote down *the bright pink flowers in Mamita's garden,* I could summon up my grandmother's back patio with the hot-pink bougainvillea dropping down through the slats of the overhead trellis. By rubbing the lamp of language, I could make the genie appear: the sights, sounds, smells, the people and places of the homeland I had lost.

I realized something I had always known lying on my stomach under the bed: language was power. Written-down language was money in the bank.

STILL, I REMEMBER the faces of those tormenting boys. The corners of their mouths were stained with egg yolk. Their eyes seemed colorless, without warmth or kindness. In their jeering voices I could hear some other voice—maybe a parent's—hurling the same kind of insults at them. I dreaded this playground gang because I could not speak *their* language clearly enough to make them understand that I was not their enemy.

"No speak eengleesh," they taunted my accent. "I'm Chiquita Banana and I'm here to say. . . ." They glared at me as if I were some repulsive creature with six fingers on *my* hands.

Sometimes the teacher caught them and gave them a talking-to or kept them after school. Finally, the pain of punishment must not have been worth the pleasure of watching me burst into tears, and they gave up picking on me and started in on someone else.

Looking back now, I can see that my path as a writer began in that playground. Somewhere inside, where we make promises to ourselves, I told myself I would learn English so well that Americans would sit up and notice. I told myself that one day I would express myself in a way that would make those boys feel bad they had tormented me. Yes, it was revenge that set me on the path of becoming a writer. At some point, though, revenge turned into redemption. Instead of pummeling those boys with my success, I began to want to save them. I wanted to change those looks of hate and mistrust, to transform the sultan's face into the beautiful face of the reclining prince on the cover of my childhood storybook.

Where did I get the idea that stories could do that? That *I* could do that?

I GREW UP hearing a different story about who I was and where I was going. Scheherazade was not the approved heroine of my childhood. Instead, the golden model I was given by my parents, my aunts, and teachers was the age-old fairytale princess: Cinderella, mixed in with lots of Sleeping Beauty and the Virgin Mary.

Once upon a time there was a sweet, pretty, passive, powerless, and probably blond (stay out of the sun!) princess who never played hooky from school or told lies about who broke the crystal ball in her grandmother's garden. The handsome (Catholic) prince of the land fell in love with her, married her, and she lived happily ever after as his lucky wife and the mother of his children.

This is the true shape of every happy woman's life, I was told. Give and take a few adjectives—maybe not so pretty, maybe not so passive—this is what you should aspire to be. Especially once I hit adolescence, I was told this story over and over.

But the problem was that there was another story in my head. In the back rooms of my mind, Scheherazade was recounting her version of my life: If I wanted to tell stories, I better get off my butt and write them down.

My mother and aunts shook their heads knowingly. "Be

smart: get married while you're still young and pretty and can attract a good man. Have your children while you're still young and energetic and have the energy for children. You can always write." That is what they said. You can *always* write, as if writing were some automatic skill you could pick up when you wanted. As if you did not have to give your whole life over to it—isn't that what Scheherazade had done? And one life might not be enough. Even Chaucer, a master of English literature, complained about how little time there was to master the craft of writing. "That lyf so short, the craft so long to lerne."

And so, I married, not once, but twice before I was thirty, searching for that right man, for that elusive happiness. With each marriage, I put aside my writing. It was nobody's fault, really. Back in those pre—women's movement days, wives were wives, first and foremost. I'd sooner have had an affair than lock myself in my room to write and leave my husband to fend for himself.

Instead I closed the door to that world of books. I wrote very little those years I was married. But she was back there in my head causing trouble, waking me up in the middle of the night with her stories of the life I could be living if I trusted myself, if I became my own woman, if I followed my heart's desire and brought forth what was inside me to bring forth.

Both marriages were brief. I was not yet thirty and I was *twice*-divorced. No one we knew got divorced at all, and only movie stars got divorced more than once. I was a true failure at the fairytale princess story. There was no way to tidy up my messy life and come out with a happy ending. No one expected much from me anymore. Mami stopped making suggestions. The aunts sighed a lot, but said nothing.

And so ironically, my two failures freed me to be whoever I was. On my customs card coming back from the Dominican Republic where I had gone after my second divorce, I wrote down *teacher* after *occupation*. Then I rethought my answer and made a slash mark and added *writer*.

"Oh?" the customs officer asked me, glancing at the card. "What have you written? Anything I've heard of?"

"Not yet," I murmured.

THAT SUMMER I enrolled in a fiction workshop and began writing stories. I set up a writing schedule and I kept to it. I began to make decisions based not on how to make my life safe and cushioned so that I could accommodate my princess fears and fantasies, but on what choices would allow me to pursue the dream in my heart. Many times I made what looked like seemingly foolish choices, giving up "perfectly good" jobs or turning down job offers because during the interview with prospective employers, it would become clear that I would have no time for writing during the school year. "You can always write summers," they suggested.

But I wanted to write *now*. And so I made a space for it in my head, in my heart, and in my working day. I wrote every morning, even if it was only for a brief half hour or hour before I turned to my stack of papers to correct or lesson plans to prepare. The days I absolutely could not write because there was no time, I felt off balance, defeated, as if I were one of the damsels who had not gotten away from the sultan. It was turning out to be true, what William Carlos Williams had said, "It is difficult / to get the news from poems / yet men die miserably every day / for lack / of what is found there."

Years went by, and I kept on writing, and teaching at whatever institution would allow me that little extra time every day to write. These jobs were mostly adjunct instructor jobs at local colleges, teaching however many sections of freshman composition would pay the rent and put food on the table and still give me time to write. As I published more, I managed to get jobs as a visiting writer. These positions were never secure, funded according to the vagaries of class enrollments or arts funding. And so I moved across America from colleges to old-age homes to poets-in-the-schools programs to private schools to universities, replacing someone on his Guggenheim or staffing an extra fiction-writing course that had been added at registration. And I continued to write, to send out my poems and stories.

Among my circle of friends, everyone had married, once, or if twice, they stayed married the second time around. Many had children and seemed to be settled down for the rest of their lives. And here I was, still on the road, supporting myself with hand-to-mouth jobs. Many nights I woke up at three in the morning in Illinois or Washington, D.C., or Delaware or Vermont and wondered if I was fooling myself. Maybe I was a deluded Scheherazade? The few single men I was now meeting looked over my shoulder at the pretty, young arrivals in the field of time. It was just as well, I told myself (not fully convinced). I had never been successful at picking a lover with whom I could be both a wife *and* a writer.

Ten years after the fairytale fiasco of my second marriage, happiness surprised me. A feisty Scheherazade-type agent found a good publisher for my first novel. I also found a true compañero for the woman I had become. The first night we went out we stayed up late telling each other the story of our lives. Since we were already middle-aged, we needed a second night to continue the narrative, and a third, and a fourth. We found that our individual narratives could be woven into whole cloth with nothing important left out.

WHAT IF SHE hadn't been in that back room of my mind, under the bedskirt of my consciousness? What if early on, I hadn't found Scheherazade's example to kindle in me the possibility of another choice? If I hadn't seen her reflection in the mirror: a woman who used words to weave a web of enchantment, a woman who was not going to be a victim, a woman who took matters into her own hands?

Maybe I would have found her anyway, because, as I mentioned earlier, I was raised in a storytelling culture. Certainly, in coming to this country and this new language, I discovered new resources and the need for self-invention. What was already a natural love of words and their music, of narrative and its enchantments might have flowered, and I would have become a writer anyhow.

But I am glad that she came so early into my life and into my imagination, so that her voice was not completely drowned out by the other voices that were telling me something else. She was my first muse long before I knew what a muse was. Early on, I began to tell stories to anyone who would listen and even to those who would not. It was just a matter of time before I, too, listened to the story I was telling myself about who I really was.

Of Maids and Other Muses

· · · · · · · ·

For a long time as a young writer I had some wrong-headed ideas. The biggest misconception was that I should be writing about something Important and Deep that would impress my readers. My voice in a poem should carry authority and weight as I spoke about the big matters that Milton, Yeats, Homer had tackled. Upon graduation, I felt as if I'd been immersed in a literal canon and now it was my turn to be blasted out from that tradition into the literary world to make a sensation.

Such wrongheaded thinking! Where did it come from? I don't know. Don't all young writers need a spare tank of ego to get them far enough down the road of self-doubt so they can't turn back anymore? I suppose I was still feeling my immigrant status. English was my second language. I was a newcomer in this literature, tradition, way of making meaning. And so I overcompensated for my feelings of literary and linguistic insecurity by making myself learn and master everything I could about the tradition. There is a saying in the old country that the traitor always wears the best patriot uniform.

Of course, there were other voices in my head, other instincts. Along the way, I met other muses whom I made the mistake of ignoring because I had never seen their faces between the covers of books. They did not seem important enough, American enough, literary enough. In silencing them, I was silencing myself. I found my voice only when I let them sing inside my work, when I sat down and finally listened to them.

I AM NOT talking now about book muses—fairytale heroines like Scheherazade or heroines in novels like Jo in *Little Women* or even writer heroines whom I fell in love with at different times in my reading life. Certain soulful passages of my George Eliot novels are marked so heavily, that I am embarrassed to lend them out. There was a time when if I loved a book, I underlined every word as if I had to physically take hold of each one. And as for poetry, I have touched certain volumes to my cheek as if they were favorite aunts who had given me a special gift.

But I'm talking now about real-life muses—ones who never wrote a book but who stirred my imagination with their pluck and sometimes with their failures; whose cheeks I really touched; who held me and told me I could do it, which is a muse's primary job. I don't know if these are the same muses Milton and Homer meant when they invoked *the muse,* but now that I am an older, chastened, and somewhat humbler writer, I know the muse is many muses, and not all of them leave paper trails.

When I read a page of my own writing, it's as if it were a palimpsest, and behind the more prominent, literary faces whose influence shows through the print (Scheherazade, George Eliot, Toni Morrison, Emily Dickinson, Maxine Hong Kingston), I see other faces: real-life ladies who traipsed into my imagination with broom and dusting rag, cookbook and garden scissors, Gladys and the tías, and the cook at Yaddo and her sidekick, the lady with the vacuum cleaner. Of them, I sing.

MY CHILDHOOD WAS spent in the bosom—an appropriate metaphor given that all who raised me were female—of my mother's well-to-do family. My mother and two uncles and grandparents and maiden aunt all lived in houses close to one another. Every day, when my grandfather and father and my two uncles left for work, this complex of houses became a stronghold of women, my mother, my tías, and an army of maids. The world was run by women—at least the immediate world I had to live in, which was the only one that mattered to me at that young age.

Of these many tías, three in particular sparked my imagination. Their passionate engagement with their lives made them seem bigger than life. The first was Tía Rosa, who had studied to be a doctor and knew how to do so many things. What most impressed me about this aunt was how she made each person feel special. Back then in the fifties, this surrender to others was a dangerous quality for a woman to have. But Tía Rosa seemed to both surrender and remain her own person. She listened to us, her nieces, with deep interest, not as if we were in the way, taking up her precious time. She noted the bent of each nature and she tried to work with it.

"Come here," she said to me one day, when she saw me struggling with a newspaper in Spanish. "You have to learn to read your own language." My mother's Americanophile family was the dominant influence. But Tía Rosa was a passionate Dominican; her great-grandfather Francisco del Rosario Sánchez had been one of the three founding fathers of the country. It was Tía Rosa who taught us the words to the Dominican national anthem. "Quisqueyanos valientes alcemos. . . ."

My maiden aunt Tití was a very different kind of aunt. She sat by herself on the couch with her legs tucked under her, reading a book. You asked her what a word meant, and she knew what it meant and a number of other things about that word as well. We were not supposed to mention that she was a jamona, an old maid, but children being what they are, my cousins and I made up a song, "Si las vacas volaran, Tití se casara." If cows could fly, Tití would marry.

But Tití didn't seem to want to marry. She refused to work at catching a husband, which should have been her primary focus as a young, nice-looking, upper-class woman. Instead, she focused on her books and her beautiful garden. Everything Tití touched seemed to sprout and branch and bud and burst with blossoms. She had green thumbs for all her fingers. In the front of my grandparents' house was a big island of almond trees bordered by clumps of anthuriums. Sassy flowers, they seemed to be cocking their pistils at me! I snatched at them when no one was looking. In the backyard, just beyond the tamarind tree, the limonsillo tree, the guava trees, was the large shed with Tití's cuttings and garden tools, and beside it, her orchid greenhouse, which given my anthurium history, I was not allowed to enter except in her company.

I loved it when Tití finally put her book down, and as if not knowing what to do with the intensity of her stirred imagination, she came out to work in her garden. The whole ginger bed had to be moved. The caprichos needed thinning. The sprinkler had to be aimed at the cayenas. The spider orchid repotted. I followed behind her, helping her with this task or that one, my mother marveling that I behaved so well with her baby sister who couldn't know the first thing about raising children because she had never had any. But I sensed Tití's passion for beauty and order, and that, more than her flowers, is what I wanted to be close to.

The most exciting tía was not a daily aunt, but a once-a-week extravaganza. Saturdays when she was in town, my godmother sent her chauffeur to pick me up for the day. I rode in the back of the big black car in a pale rose organdy dress that Tía Amelia had brought me from some place over in Europe and waved languidly at my envious cousins as if I had been born with a whole silverware-drawer of silver spoons in my mouth.

Tía Amelia was a beautiful, rich widow who lived all alone in a mansion by the ocean. Actually, she wasn't alone at all but had half a dozen servants, a priest who came daily to say mass, and a host of interesting visitors, many of whom were artists. She had her very own private chapel inside her house with a coat stand hung with rosaries from all over the world, some even blessed by the pope! You got a special dispensation if you said prayers on such blest rosaries, so she told me. During mass, Tía Amelia's beautiful face would be transformed with religious passion, her sky blue eyes rolled upwards, her mouth just slightly open. I watched her closely, wondering what feeling in her heart went with that astonishing look on her face.

All day, while Tía Amelia busied herself with dressing, answering calls, receiving guests, I had the run of the house and the garden with its enormous lawns. I always hoped my glamorous Tía Laura, my godmother's daughter, and her handsome American husband with movie-star looks, Tío Raymond, would drop by. "Hi, there, gorgeous," he'd say to me in English. "How's my girlfriend?" I'd take off at a run across those lawns, overcome by the violence of my feelings. I think I was almost hoping that Tío Raymond would take off after me.

In the early afternoon we had lunch in the upstairs living area, which was more informal than the innumerable, somber parlors downstairs with heavy drapes that were always drawn to "save the furniture." Light and airy, the upstairs opened onto a large balcony. I could see the ocean, blue and festive in the distance, and if there was a pause in the conversation, I could hear the waves dashing on the cliffs. The food came up to us on something my godmother called *el dumbwaiter.* I waited, fascinated, hoping to catch a glimpse of some idiot butler with drool on his chin in a black jacket showing his face in the shaft she pointed to in the wall.

The other guests, all adults, talked and laughed and clinked glasses, and mostly ignored me. Every once in a while one or another would say something, and there would be an abrupt pause, and my godmother would glance at me and say, "Remember, there are Moors on the coast." Quick, I'd look out the window for a ship, loaded with swashbuckling pirates with eye patches, waving their swords. But I never saw these Moors who always seemed to show up when the adults were saying interesting things.

As soon as the cafecitos had been served, Tía Amelia would turn to me and ask me to recite. "Este era un rey que tenía . . ." ("There was once a king who had . . .") "La princesa está triste. . . . ¿Qué tendrá la princesa?" ("The princess is sad. What's wrong with the princess?") Mid-recitation, I would glance towards Tía Amelia to see how I was doing. There was that look again: the pale face transfigured with emotion, the lips parted. What was she feeling? Would words ever do that to me?

Among the blur of faces, the dozens of aunts, the smell of perfume, the caress of their skirts as I wandered underfoot, these three tías stand out. And yet, though these women seemed queens to me, in charge of households and gardens and large staffs, I began to sense that they really had few options at their disposal. Why couldn't Tía Rosa go out and deliver babies? Why couldn't Tití leave the garden and fly to the moon on a cow and come back with a husband? And with as much money as she had, why couldn't Tía Amelia travel around the world and surprise the Moors in their own country? At such moments, when I sensed the circumscribed world awaiting me, some rage or deep desire would propel me out to the garden to tear off the pistils from my aunt's anthuriums or to gallop across the lawn even if Tío Raymond wasn't around to run after me.

· · ·

BUT TO TELL you the truth my deepest identification was not with any of these *tías* but with the maids. All day long, while Mami and my aunts played canasta or visited with each other or supervised this or that project (the making of pastelitos, the planting of orchids, the visiting of the sick, and so on), it was the maids who took care of my sisters, my cousins, and me. They were the ones who more often than not picked us up if we fell, soothed us when we woke up in the middle of the night with a nightmare, spooned warm sopitas they had made us in our mouths when we were too sick with fever to want to eat anything at all.

My favorite of all the maids was Gladys. She was the pantry maid, light-skinned and pretty, with a beautiful voice and a repertoire of songs, many of them Mexican mariachi songs, which she taught me to sing. Brooms in hand, the two of us would dance-sweep across the galería, singing, "Con tu amor, soy feliz y seré toda la vida. Yo soy el aventurero. La mujer que quise se me fué con otro."

From Gladys and the maids I learned what leaves to boil for what ailment, what days I could safely wash my hair, what to do if a cuco appeared to me in the middle of the night wanting to cut off my sucking thumb. I learned what saints were good for what protection and what lay between a man's legs and what would happen between mine when I reached puberty and later when I had a baby. These women were the guardians of those secrets and were connected to a world much more vibrant than the polite, upper-class world of my mother and aunts with their litany of keep-your-legs-together, did-you-wash-your-hands, did-you-chew-that-enough. Of course, as I grew older, I began to see how severely the maids' lives were limited by poverty and how little freedom they had. Grown women, and they couldn't do the simplest things like live in their own houses or eat a nice cut of the meat they had prepared for the big table with the high-back chairs in the formal dining room with the Gauguin painting of two native girls hanging on the wall. Even pretty ones like Gladys who married "well," a chauffeur or guardia, left their positions as family maids to become wives and mothers, handmaidens to their own families. In fact, both classes, the maids and the tías—I began to see—were circumscribed either by poverty or social restrictions, and both were circumscribed by their gender.

Early on, I realized that the boys in our family were the preferred ones. "So many girls," visitors would shake their heads, as if to say, "so many mouths to feed." As they grew older, boys were allowed to stay out late, to come and go as they pleased, to receive higher educations that prepared them for "the real world." Meanwhile, I was belting out boleros with Gladys in the galería.

But something was happening to the little girl as she sang her way through Gladys's housekeeping chores. Something was happening to the little girl who snuck into her aunt's orchid hothouse or recited poems at her godmother's knee. A seed was being sown in the fertile soil of my imagination. It took coming to this country for that seed to grow beyond the limited options that these early muses represented for me.

WHEN WE LANDED in New York City, we became spics who spoke English with an accent. In fact, it became clear that by being Latinos we had entered the American servant class.

"You're from Portorico?" one classmate asked, trying to place me somewhere in her world. "We have a Portorican lady who comes cleans our apartment."

What I didn't realize back then was that by losing everything I had escaped the entrapment of my Dominican social class. The golden handcuffs, as I like to call those positions of privilege that often trap us women into denying our bodies, our desires, our selves—and what is worse or just as bad, into denying the souls of others. Those golden handcuffs can look to all the world like expensive, heavy bracelets, but in fact, they manacle the hands that could otherwise be holding a paintbrush or a pen or unlocking the handcuffs of others.

In this new culture, my sisters and I had to find new ways to be, new ways to see, and—with the change in language—new ways to speak. It was this opportunity to create ourselves from scratch that led me to become a writer.

The seed was there from Gladys and the tías, as I mentioned. But what got me interested in language rather than singing, say, or horticulture, like my aunt Tití, was having to master a new language at the age of ten: the spoken, fast-paced, living language of a New York City street. Where did one word end and another begin? Why did the Americans say *under the weather* instead of *sick*, why *pleasant* instead of *nice* instead of *friendly* instead of *amiable* instead of *kind*? Every writer has to do this kind of fine-tuning in her own native language, but I was doing it as a ten-year-old struggling with a second language. And this process made me interested in how words can contain and hold and pinpoint experience, how words can help us know what we are thinking and feeling, how words can make us feel intimate with ourselves and with strangers.

We arrived with the idea that we would be going back as soon as the dictatorship was over. But once Papi got his license, he started to earn good money and the lure of America caught. Our severe homesickness passed. With each year, the strong and lively current of American culture swept us forward, carrying us along even as we felt "out of it." We had arrived before the waves of Dominican immigrants created a Washington Heights or a Lawrence, Massachusetts. Where we lived in Jamaica Estates and later as students in our New England boarding school, my sisters and I were "the only ones," surrounded by los americanos. We felt even more foreign, even less affirmed as Latina girls.

Luckily, I found new muses who kept me in touch with my roots. One was a Dominican woman named Ada, who had come to the United States to work for the family of the ambassador in Washington. When the ambassador's term was over and he went back to the Island, Ada came to work at our house as our live-in maid. She was a large, sassy, café-con-leche woman, who provided the extra mothering that the extended familia and maids had provided back home.

The basement, where Ada lived, was a den of Dominicanness. Down there, Ada played "her" music, teaching my sisters and me how to merengue, reminding us that we must not forget what las americanas seemed to have forgotten: that we had hips and fundillos that should be used for dancing. In the laundry room, she had her altar to her santos and kept her lit velones in the deep sink to avoid a house fire. In that same sink, she sometimes brewed the special baths she sponged over herself to make the good luck come. She had a gift for reading coffee grounds and could predict the arrival of letters, the fate of a crush, the general score on an SAT exam. Her special gift was storytelling, which is why I helped her clean house whenever I was home from school. I knew the whole dramatic, complicated saga of her family and even kept pictures of her three kids and lifelong flame, Dinol, in my wallet. The stories were updated daily, for Ada had a friend in the phone company who connected her to the Island for free. Often, I would be put on to converse with her daughter or her mother or Dinol while Ada popped upstairs to season the habichuelas or take her pastelón out of the oven.

The other muses, also Latinas, worked as nurses in Papi's office, where I spent my summers and school vacations. These young women were the only models I had of what it might be like to be a professional woman and a Latina in this country. Two of the "nurses" were actually doctors in their native countries and were hoping, like Papi, to earn their American license and work as MDs in the practice.

My favorite of the nurses was Belkis, who was the oldest of the bunch, in her early thirties. She was large-bodied and expressive, with a raucous laugh and a string of boyfriends; the phone rang as often for her as for the doctor. (When years later I read Chaucer's *Canterbury Tales*, I met Belkis's Anglo match in the Wife of Bath.) Belkis was so wild, I know my mother would not have let me work at the office if she had known the education I was getting. Suffice it to say that I learned from Belkis almost everything I didn't know by then and everything I've needed to know ever since then about sex. I heard off-color jokes that put color on my cheeks. If a young man needed a shot, Belkis insisted that a needle in the bottom didn't hurt as much as one in the arm. She'd invite me to assist her. "Come help me hold him down," she'd tease. The young men always laughed.

When I went away to boarding school and then college, I saw less of these two women. Belkis, in fact, lost her job when my father got wind of some of her shenanigans. Away at school, I met American muses, who like my aunt Tití, were handmaidens of the written word. Miss St. Pierre and Miss Stevenson, my English teachers, were both single, both young, both passionately in love with books.

They encouraged me, not just to receive the language passively, but to actively engage it. In other words, not just to read, but to write. I wrote essays, poems, stories. I kept a journal. For my senior project, I put together a handwritten manuscript of poems and drawings, and with Miss St. Pierre's blessing, I carried it to a New York publisher when I was home for vacation. The editor, Gene Young, was actually a friend of my aunt Tití's who had been to boarding school with her. Gene very nicely offered to read the manuscript and then took me on a tour of the Harper & Row building, introducing me to her coworkers as "a talented young poet." I glowed with pride—though it did occur to me that she had not, as yet—read any of my poems. Oh well, maybe editors could tell ahead of time that someone was going to be a good writer? The book, titled *Thoughts,* dealt with important, well, thoughts: Death, Loneliness, the Meaning of Life. Nowhere was there a trace of Belkis, Ada, Gladys, or any of my Dominican tías—a good sign, I thought, that I sounded "so American." A few weeks after my visit to Harper & Row, my handwritten book was returned in the mail with a nice note from Gene advising me to "keep writing, you'll find your voice."

This discovery of a voice did not come easily. I was in school before women's studies or multicultural studies or anything but the CANON became the norm. We read the great writers, Yeats, Milton, Shakespeare, Chaucer, Whitman, with a sprinkling of female exceptions. I do not regret having had these models. They taught me my craft; they forced me to go outside my own experience and background. But it was difficult to find or trust my own voice using only these male models.

I can still remember the first time I heard my own voice on paper. It happened a few years after I graduated from a creative writing master's program. I had earned a short-term residency at Yaddo, the writer's colony, where I was assigned a studio in the big mansion—the tower room at the top of the stairs. The rules were clear: we artists and writers were to stick to our studios during the day and come out at night for supper and socializing. Nothing was to come between us and our work.

I sat up in my tower room, waiting for inspiration. All around me I could hear the typewriters going. Before me lay a blank sheet of paper, ready for the important work I had come there to write. That was the problem, you see. I was trying to do IMPORTANT work and so I couldn't hear myself think. I was trying to pitch my voice to "Turning and turning in the widening gyre," or, "Of man's first disobedience, and the fruit of that forbidden tree," or, "Sing in me, Muse, and through me tell the story." I was tuning my voice to these men's voices because I thought that was the way I had to sound if I wanted to be a writer. After all, the writers I read and admired sounded like that.

But the voice I heard when I listened to myself think was the voice of a woman, sitting in her kitchen, gossiping with a friend over a cup of coffee. It was the voice of Gladys singing her sad boleros, Belkis putting color on my face with tales of her escapades, Tití naming the orchids, Ada telling me love stories as we made the beds. I had, however, never seen voices like these in print. So, I didn't know poems could be written in those voices, *my* voice.

So there I was at Yaddo, trying to write something important and coming up with nothing. And then, hallelujah—I heard the vacuum going up and down the hall. I opened the door and introduced myself to the friendly, sweating woman, wielding her vacuum cleaner. She invited me down to the kitchen so we wouldn't disturb the other guests. There I met the cook, and as we all sat, drinking coffee, I paged through her old cookbook, *knead, poach, stew, whip, score, julienne, whisk, sauté, sift.* Hmm. I began hearing a music in these words. I jotted down the names of implements:

Cup, spoon, ladle, pot, kettle,
grater and peeler,
colander, corer,
waffle iron, small funnel.

"You working on a poem there?" the cook asked me.
I shook my head.
A little later, I went upstairs to the tower room and wrote down in my journal this beautiful vocabulary of my girlhood. As I wrote, I tapped my foot on the floor to the rhythm of the words. I could see Mami and the aunts with the cook in the kitchen bending their heads over a pot of habichuelas, arguing about what flavor was missing—what could it be they had missed putting in it? And then, the thought of Mami recalled Gladys, and that thought led me through the house, the mahogany furniture that needed

dusting, the beds that needed making, the big bin of laundry that needed washing.

That day, I began working on a poem about dusting. Then another followed on sewing; then came a sweeping poem, an ironing poem. Later, I would collect these into a series I called "the housekeeping poems," poems using the metaphors, details, language of my first apprenticeship as a young girl. Even later, having found my woman's voice, I would gain confidence to explore my voice as a Latina and to write stories and poems using the metaphors, details, rhythms of that first world I had left behind in Spanish.

But it began, first, by discovering my woman's voice at Yaddo where I had found it as a child. Twenty years after learning to sing with Gladys, I was reminded of the lessons I had learned in childhood: that my voice would not be found up in a tower, in those upper reaches or important places, but down in the kitchen among the women who first taught me about service, about passion, about singing as if my life depended on it.

So Much Depends

· · · · · · · ·

I remember discovering William Carlos Williams's poetry in my anthology of American literature over twenty-five years ago. It was love at first sight:

> So much depends
> upon
>
> a red wheel
> barrow
>
> glazed with rain
> water
>
> beside the white
> chickens.

"What a curious syntactic structure," our teacher noted, " 'So much depends . . .' So much *what* is depending on the wheelbarrow and the chickens?"

But the syntax seemed familiar to me. I had heard a similar expression all my life, *todo depende*. Everything depended on, well, something else. It was our Spanish form of "maybe."

Scanning a collection of his poetry in the library, I found a half-dozen Spanish titles—even a volume named *Al Que Quiere*! But there was no mention in my anthology of the why of these Hispanicisms. It was only later that I came to find out that William Carlos Williams was—as he would be termed today—"a Hispanic American writer."

His mother was Puerto Rican—upper-class Puerto Rican with a Paris education, but still . . . She married an Englishman who seems to have lived everywhere, including some years in the Dominican Republic, my homeland. The two moved to Rutherford, New Jersey, where they raised their two sons. Growing up, William Carlos never had a close association with Puerto Rico. In fact, he did not see the islands until he was almost sixty and had a deep longing to try to understand what his own roots really were. His was an American boyhood indeed, but with the powerful and sometimes baffling presence of his mother, who spoke Spanish in the home and who terrified and embarrassed her sons by going into trances and speaking to her Caribbean dead, especially while she played the organ during Unitarian church services. Williams did not phrase or even seem to understand his divided loyalties in terms of ethnicity. Still, as a first-generation American, he often felt "the islandness in him, his separateness," as his biographer Whittemore has described it.

His friend Ezra Pound didn't help things. "What the hell do you a blooming foreigner know about the place," Pound taunted. "My dear boy, you have never felt the swoop of the PEEraries." But it was Pound who jumped ship and fled to Europe in search of classical models. Williams stayed, in New Jersey, and struggled to set down "the good old U.S.A."

AS AN ADOLESCENT immigrant, I, like Williams, wanted to be an American, period. I was embarrassed by the ethnicity that rendered me colorful and an object of derision to those who would not have me be a part of their culture, at least not without paying the dues of becoming like them. And I was encouraged to assimilate by my parents and teachers, by the media and the texts I studied in school, none of which addressed the issues I was facing in my secret soul. So much of who I was seemed to have no place in this world and culture—and so I started to have a secret life, which no doubt contributed to my becoming a writer.

My family did not move into a comunidad in this country, where a concentration of Dominicans or Latinos would have kept alive and affirmed the values and customs, the traditions and language that were an increasingly hidden part of me. Jamaica Estates was a pretentious—back then, anyway—area in Queens for solidly middle-class families and for up-and-coming white European immigrants—many Germans, some Italians, some Jews, and a couple of us Hispanics.

My father did have the other comunidad in his work life. Every morning he left the Estates for his Centro Médico in a Latino area in Brooklyn, a place my mother called, "a bad neighborhood." The summers I worked at his office, I drove with him through block after block of brick apartment buildings bracketed by intricate fire escapes, a city of concrete. But the lively and populous street life was a lot more enticing than the lonely, deserted lawns back in Queens. At the Centro Médico the nurses were all Dominicans or Puerto Ricans with sometimes an Argentinian or Chilean lording it over us with her Castillian lisp and blond hair. No matter. Papi was boss, and I was la hija del doctor. His patients brought me pastelitos and dulce leche. The guys flirted with me, tossing out their piropos. ("Ay, look at those curves, and my brakes are shot!") I loved the place, though I admit, too, that I was very aware of my difference. At night, we drove back home to a welcome of sprinklers waving their wands of water over our look-alike lawns. We were of another class, in other words, a difference that was signaled the minute I walked into our house and my mother instructed me to wash my hands. "You don't know what germs you picked up over there."

But any comunidad we might have joined would have been temporary anyway. Worried about the poor reception and instruction we were receiving at the local school, my mother got scholarships for us to go away to school. We were cast adrift in the explosion of American culture on campuses in the late sixties and early seventies. Ethnicity was in. My classmates smoked weed from Mexico and Colombia and hitchhiked down the Pan American highway and joined the Peace Corps after college to expiate the sins of their country against underdeveloped and overexploited countries like, yes, the Dominican Republic. More than once I was asked to bear witness to this exploitation, and I, the least victimized of Dominicans, obliged. I was claiming my roots, my Dominicanness, with a vengeance.

But what I needed was to put together my Dominican and American selves. An uncle who lived in New York gave me a piece of advice embedded in an observation: "The problem with you girls is that you were raised thinking you could go back to where you came from. Don't you see, you're here to stay?"

He was right; we were here to stay. But the problem was that American culture, as we had experienced it until then, had left us out, and so we felt we had to give up being Dominicans to be Americans. Perhaps in an earlier wave of immigration that would have sufficed—a good enough tradeoff, to leave your old country behind for the privilege of being a part of this one. But we were not satisfied with that. The melting pot was spilling over, and even Americans were claiming and pro-claiming, not just their rights, but the integrity of their iden-tities: Black is Beautiful, women's rights, gay rights.

What finally bridged these two worlds for me was writing. But for many years, I didn't have a vocabulary or context to write about the issues I had faced or was facing. Even after I discovered female models and found my own voice as a woman writer, I did not allow my "foreignness" to show. I didn't know it could be done. I had never seen it done. I had, in fact, been told it couldn't be done. One summer at Bread Loaf, a poet stated categorically that one could write poetry only in the language in which one had first said *Mother*. Thank God, I had the example of William Carlos Williams to ward off some of the radical self-doubt this comment en-gendered.

How I discovered a way into my bicultural, bilingual experience was paradoxically not through a Hispanic American writer, but an Asian American one. Soon after it came out, I remember picking up *The Woman Warrior* by Maxine Hong Kingston. I gobbled up the book, and then went back to the first page and read it through again. She addressed the duality of her experience, the Babel of voices in her head, the confusions and pressures of being a Chinese American female. It could be done!

With her as my model, I set out to write about my own experience as a Dominican American. And now that I had a name for what I had been experiencing, I could begin to understand it as not just my personal problem. I combed the bookstores and libraries. I discovered Latino writers I had never heard of: Piri Thomas, Ernesto Galarza, Rudolfo Anaya, José Antonio Villareal, Gary Soto. But I could not find any women among these early Latino writers.

The eighties changed all that. In 1983, Alma Gómez, Cherríe Moraga, and Mariana Romo-Carmona came out with *Cuentos: Stories by Latinas*. It was an uneven collection, but the introduction, titled "Testimonio," was like a clarion call:

> We need una literatura that testifies to our lives, provides acknowledgement of who we are: an exiled people, a migrant people, *mujeres en la lucha*. . . .
>
> What hurts is the discovery of the measure of our silence. How deep it runs. How many of us are indeed caught, unreconciled between two languages, two political poles, and suffer the insecurities of that straddling.

The very next year Sandra Cisneros published her collection of linked stories, *The House on Mango Street;* Ana Castillo published her book of poems, *Women Are Not Roses;* I published *Homecoming.* At Bread Loaf, I met Judith Ortiz Cofer and heard her read poems and stories that would soon find their way into her books of poems, stories, and essays, and her novel, *The Line of the Sun.* Lorna Dee Cervantes, Cherríe Moraga, Helena María Viramontes, Denise Chavez. Suddenly there was a whole group of us, a tradition forming, a dialogue going on. And why not? If Hemingway and his buddies could have their Paris group, and the Black Mountain poets their school, why couldn't we Latinos and Latinas have our own made-in-the-U.S.A. boom?

STILL, I GET nervous when people ask me to define myself as a writer. I hear the cage of a definition close around me with its "Latino subject matter," "Latino style," "Latino concerns." I find that the best way to define myself is through the stories and poems that do not limit me to a simple label, a choice. Maybe after years of feeling caught between being a "real Dominican" and being American, I shy away from simplistic choices that will leave out an important part of who I am or what my work is about.

Certainly none of us serious writers of Latino origin want to be a mere flash in the literary pan. We want to write good books that touch and move all our readers, not just those of our own particular ethnic background. We want our work to become part of the great body of all that has been thought and felt and written by writers of different cultures, languages, experiences, classes, races.

At last I found a comunidad in the word that I had never

found in a neighborhood in this country. By writing power-
fully about our Latino culture, we are forging a tradition
and creating a literature that will widen and enrich the existing canon. So much depends upon our feeling that we
have a right and responsibility to do this.

Doña Aída, with Your Permission

. . . .

A few years ago the Caribbean Studies Association had its annual meeting in Santo Domingo, and they asked me if I would be its keynote speaker as a Dominican American writer along with Aída Cartagena Portalatín, the grand woman of letters in the Dominican Republic. She read in Spanish, and then I read in English, and then—as a kind of crowning moment—we were both brought together on stage to meet each other in front of everyone.

Doña Aída embraced me, but then in front of the mikes, she reamed me out. "Eso parece mentira que una dominicana se ponga a escribir en inglés. Vuelve a tu país, vuelve a tu idioma. Tú eres dominicana." ("It doesn't seem possible that a Dominican should write in English. Come back to your country, to your language. You are a Dominican.")

Since she was grand and old—and I was raised to have re-speto for the old people—but also because she was arguing in Spanish—and I can usually only win my fights in En-glish—I kept my mouth shut. What is it that I would have said?

This is what this short essay is about.

Doña Aída, con su permiso. Doña Aída, with your per-mission.

I am *not* a Dominican writer. I have no business writing in a language that I can speak but have not studied deeply enough to craft. I can't ride its wild horses. Just the sub-junctive would throw me off. I know the tender mouth of English, just how to work the reins. I've taken lessons from Emily Dickinson and Walt Whitman and Toni Morrison and William Carlos Williams, whose Mami was Puerto Rican. And though I have read Pablo Neruda and César Vallejo and Julia de Burgos and Ana Lydia Vega and Aída Cartagena Portalatín, I can only admire what they do in Spanish. I cannot emulate their wonderful mastery of that language.

No, I am not a Dominican writer or really a Dominican in the traditional sense. I don't live on the Island, breathing its daily smells, enduring its particular burdens, speaking its special dominicano. In fact, I would tell a different story and write poems with a different rhythm if I lived and worked there, ate there, made love there, voted there, dried my tears there, laughed my laughter there. If daily what I heard was *Ay* instead of *Oh,* if instead of that limited palette of colors in Vermont, gray softening into green, what I saw were colors so bright I'd have to look twice at things to be-lieve that they were real.

Doña Aída, with Your Permission

But, you're right, Doña Aída, I'm also not una norteamer-icana. I am not a mainstream American writer with my roots in a small town in Illinois or Kentucky or even Nuevo Méx-ico. I don't hear the same rhythms in English as a native speaker of English. Sometimes I hear Spanish in English (and of course, vice versa). That's why I describe myself as a Dominican American writer. That's not just a term. I'm map-ping a country that's not on the map, and that's why I'm try-ing to put it down on paper.

It's a world formed of contradictions, clashes, cominglings —the gringa and the Dominican, and it is precisely that tension and richness that interests me. Being in and out of both worlds, looking at one side from the other side— thus the title of one of my books of poems, *The Other Side/ El Otro Lado*. These unusual perspectives are often what I write about. A duality that I hope in the writing transcends itself and becomes a new consciousness, a new place on the map, a synthesizing way of looking at the world.

And I would propose that this multicultural perspective— and forgive me that word because it has become such a catchphrase, a lap for every baby—this multicultural per-spective is the perspective of some of the most interest-ing writers of this late twentieth century: Salman Rushdie in London, Michael Ondaatje in Toronto, Maxine Hong Kingston in San Francisco, Seamus Heaney in Boston, Bharati Mukherjee in Berkeley, Marjorie Agosin in Welles-ley, Edwidge Danticat in Brooklyn. We're a mobile world; borders are melting; nationalities are on the move, often for devastating reasons. A multicultural perspective is more and more the way to understand the world.

So Doña Aída, I'm a mixed breed, as are many of us

U.S.A. Latino/a writers. With our finger-snapping, gum-chewing English, sometimes slipping in una palabrita o frase español. With our roots reaching down deep to the Latin American continent and the Caribbean where our parents or abuelitos or we ourselves came from. With our asabaches and SAT scores; our fast-paced, watch-checking rhythms combining with the slower eternal wavings of the palm trees.

And though I complain sometimes about the confusion resulting from being of neither world, and about the marginalizations created on both sides—the Americans considering me a writer of ethnic interest, a Latina writer (meaning a writer for Latinos and of sociological interest to mainstream Americans), or the Dominicans reaming me out, saying she's not one of us, she's not Dominican enough —though I complain about the confusion and rootlessness of being this mixed breed, I also think it's what confirmed me as a writer, particularly because I am a woman.

This is probably true for many of us Caribbean women writers. Our emigrations from our native countries and families helped us to achieve an important separation from a world in which it might not have been as easy for us to strike out on our own, to escape the confining definitions of our traditional gender roles. We also, many of us, achieved a measure of economic security, jobs in universities, say, that released us from the control of our papis and brothers and husbands and a patriarchal system that doesn't even pretend to be something else. For me, anyhow, as a writer, I had to free myself from certain restrictions—physical and mental—of being a Dominican female before I could rediscover and embrace the Latina in my writing.

Doña Aída, with Your Permission

"So what are you doing here in Santo Domingo?" you ask me, Doña Aída.

To know who I am, I have to know where I come from. So I keep coming back to the Island. And for fuerza, I go back to this thought: it really is in my Caribbean roots, in my island genes to be a pan-American, a gringa-dominicana, a synthesizing consciousness.

Think of it, the Caribbean . . . a string of islands, a sieve of the continents, north and south, a sponge, as most islands are, absorbing those who come and go, whether indios in canoes from the Amazon, or conquistadores from Spain, or African princes brought in chains in the holds of ships to be slaves, or refugees from China or central Europe or other islands. We are not a big continental chunk, a forbidding expanse that takes forever to penetrate, which keeps groups solidly intact, for a while anyhow. Our beaches welcome the stranger with their carpets of white sand. In an hour you reach the interior; in another hour you arrive at the other coast. We are islands, permeable countries. It's in our genes to be a world made of many worlds. ¿No es así?

Ay, Doña Aída, you who carry our mixtures in the color of your skin, who also left the island as an exile many times and so understand what it is to be at home nowhere and everywhere, I know I don't really have to ask your pardon or permission. Beneath our individual circumstances and choices, we have fought many of the same struggles and have ended up in the same place, on paper.

Have Typewriter, Will Travel

· · · · · · · ·

I remember a teacher once saying that revolutionaries don't die; they grow up and become lawyers and bankers. Having come of age in the sixties and early seventies, I can attest to that. Many of my radical college classmates who led strikes against the Vietnam war or burned their bras or smoked dope and inhaled are now working for fancy firms or designing sports clothes or running for governor.

But what happens to struggling writers when they grow up—those starving writers who didn't starve, turtlenecked English majors who were going to write the great American novel by the time they were twenty-five? Am I talking about myself? You bet!

Struggling writers grow up to become college teachers with one or two slim volumes and occasional sabbaticals.

They grow up to be editors and self-employed freelancers who do word-processing at home between babies and novels. A few become Famous Writers, which means that you see their pictures, if not their writing, in glossy magazines. But some of these seemingly successful writers never get over having been a struggling writer, especially if the struggles went on and on and on, for over two decades, say, and a dozen teaching jobs.

Am I talking about myself? You bet.

First, let me explain that by struggling writer I am referring to the livelihood struggles every writer who doesn't have a trust fund or a well-heeled partner must go through. The other struggle—mastering the craft—is never over. Writing does not hand out any lifetime guarantees. The fact that you've written one good book or one successful book does not guarantee that you've got the craft "in the bag." The apprenticeship continues and continues and continues from your first poem on a plywood-plank table in a one-room attic apartment to a sixth book in a large, sunny study about the size of that whole first apartment.

Recently, a friend noted that although I have achieved the success and security I was looking for as a writer with published books, I am still full of the same self-doubts I had when we first became friends, and I was living in her attic as a boarder. "The past is over. Time to do a little housecleaning," she urged me, nodding gently the way I've seen her nod at the messy room over her daughter's shoulder. This essay is meant to be that housecleaning, a coming to terms and setting to rights of some of the fears that haunted me when I was a struggling writer.

I had every reason to doubt myself back then. I was

twenty-five, I was thirty, I was thirty-five, and then I was almost forty. With no major publications and no steady job in sight, I was constantly on the move. I used to joke that I should get vanity plates that read, HAVE TYPEWRITER, WILL TRAVEL, because I would take a job anywhere that would hire me as its visiting writer. I lived in the South, I lived in California, I lived in the Midwest, New England, some of the mid-Atlantic states, you name it. One time, I counted them and figured out I had had eighteen different addresses in fifteen years (the last three within the same town). Mine was definitely the re-re-revised entry in my friends' address books.

In my wake, were two divorces, friendships lost to too much mobility, books stored in garages and attics across America. Sometimes during those knockabout years, I would wake up in the morning, and like a jet-lagged traveler, I'd have to figure out where it was that I had slept. Driving home from the grocery store, I'd make the wrong turn because it would have been the right turn in the last town I had lived in. Horns beeped at me. "Oh," I would think. "That's right. I'm in Illinois now. I can turn right on a red after a full stop."

These are small details, but as we all know, small details are the stuff of our lives. The hardest details were those that came of having to curb a built-in impulse to return favors. It was difficult to repay the countless hosts and hostesses who let me stay in their houses while I found a place to live in a new town or invited me to their supper parties once I was settled so I could meet my neighbors and colleagues. One-room efficiencies do not have guest rooms and as for dinner parties—I didn't really know how to cook "meals." Once, when I gave a dinner for a department chairman who had been very kind to me, I hired a Puerto Rican woman I met in a laundromat to cook us up something Caribbean. I don't know if the money I gave her for groceries wasn't enough or if her culinary skills were not what she had boasted they were, but the big pot of rice hardly had any beans in it. The side platter of chicken was all scrawny wings and drumsticks. I had come from a Latino culture of lavish gestures where there was always room for one more at the table. Here I was living in an efficiency where the dining-room table doubled as my desk, and if I had friends over, the supper plates had to be collected from underneath my potted geraniums.

Although my parents could have helped me, I was too ashamed to ask them for a handout. After all, they had already predicted the bad consequences of most of the choices I had made. And so I lived skinny—as I called it back then. I learned to read library books, call everyone on weekends or after eleven, shop in used-clothing stores or during sales, debating the necessity of any purchase until a terrible indecisiveness would set in. Held up to the harsh light of *Do I really need this?* the floor-length black coat or tooled cowboy boots were luxuries. My Volkswagen literally rusted out from under me—I could see the road through a hole in the floor. During one of my visits back to my college town, an old professor of mine welcomed me at the door of his country house. He had heard the roar of the bad muffler I couldn't afford to replace coming up his mile-long driveway. Before I left that day, he suggested I talk to my father about buying me a new car.

"Why?" I asked. My eyes were burning with shame at the poverty I could not hide.

"It would help," he said vaguely.

I do not know if he meant that it would help my morale or that it would give off a better impression when I went look-ing for jobs—what my chef sister calls the importance of presentation when serving people fine food. With my uncut hair and shapeless jersey dresses and a car that seemed like something an incorrigible hippy might drive to prove a point, my presentation was in the negative numbers. I looked like the failure I was secretly afraid I had become.

All around me my contemporaries and colleagues seemed launched into successful lives. Those of my college class-mates who, like me, had majored in English but gone on for their Ph.D.'s were now landing their first tenure-track jobs or deciding wisely to go into business because there were too few of those jobs. I, on the other hand, had debated and de-layed going for a doctorate because I didn't really want to be an academic, but a writer. Some of my friends had gotten married and were now beginning to have their children and buy their first houses and talk about what they were going to do once their kids were in school. "What are you up to?" they would ask at reunions or during catch-up phone calls. "I'm not sure," I'd answer.

Actually, I was sure what I wanted to do: I wanted to write, but nobody would pay me to do it. Oh, once a year, my par-ents gave me fifty bucks to write the poem they put in their Christmas card. Once I got eighteen dollars for two poems in *Poetry* magazine. Usually I got two complimentary copies, one of which I mailed off to my parents, book rate, so they could see how my career was on the upswing. On the strength of these few publications, small colleges and large universi-ties and prep schools seemed willing to hire me on a semester basis to teach writing workshops. "What you need," my mother kept telling me again and again, "is to get your teaching certificate. It would be perfect. You'd have summers off to write."

She had been making this suggestion since college, when the perk was that I'd have summers off to spend with my children. My mother had given up on a conventional, happy life for me. But she did want me to be solvent.

As much as I admired the profession and as much as I had enjoyed teaching at a boarding school for two years, I did not want to be a high-school teacher—the job was too consuming. I already had a full-time job, as I kept explaining to my mother and my friends. I was writing.

The problem was that this inner certainty was beginning to erode. Perhaps I was fooling myself? I still own the anthology of contemporary American poets in which a key notation on every margin is the age at which these poets published their first, second, third books. One of the most anxiety-producing entries was Joyce Carol Oates: she really had published over ten books by the time she was my age, thirty-five! As for my friends, many had lives that made me think of them as people of my parents' generation: people with garages and matching silverware and sit-down meals and families. Everyone else seemed to know how to work the controls in their life. I felt as if I couldn't even reach the gas pedal.

That feeling was strongest whenever I visited my cousins in the Dominican Republic. Every year, my parents offered me a trip "home" to see the family, the one handout I always took. Sitting on the white wicker rockers on terrazas hung with baskets of orchids and birds of paradise, listening to cousins my age complain about their maids, I felt like the poor relation. But what I most lusted for was not their luxuries, but their lives of certitude. They seemed so unshaken by the self-doubts and life decisions that were buffeting me. "What you need is a rich Dominican," one of my cousins suggested—as if any self-respecting rich Dominican would marry me to produce poetry, not progeny.

Everyone was full of advice, but I already knew what I needed was to keep writing, which I did, every day, from wake-up time till two or three in the afternoon, or on teaching days, from waking time until I had to prepare for class. I kept reminding myself of that famous remark about writing attributed to Hemingway: "It's one percent talent, ninety-nine percent applying the seat of the pants to the seat of the chair." But the seat of my pants was getting mighty threadbare.

During bad days, I would actually turn the Hemingway quote against myself. What did Hemingway have in common with me? He was an American, I was not. He was a man, I was not. Maybe he had been bad at math, and his calculations were off, and it was more like ninety-nine percent talent and one percent hard work. And besides, he had ended up shooting himself, leaning against a shotgun as if to shoot down—what else? Self-doubt, you can be sure!

In this sense I was like other women of my generation: women who had grown up with mothers we could no longer use as models for the lives we were living. And so we stumbled ahead and invented ourselves. In the case of my sisters and myself, the confusion was compounded by the fact that, having come from a so-called Third World country and from a very traditional Latino culture, our female prede-

cessors were not just one but two or three generations behind the women we were now becoming: old-fashioned tías
who believed too much education could ruin a girl for marriage. By coming to this country, my sisters and I *had* come
a long way, baby: from nineteenth-century sheltered Dominican convent-school girls to twentieth-century career
women. No wonder we made so many mistakes! Even my
mother, who entered the job market long after her children
had grown up and moved out of the house, had models for
being a career woman: her own daughters, who had picked
themselves up from their many falls, dusted themselves off,
and become a chef, a social worker, a psychologist, and a
struggling writer.

By then, too, many of my girlfriends who had gone into
early marriages were starting to go through their own divorces and life crises. Suddenly, from being one of a few
single women in my early thirties, I had a handful of divorcing or recently divorced women friends who were setting up reading groups, writing groups, political action
groups. We gave each other lots of support, put together our
combined dishes and threw lavish potluck supper parties.
We lived on the edge, but because by now I was settled in
Vermont, that lifestyle didn't feel marginal but middle of
the road.

Slowly—so slowly I hardly noticed it, and accidentally, for
I hardly planned it—I found myself dead center in an established life. I landed a tenure-track teaching job. I met my
husband, and we built a house in the country. My oft-
rejected manuscript finally found a publisher, and two
months after my forty-first birthday, my first novel was published. Three years later, my second. Young struggling writ-

ers came up to me at readings or wrote me letters asking for my advice on how to make it. Every time it happened, I wanted to say, "Just wait a while."

After the gypsy habits of twenty years, getting used to settling down took some getting used to. I kept my distance from colleagues because an internal clock that had still not adjusted itself to these changes told me I would be gone in a year. Building our own house on eleven acres made me nervous—a whole house? It was too much space. For years, whenever my husband left on business trips, I moved into my study, sleeping and eating there because it felt more familiar and cozy than wandering around in so many rooms by myself. Before I was awarded tenure, I kept warning my husband that we might end up in a commuting marriage. "Where are you going?" he asked me. "To another job if I don't get tenure," I explained. The idea of staying put and just writing never crossed my mind. I had to earn a living! "But you *are* earning a living with your writing," my husband reminded me. It could have been monopoly money for all I believed him.

Though the past is over, as my friend keeps telling me, the habits of those years are still with me, habits of second-guessing, of tentativeness, of believing the fat of the land belongs to others. And behind the personal struggle of those years lies the lesson of immigration: that success is fickle, that a well-off life can suddenly turn into a life of struggle and uncertainty. But that life of uncertainty can also create a sense of compassion for those on the margins who now might be watching me with their noses pressed to the window, thinking, "She's lucky!"

In a way, I am, for a happy ending redeems the past and

makes the struggles meaningful. Still, the shadow of the lean years falls on the present like dust motes in a shaft of sunlight even after a thorough housecleaning. After so many years living on the shaky side, you never quite believe what other people keep telling you, that you've arrived.

A Vermont Writer from the
Dominican Republic

. . . .

Recently, I've been receiving invitations to come speak or give readings at gatherings where I am billed as a Vermont writer. After a lifetime of wanting to belong, I'm not one to argue when people finally choose me to be on their team. Vermont wants me to be one of its writers, that's okay with me. I'm joining good company: Robert Frost and Shirley Jackson and Grace Paley and Jamaica Kincaid and Howard Norman and Jane Shore and, up to a few years ago, Aleksandr Solzhenitsyn.

Wait a minute! Aleksandr Solzhenitsyn, a Vermont writer? Jamaica Kincaid? Or for that matter, Grace Paley? Even the quintessential Vermont poet Robert Frost was born in California. Certainly none of us are Vermont writers in the way my old-time Vermont neighbor defines the term. Hearing my husband describe his two daughters, who grew up here and are now in their mid-twenties, as Vermonters, this old-timer corrected him, "Just cause your cat went and had her kittens in the oven, you wouldn't call them biscuits, now would you?"

Given such stringent qualifications, I don't even qualify as a biscuit Vermonter. I wasn't born or bred here. I didn't raise a family here. I have buried one beloved friend here, but since the funeral was actually only a scattering of her ashes rather than an actual putting into the ground, I'm not sure this counts. And yet, I do consider myself a Vermonter—even if real Vermonters, who have been here a couple of generations, would turn even paler to hear a dark-haired, olive-skinned Hispanic woman say so. "You from New York?" the same old-timer neighbor asked when he first met me. Foreign to him was just someone from another state, not from a whole other country—a tropical island, no less, where the light is so bright and summers so hot, you can almost believe you are in an oven and someone has turned the broiler on.

Still, I'm not going to renounce my claim to my home state so easily. Maybe because for most of my life in the United States I have been such a migrant—living briefly in almost every region of the country—I cling to my new roots. And they're not so new. I first came to Vermont in the summer of 1961, my first summer in this country. My grandfather had heard about a famous camp, École Champlain, where youngsters could learn French. And so, barely one-American-year-old, I boarded a train for Vermont. My first impression of these green mountains, after the grays of New

York City, was that I had been sent back home to my beloved tropical island.

The attachment to the state had begun. I kept returning. I attended Middlebury College, and then during my roving teaching years, I got a job as a visiting writer at the University of Vermont. Finally, nine years ago, I returned to Vermont with a job at Middlebury College. If we add them up, I've lived in Vermont fourteen years, the longest I've lived anywhere. In fact, fourteen years is four years more than my first ten years in my native country. Surely that adds up to the fact that I am from Vermont, even if my roots are in the Dominican Republic.

But it's not just the math that makes me a Vermonter; it's the feelings that the place calls up. A rush of gratitude that makes me want to clap when that little commuter plane lands in Burlington and not just because we miraculously made it on what looks to me like the mechanical equivalent of the dragonflies over our pond. Coming home from a trip, I crest the hill on our road, and I see the weathervane angel on our barn blowing her trumpet, and it might as well be the Second Coming. I feel a flash of joyful exultation, even if she's not the real thing but store-bought. I remember the day we hired Chuck to put her up on top of the then new barn: how I was so worried that he'd fall, how I said a silent prayer to *his* guardian angel, how he didn't fall, how afterwards we watched as a welcome breeze came from the west and the angel turned, squeaking, on her pivot. Much of this feeling of belonging comes from an accretion of all these little moments.

My last nine years in Vermont include some of the happiest and luckiest moments of my life. I met my husband Bill here. At our wedding, we danced on the floor of the unfinished house with friends, many of whom had come from all the areas of the country I had lived in. Three years later, I earned tenure at Middlebury; my friend and colleague John Elder hand-delivered the letter to me in my seminar in the library. My "babies," as I call my students, from my first classes at the college are now returning with their own babies for reunions. The two locust trees that shade my study in the summer were put into the ground by my own hands— with a little help from my farming husband, of course. I've watched our birch seedlings grow into trees; in fact, I saved them their second winter, shaking the heavy coating of ice from their young branches when they were at the point of snapping after the kind of ice storm I had learned about from a Frost poem. But perhaps, what makes me lay the deepest claim to Vermont as my home state is that this is where I've written most of my books.

In fact, this is truer than I myself thought when I first made my calculations. All my novels were written here, beginning with *How the García Girls Lost Their Accents,* published in 1991, which was actually my second book. My first book, *Homecoming,* a book of poems, was written in a ground-floor apartment in Burlington, where I lived while I was teaching at the University of Vermont. I've written stories and poems in many other temporary home states—Kentucky, North Carolina, California, Illinois, Arkansas—but the bulk of my writing, and certainly all of the polishing and revising that goes into finishing a book, happened here.

What is it about Vermont that has inspired me as a writer? You might be surprised that I don't launch immediately into the beauty of the Green Mountains as the source of my in-spiration—although I admit that a landscape that stirs my imagination does make me want to reciprocate on paper. But what has been most inspiring about Vermont, plain and simple, is that I've been able to stay put here. Nothing is as good as stability for getting your work done. "The writer needs an address, very badly needs an address—that is his roots," Isaac Bashevis Singer, himself an immigrant and a writer, once noted. If your hands are busy packing boxes rather than putting pen to paper, and if your imagination is absorbed with nest building rather than the color of your character's hair, you are not going to get much writing done. At least I didn't.

But of course, the reason I stayed put—besides the steady job and marriage (big reasons, indeed)—is that the place is hospitable to my lifestyle and my writing style. Incredulous writer friends from New York often ask me how I, a person who once lived in the city, can stand to live in Vermont. And I always wonder back, how can you get work done when in a space of a few blocks there are three or four movies you want to see, restaurants you want to try, stores where you want to shop till you drop—or your credit card bounces. How can you get writing done when there are dozens of readings going on by writers whose work you don't have time to read because there are so many book parties and publishing par-ties and just plain parties you want to go to? As for Do-minican writer friends who ask how I can stand to live in such a forbidding climate, I ask back, how can you stay in-doors writing when the world is bathed in sunshine and the ocean is a stone's throw away with water warmer than our Vermont pond even on the hottest day of the summer?

So, I am glad that I live in a state that doesn't overstimulate me with choices and temptations, with distracting colors and sights and sounds. Here, I can plumb deep into my own resources—which is how most writers I know begin writing. In fact, for me the best muse is having the time and the solitude in which *to* muse. And I have plenty of this quiet musing time in Vermont. Especially during those five or so months when the snowy fields blur into the snowy air so that the world out there looks like a blank page I want to fill up with words.

Now people who ski and ice skate and do all manner of foolish outdoor things in the winter (their brains no doubt affected by the cold) might not agree that Vermont has nothing to offer but inner recreation from November to April. But a ski slope and a frozen pond are not hundreds of movie theaters, four thousand restaurants, a dozen parties, galleries, museums. And they are not a tropical ocean and a sun so radiant you feel like you died and went to heaven. (So why write *Paradise Lost,* for heaven's sake?) And even if you are a skier, you can only stand a few hours on top of Mount Killington. (Why do you think they call it Mount *Kill*ington?) Plenty of time left over for writing.

But it's more than climate that roots so many writers here. If the muse were just cold weather, we could all hole up in Labrador and "enjoy" nine or ten months of writing instead of Vermont's five. The appeal of this state goes deeper than climate. In an age when everything seems malled in and part of a chain, Vermont is still a place connected to the land and its uses. In my part of the state, almost every town is bordered by working farms. People actually throw spring parties and summer solstice parties (some friends even have an annual firefly party), and the talk is as much about gardens, bluebird houses, what didn't make it through winter as it is about the bond market or new software for the computer. In fact, this rural aspect of Vermont reminds me very much of the Dominican Republic, a country which is still primarily agricultural. Both here and there, the flora and fauna are the focus of attention—there, because with its lushness and brightness, the outdoors intrudes upon the attention; here, because far from the hurly-burly of cities and the roar of highways and the flash of lights, we look and listen closely to what the land is trying to tell us.

Being connected to the large, mysterious forces of nature keeps a writer in tune with the deepest rhythms of being alive. And face it, a farm schedule is also a good writing schedule. A light on downstairs is a rare sight in houses on my country road on a weeknight after ten. After eleven, maybe only one bedroom light is still on (a teenager's?) and after midnight, I think a Vermont equivalent of Cinderella's fairy godmother comes around and unplugs everything. You go to bed early, you get up early, you get your work done in Vermont. (I think it's a law still on the books here.)

But it's not all work and isolation. I don't think I've ever lived anywhere else in the United States where community is so important. In fact, Vermonters "invented" town meeting day, one day a year when members of a community gather together to hash out the problems and issues that affect them. Since the state is small and rural, the citizens interact closely with each other. What often brings me together with my neighbors in Vermont are the commonplace but profound moments of a life: births, deaths, the raising of children, the marrying of the young people, the taking care of the sick, the planting of the garden. We connect with each other over the nitty-gritty, which is what literature is all about.

This sense of community also reminds me of my native country—the aspect of it I missed most in my many years of anonymous city living and moving from place to place. Just as Vermont is a small state, the Dominican Republic is a small country. On the flight down from New York to Santo Domingo, I usually know at least one other person well, and I'm often acquainted with several more. And even if I don't know them, they often know me or my family. They remember when I was this high, when I climbed the tamarind tree and instead of picking the fruit picked a wasp's nest by mistake, when I fell into the fish pond and almost drowned, and so on. Having a history—a connection over time—with the people around you deepens and enriches any interaction. Of course, this connection comes, in part, from being settled down in a place, but a lot also depends on the openness and attitude of the people you find there. And Vermonters are known for their neighborliness. Strangers quickly turn into neighbors—even if they don't live next door to you. My mother-in-law bakes a welcome dish for any newcomer in her condo development. And she delivers it along with my father-in-law, who has his toolbox ready in case you need to connect something to something else and what you've got to connect it with is still packed in a box somewhere.

I admit that at first the small-town aspect of Vermont life was hard to get used to. Seemed like I couldn't shop for my groceries efficiently without getting into some conversation or other. If I had a bad day and was a little short with the teller at the drive-in bank, I was bound to bump into her at farmer's market on Saturday. Taught me to hold my tongue, all right. Count to ten, and on those bad days, to twenty-five. I'm not sure a lack of anonymity makes me a better writer, but it can't help but improve my character. I can't get away with much in a small town, no sir. In fact—and no offense to my fellow Vermonters—people here snoop. I jog by a house, and the curtain lifts. I bend to check out a flower, and a door clicks open. With the lack of urban distraction and excitement, Vermonters provide each other's entertainment. We pay attention to details and to each other. If as García Lorca professed, the poet is the professor of the five senses, then most Vermonters I know have doctorates.

I, too, am curious about the details of my neighbors' lives. Did so-and-so really do such-and-such with so-and-so? I, too, read the local papers and can't believe little so-and-so is already graduating from high school. If this just sounds like low-grade gossip to you, I'm here to insist that's where high-quality fiction comes from. Did you hear about the poor indecisive guy whose father died unexpectedly, and then his mother went and married her brother-in-law, so that the funeral meats did coldly furnish forth the marriage table? Shakespeare would fit right in with the rest of us biscuit Vermont writers.

So, yes, although I am from a tropical island, I am also a Vermont writer. After nine years, even my old-timer Vermont neighbor has warmed up to me, and though he hasn't yet come out and said he has read my books, he has complimented me by saying that he has "seen them" in the papers. As for his always greeting me on a forbiddingly frigid day with, "Cold enough for you?" I've learned that the remark isn't directed personally at me, as if he's earmarked me as a weather wimp because I'm from the tropics. He says it to everyone. It's his winter's hello if he happens to meet you in town or on the road.

"It's not so bad," I've learned to say back to him through chattering teeth. "Perfect writing weather."

Chasing the Butterflies

. . . .

I first heard about the Mirabal sisters when I was ten years old. It was four months after we arrived in this country. My father brought home a *Time* magazine because he had heard from other exiles in New York City of a horrifying piece of news reported there. My sisters and I were not allowed to look at the magazine. My parents still lived as if the SIM might show up at our door any minute and haul us away.

Years later, doing research for the novel I was writing, I dug up that *Time* article. I stared once again at the picture of the lovely, sad-eyed woman who stared back from the gloom of the black-and-white photo. As I read the article, I recovered a memory of myself as I sat in the dark living room of our New York apartment, secretly paging through this magazine I was forbidden to look at.

Declarations

It was December 1960. My first North American winter. The skies were gray and my skin was turning a chapped, ashy color that made me feel infected by whatever disease was making the trees lose all their leaves. Every evening my sisters and I nagged our parents. We wanted to go home. They answered us with meaningful looks that we couldn't quite decipher. "We're lucky to be here," my mother always replied. "Why?" we kept asking, but she never said.

When my father read of the murder of the Mirabal sisters, he must have felt a shocking jolt at what he had so narrowly missed. Patria, Minerva, and María Teresa were members of the same underground he had bailed out of in order to save his life. Here, just four months after we had escaped, they were murdered on a lonely mountain road. They had been to visit their jailed husbands, who had been transferred to a distant prison so that the women would be forced to make this perilous journey.

And so it was that my family's emigration to the United States started at the very time their lives ended. These three brave sisters and their husbands stood in stark contrast to the self-saving actions of my own family and of other Dominican exiles. Because of this, the Mirabal sisters haunted me. Indeed, they haunted the whole country. They have become our national heroines, and November 25, the day they were killed, has been declared by the United Nations the International Day against Violence against Women.

I DID NOT become personally involved in their story until a trip I made to the Dominican Republic in 1986. A woman's press was doing a series of postcards and booklets about

Latina women, and they asked me if I would contribute a paragraph about a Dominican heroine of my choice. The Mirabal sisters came instantly to mind. Looking for more about them, I visited several Dominican bookstores. But all I found on that first trip was a historical "comic book." How disconcerting to read about heroines with balloons coming out of their mouths! On the other hand, any shoeshine boy on the street or campesino tilting his cane chair back on a coconut tree knew the story of the Mirabal sisters. Las muchachas, everyone called them. The girls.

When I complained to a cousin that I couldn't find enough formal information about them, she offered to introduce me to someone who knew someone who knew one of the Mirabal "children." Six orphans—now grown men and women—had been left behind when the girls were murdered. That's how I met Noris, the slender, black-haired daughter of the oldest sister, Patria. In her early forties, Noris had already outlived her mother by six years.

Noris offered to accompany me on my drive north to visit the rich agricultural valley where the girls had grown up. She would take me through the museum that had been established in their mother's house, where the girls had spent the last few months of their lives.

What happened on that trip was that the past turned into the present in my imagination. As I entered the Mirabal house, as I was shown the little patio where Trujillo's secret police gathered at night to spy on the girls, as I held the books Minerva treasured (Plutarch, Gandhi, Rousseau), I felt my scalp tingle. It was as if the girls were watching me. Here is a page from the journal that I kept on that trip:

In the bedroom: The little clothes that the girls had made in prison for their children are laid out on the beds. Their jewelry—bracelets, clamp earrings, the cheap costume type—lies on the dresser under a glass bell that looks like a cheese server. In the closet hang their dresses. "This one was Mami's," Noris says holding up a matronly linen shift with big black buttons. The next one she pulls out she falls silent. It's more stylish, shirtwaist style with wide blue and lavender stripes. When I look down, I notice the pleated skirt has a blood stain on its lap. This was the dress Patria carried "clean" in her bag the day she was murdered so she could change into something fresh before seeing the men.

María Teresa's long braid lies under a glass cover on her "vanity." There are still twigs and dirt and slivers of glass from her last moments tumbling down the mountain in that rented Jeep. When Noris heads out for the next room, I lift the case and touch the hair. It feels like regular real hair.

We walk in the garden and sit under the laurel tree where "the girls used to sit." Noris says it is too bad that I am going to miss meeting Dedé.

That is the first I hear there is a fourth sister who survived.

Dedé was away in Spain and wouldn't be back until after I had returned to the States. Maybe the next trip, Noris said. "Meanwhile, there are a lot of people you can meet now."

"It's just for a paragraph on a postcard," I reminded her, for I was a little ashamed to be taking so much of her time.

She waved my politeness aside. "It will inspire you," she promised me. Maybe she could sense that more than a post-card was already cooking in my head.

One of the people I met was the dynamic and passionate Minou, daughter of Minerva Mirabal. She was four years old on the day her mother was killed. *I remember her sitting in that chair. I remember her leaning down to kiss me, laughing.* Eventually, Minou would show me a folder of the love letters her parents had written each other during their many separations. Among them, letters they had smuggled back and forth in prison:

My life, I send you this pencil so you can write me. Tell me everything. Don't keep a sorrow from me.

Adored one, how many times haven't I thought about our last night together, how full of presentiments we were. I've asked myself a thousand times if I should-n't have done something to escape capture. What a painful experience this has been. ¡Dios mío! And then, when I knew you and your compañeras had been caught, I wanted to die. I could not bear that large, cruel moral torture of knowing you were suf-fering what I was suffering. *Ay*, what long days, what interminable days. All I can do is fill myself with il-lusions. To be asleep in your arms, my head on your breast. ¡Vida mía! Tu Manolo.

I also met Marcelo Bermúdez, another member of the underground who was in the torture prison along with the other men. Again, from my journal:

Marcelo tells the story of the day the girls were cap-tured and brought to the torture prison. The men were already there, naked, packed in cells behind thick walls of stone, silent and afraid. All of a sudden, the girls spoke out in code and the prisoners took heart. "We are the Butterflies!" (Las Mariposas, their code name.) "We are here with you. If any of you would like to identify yourselves, do so now." Marcelo said that voices started to call out, "I am the Indian of the Mountains." "I am the Hunter of the North Coast." And so on. That's how the group found out that people believed long dead were still alive.

Back in the capital, I recounted the story for my aunt and cousin. "What did the guards do?" my aunt asked me.

I had been so caught up in Marcelo's story that I couldn't remember what he had said had actually happened. "Let's see," I told my aunt. And I think that's when I realized that I was bound to write a novel about the Mirabals rather than the biography I had been vaguely contemplating.

BUT AFTER I wrote my Latina postcard paragraph, I put the project away. The story seemed to me almost impossible to write. It was too perfect, too tragic, too awful. The girls' story didn't need a story. And besides, I couldn't yet imagine how one tells a story like this. *Once upon a holocaust, there were three butterflies.* A paragraph of this stuff was quite enough.

What I was forgetting—and not forgetting—was the fourth sister. It was my curiosity about her that led me back to the Mirabal story. In 1992, during my annual trip "home," I met her—the surviving sister. Dedé, as everyone calls her, invited me out to the house where she and her sisters had grown up and where she still lives.

It was late afternoon, the light falling just so, a deepening of colors in the garden, the rockers clacking on the wooden patio floor. Dedé, very modern in black culottes, a hot-pink shirt, wire-rimmed glasses, recalled this and that in a bright, upbeat voice as if it were the most normal thing, to have had three sisters massacred by a bloody dictator and live to drink a lemonade and tell about it. I realized this was her triumph. She had suffered her own martyrdom: the one left behind to tell the story of the other three.

It was after this meeting that I decided to write a novel about the Mirabal sisters. I wanted to understand the living, breathing women who had faced all the difficult challenges and choices of those terrible years. I believed that only by making them real, alive, could I make them mean anything to the rest of us.

And so I began to chase the butterflies. With my husband, Bill, at the wheel of our rented car, we traversed the Island, meeting the people and visiting the places that had been a part of the girls' lives. There were always surprises.

In the National Archives I combed for information about the Trujillo regime. I found many volumes missing and the blaring radio distracting. The "librarians" (two young girls doing each other's nails and singing along with the radio) offered to help. We found a stack of yellowing *El Caribes*. In the one published the day the girls were killed, November 25, 1960, a warm day was forecast throughout the Island with possible rains in the north. A Japanese doctor had registered a machine that proves that humans snore in thirty different patterns. In "Confidencialmente," it was reported that everyone has the same measurement at the fattest part of the calf as at the neck. María Teresa, the youngest sister, might have read her horoscope for the day: *Libra, Do you realize how much effort and materials you've lost? Try to find a way to save your efforts.* Her two sisters had better luck predicted: *Pisces, This is your lucky time. Neptune is now in a benevolent angle for your sign.*

Leaving the capital and driving north, we stopped at Salcedo. I wanted to see the church where the girls had gone to mass. A gray adobe with a red bell tower, it looked quaint and pretty, a place for fairytales. We wanted to see the inside, but the big wooden doors were locked. We stopped an old man who asked Bill in Spanish if he was a priest. Cura, one who cures? Bill deduced. Bill, a doctor, nodded, "Sí, yo cura." No, I shook my head. "Honey, he's asking you if you're a priest."

"He's not a priest," I said. Then, more bluntly. "He sleeps with me."

"That's okay," the old man said, slapping Bill on the back. Way to go.

We found out why priesthood and pleasure didn't necessarily jar the old man. In order to get inside the locked church, we had to find the priest with the key. He wasn't in the rectory, the old man told us, but over in the discotheque. Bill and I looked at each other, daring each other not to laugh.

A young woman came out on the sidewalk. Her mother owned the pharmacy behind us. Did we want to come in and get out of the sun? Many thanks, but we were headed to the discotheque to find the priest so we could get inside the church. She was too polite to ask what we were up to. But I offered her our story. I was interested in the Mirabals. I wanted to visit the church where they had been married and had gone to mass. The mother came to the door from behind the counter. If you're interested in the Mirabals, why don't you go talk to Doña Lesbia. She lives right across the street.

Who's Doña Lesbia? my look said.

"Their aunt. She knew the girls since they were this high." The proprietress of the pharmacy held her palm flat near her knees.

"Let's go," Bill said. He had understood enough Spanish to know we were being invited into another story.

So, that's how we met the girls' aunt, and how we met many others who had been important to the Mirabal sisters. We even got the priest to come out of the discotheque. ("I get invited to these darn things I have to go to," he explained himself.) He opened the church doors, chatting all the while about his parishioners. "By the way," he asked—and my ears had learned to perk up at the phrase in Pavlovian anticipation of a choice tip or tidbit—"do you know one of Minerva's compañeras in prison lives in town? Doña Sina. Shall I give you an introduction?"

Just past the town of Salcedo, we turned off the main road and headed down a dirt road shaded by a canopy of interlacing amapola branches. Here and there we stopped to admire one of the lovely ranchos, small wooden houses, painted bright island colors with Victoriana bric-à-brac on the gables and shutters of tiny wooden slats for windows. A man, and in a moment, a woman, who had been tying a scarf stylishly around her head, stepped out of one of the ranchos. Her makeup matched the extravagant colors of some of the houses: bright lipstick and heavy eyeliner with little tadpole tails at the corners of her eyes. Did we want to come inside the gate?

We sat on their verandah and told them what we were

after. We had heard that down this road we'd find Patria's husband's farm. It had been a magnificent, thriving spread, but when the girls were captured, the house was destroyed and the farm confiscated. Did they know where the place was?

Why, of course they knew where the González farm was! "We're all related," the woman explained. "Their mother and my paternal grandmother . . ." They went on to recount how the girls' deaths was reported the very next day in *El Caribe* as a car accident. "We felt those girls' deaths. Trujillo pretended his hands were clean. Such a tragic accident, he said when he was here. Oh yes, he was here. He made us throw him a big party. And the girls not a month in the ground. Imagine, all of us dressed up like there was something to celebrate, our hearts so heavy, ay."

They directed us to follow the road till it came to a dead end. There we would find what was left of the farmhouse.

You can't miss it: seven concrete pillars stand in the middle of a field. In what would have been the backyard, we could make out the water tank. We climbed over the barbed wire, walked towards the front steps, still visible, past two toppled concrete urns where I imagined Patria grew her sweet-smelling jasmine. She loved flowers.

Bill and I stayed close, stunned at the sight of a great house fallen. Wandering back towards the fence, we found a grapefruit tree with low-hanging branches. We picked one, peeled it, and ate the bittersweet fruit.

At the opposite end of the island in the dry and desert-like Northwest, we visited Monte Cristi, the hometown of Manolo Tavárez, Minerva's husband. After they were married, Minerva and Manolo lived there, first with his parents, then alone in their own humble casita. It was from their own house, one they would never return to live in, that both were taken into custody by the SIM. We walked the hot, dusty streets wondering how we would ever find the house. At the square, we approached a seated, elderly gentleman wearing a Panama hat and smoking a cigar. Would he happen to know the house where Minerva Mirabal and her husband, Manolo Tavárez, had lived? He looked us over, deciding. Then, he pointed across the street at a tiny pea-green house. "They lived there!" My mouth dropped.

He let that sink in a minute. Then, patting his guayabera pocket as if to make sure he was all there, he stood up. "Come on, I'll show you the place. I live there now."

And so it was that we went inside the house in which Minerva spent the last of her married days. Everywhere we went, it seemed we could reach out and touch history. And always there were plenty of living voices around to tell us all their individual versions of that history.

Even the grim trip on the mountain road where the girls were killed brought out the storytellers. On this road Trujillo had built one of his many "mansions," kept fully staffed and ready in case El Jefe should decide to drop in without notice. Usually he brought a young lady guest he wanted to try out.

We parked in a shallow ditch off the narrow road and looked up at the crest of the hill and the abandoned house. The gate with the five stars was locked. Two young men appeared out of nowhere: a tall one in a gaudy, disco fever—type shirt and another one with a crippled foot. He walked with a crude crutch, maneuvering easily to show us the way up an incline to a break in the wall. We climbed the mossy, cobbled driveway that had once, I'm sure, been scrubbed by caretakers on hands and knees.

It was here, the boys told us, that the girls were brought after their Jeep had been stopped on the mountain road. El Jefe was waiting for them inside, the boys told us. He wanted to have his way with them, especially with the one who had slapped him when he was fresh with her at a dance.

"That would have been Minerva," I said.

"Then, they say, he gave each sister to one of his SIM to terminate."

"Which one went first?" I wanted to know.

"We don't know things like that," the tall, more self-assured one told me.

"Over there." They pointed into the lower garden full of tall grass. "Some stories say they were killed there. Then, they put them in the Jeep with their dead driver. And they drove it up that road there, see." They indicated a steep road that led from the few side-by-side thatched huts they called "the town."

"It was already dark by then," the one on the crutches said. "They pushed the Jeep over the side of the mountain to make it look like an accident."

"Many of the old people heard the crash," the tall one said. "You want to talk to someone who remembers?"

My heart was too full in this grim place. The night was falling. The overgrown garden, the brick buildings, the padlocked doors, the mossy stones that rang with our foot-steps were ominous. I said we had to go.

Down below, on the road, the villagers swarmed around our car. Two giggly girls with spreads of missing teeth ap-proached us. Somebody had told them the gringo and his lady were going to make a movie about the Mirabals. "This town needs money," an old grandmother nodded at me. "Let us all be in the movie."

"Okay," I promised them. "If they make the movie, you can be in it." There was general applause, good-bye slaps on the car as Bill and I drove away.

As we descended the mountain, I felt as if we had traveled the whole route of their lives to the place where they had been struck down. And now that I had come to love the girls in my head, I didn't want them to be dead.

"Where to tomorrow?" Bill asked. Maybe a plan would brighten both our spirits.

"Home," I said. I meant Vermont. It was time to hole up and write the novel about the Mirabal sisters.

¡Que vivan las Mariposas!

Goodbye, Ms. Chips

. . . .

This spring, after twenty-two years of teaching, I decided—a euphemism if ever I heard one for the
messy and anguishing process that brought me to this con-
clusion—to give up tenure. Of those twenty-two years, only
the last six have been tenured, the previous eighteen had
been spent teaching across America, looking for a tenure-
track position. Eventually, I found such a position and
earned tenure, and then, just a few years later, to the raised
eyebrows of friends and acquaintances who had followed
my weary migrancy from one teaching job to another, I gave
it up.

Please note that I am saying I gave up tenure, not teaching. Even if I don't continue teaching at my current college,
I will find a way into a classroom to practice a craft that is,

for me, as fascinating and difficult as writing. But after consulting and reconsulting that internal Solomon that helps us decide between impossible choices, I handed the baby over. I gave up tenure because, in fact, I love teaching, and I didn't know how to give it less than my all, now that I wanted to devote more of my time to writing.

A good friend, still in academia, encouraged my choice by quoting Shaw's famous dictum, "He who can, does. He who can't, teaches." She added her own version, "Those who can't write, teach creative writing." But I had to disagree with her. Some great writers have been magnificent teachers: John Gardner, Theodore Roethke, Patricia Hampl, Fred Chappel, Annie Dillard, Wallace Stegner, Lee Smith, Charles Baxter, June Jordan, Gwendolyn Brooks, Sandra Cisneros, Grace Paley, among others. No, my problem is that I have never been able to hold down two full-time passions. Part of being older and wiser is learning to work with the nature you've been given.

So, good-bye, Ms. Chips. Hello, full-time writer.

THERE IS, OF course, more of a story behind this plucky decision. I didn't so much "give up" tenure as I had to give up tenure. I teach at a small, liberal-arts institution where years ago the faculty voted in the rule that one could not retain tenure on a part-time arrangement. (A vote that I, even as I fall victim to it, agree with. I keep remembering John Ciardi's famous quip that a "university is what a college becomes when the faculty loses interest in students.") The very spring I earned tenure, my first novel came out. I had been writing and publishing in small magazines for over twenty years. If I belonged to any school of writers, it was to the fringe-school writers who "prided themselves" on never having been published in *The New Yorker*.

That first novel took me over ten years to write. I wrote a chapter here and there, whenever I could, during summers, school vacations, between moves, job searches, eager students. After all, I was a teacher who wrote "on the side," even though I chafed against relegating my writing to this second-class status. Still, I had to earn a living. And the truth was that teaching had also become a passion. I yearned for tenure and tenancy, "a room of my own" in the academy. Serendipitously, I signed the contract for my first novel the very year that I was being reviewed for tenure. I thought of that first novel very much as the book that might earn me tenure rather than the book that might bring me autonomy as a writer.

But the latter happened, and suddenly I found myself with an encouraging readership ("When's your next book coming out? What are you working on now?") and with enough money to take time off to do more writing. I'm sure some colleagues felt that I had been waiting in the wings, all along, to earn tenure and start misbehaving. But this was truly a quirk of timing—writing success came at the same time as academic success. The tension that had always been there between these two profoundly gratifying and absorbing vocations suddenly burst to the fore. One vocation was no longer in hock to the other: I no longer *had* to teach to support my habit of writing. So the contest was finally equal and fair, which one would gain the ascendancy. Which one would get to keep the baby?

For years, my emphasis had been on the teaching. Now, fate and luck had put this other possibility before me. I decided to turn the tables and give the writing life the same kind of full-time attention I had given the teaching. I would teach "on the side."

I pulled out a piece of paper and wrote out my letter to the vice president of the college, then read it over, and crossed the first paragraph out, replaced it with a simple, succinct sentence; then I reread the revision, which suddenly sounded too clipped and cold and ungrateful; so I elaborated, choosing an alternative word for *regret,* but dissatisfied with the alternative, returned to *regret,* then tried *sorry,* then a few other alternatives, chewing off the cap on my pen, settling finally for *regret;* at which point, I reread the letter, crushed it up, started a new version—a process I repeated several times. It took a whole afternoon to draft my resignation letter.

I was already embarked on my full-time profession of writing.

LIKE THE IMMIGRANT who is constantly tempted to cast a lingering backward look to see what it is she has left behind, I keep looking behind me at my twenty-plus years of teaching. Why is it that even though I am happy with my new life, still, when I drive by the college on a brisk autumn day and see the students going up the walk on their way to class, I feel a surge of homesickness, as if I were passing by my old childhood house back on the Island?

I know no other way of explaining it but that the academy has always been my home in the United States. Leaving it is my second big emigration into the blank sheet of paper. Once we arrived in this country, my sisters and I had no guides, no models in the family or among our acquaintances whom we could follow into this new culture. Especially at the beginning, my parents discouraged friendships with classmates and neighbors. These natives were "foreigners" to us. We didn't know what kind of families they come from, Mami said. As for absorbing the culture via the media: the new color television was in my parents' bedroom; the old black-and-white one was in the basement and unofficially "belonged" to Ada, our live-in Dominican maid. Her only pleasure in her hard and homesick life was keeping up with her novelas on the Spanish language channel. No one would think of depriving her of that to watch the Beatles on *Ed Sullivan* or *Patty Duke* or *Father Knows Best* or *Ozzie and Harriet,* shows that might have filled us all in on life in these United States of America.

So my sisters and I had to rely on school to pick up the culture. Not that school was the friendliest place, with kids taunting our clothes and our accents. But from the beginning, I had the good luck of running into some fine teachers: a generous nun in parochial school; a wonderful spitfire biology teacher my first year in high school; Mr. Barstow at a summer school camp; Miss Stevenson and Miss St. Pierre at boarding school; Bill Meredith, and as a brief visitor, June Jordan, at Connecticut College; Robert Pack at Middlebury; Philip Booth and Donald Dike at Syracuse. As I mention each name, I feel a shiver of recognition: each one passed me on to the next and the next until I reached the end of my apprenticeship and became, like them, a teacher.

IT HAPPENED, OF course, like most things in my life, by accident. That is, I followed along, teacher to teacher, high school to college to graduate school. At each juncture, my parents questioned whether they should let their daughters continue to educate themselves out of a Dominican future as wives and mothers back on the Island. But by that time, we all knew in the back of our minds that our lives were going to happen in this country. An education was the only guarantee of a secure future here.

So, education became sacrosanct in our immigrant household. Our otherwise strict old-world parents would allow and even pay for any activity if my sisters and I could put an educational spin on it. We'd ask for permission to go to the 42nd Street Library on a Saturday afternoon, but in fact, we were headed to the Village to see hippies and maybe even meet a few. In college, on Saturday nights, my parents' preferred calling time, we would leave a message with the dorm receptionist: if our parents call, please tell them we're at the library, studying. And in fact, seven times out of ten, we were actually at the library. It had been drummed into us: our true green card in America was an education—a high school diploma, a college degree, a teaching certificate. My father had a veritable accordion of cards in his wallet, proving that he was a member of one organization or another: the Royal Academy of Medicine, the American College of Surgeons, the American Medical Association; that he held surgical privileges at three New York hospitals; that he had completed any number of courses at association meetings.

Suddenly, it seemed, the whole family was studying. My mother began taking evening courses at the local college for her real estate license. My physician father signed up for more than the required hours of continuing education courses. He also started taking German and Chinese, "just in case," though he never explained what eventuality he was preparing himself for. I, who had been a terrible student back home, a hooky player and a cutup in class, failing every grade through fifth and having to make up the difference during summer school, suddenly became a serious, but sadly anxious, student.

I've tried to understand where such enormous pressure came from. When we first arrived, my mother used to warn us that unless we behaved ourselves in this country, our family would be sent back. Good behavior meant, of course, that my sisters and I had to earn good report cards—for how else could the Americans judge our merits in being allowed to stay? Though I wanted to go back home more than anything in the world, by this time I knew about the horrible dictatorship. Each A I earned was not just a personal accomplishment but a way to save my family and to prove our worth to the Americans. When, a few years later, I started to panic and walk out of exams, the school counselor diagnosed my stress level around tests and papers as so high that I could literally not hear myself think. My teachers, Miss Stevenson and later Miss St. Pierre, found the solution in allowing me to write "creatively" about what I was learning— essays, poems, stories, journals, which I could work on in my room and hand in without the dreaded clock incapacitating me.

I mention this incident because already it was my teachers who were helping me find solutions to the problems and pressures of a home divided by new-world pressures and an old-world style. To the maid, Ada, I confessed my heart every time I came home for vacations, but to my teachers, I divulged my dreams. Being women who had followed their

dreams, they presented me with proof that such a translation was possible, maybe even for me.

As the end of college rolled around, my parents began
suggesting that my older sister and I come back home to live
with them until such time as we would marry. Even better,
why didn't we consider going back home where we would
meet someone suitable? Of course, the security of the offer
was alluring. My Dominican girl cousins were all getting engaged, marrying, establishing themselves in traditional lives
of their own. But once back on the Island, I found myself
getting into arguments with my aunts, interrupting the men
to debate some pronouncement they had made, befriending
the maids, scandalizing everyone with my American ways. If
I went off on my own to read and write, my family found
such self-imposed solitude troubling. (¿Qué te pasa? ¿Estas
triste?) My American education had spoiled me for life in
my native country.

Also, unlike many of my Island cousins, I did not have a
private income. We had started over when we came to this
country—not that my father had ever had a whole lot of
money back home. It was my mother's family who were well-
to-do, and though we could benefit from her family's status
there, her name and connections meant nothing here. My
sisters and I had to earn our livings and make our own way
in this country. I already knew I wanted to be a writer, but
writing had to be combined with a "real job" to put bread
and butter on the table. So, of course, I thought of teaching. There was also the other option: working in a publishing house, which, because it was closer to the wheels of
actual publication, sounded much more promising.

Soon after graduation from college, I moved back in with

my parents in Queens and landed a "publishing" job in New York City. Every day I took the subway in to an office across the street from the 42nd Street Library. (A touch of poetic justice to have as my daily destination the place I had used as an alibi for so many years!) My job was to put together a weekly newsletter for libraries and businesses on the topic of ecology. Special Reports, Inc., my employer, comprised two men, one of whom I never met, and another one who came in several times a week to see how we were doing. "We" was myself and a talkative, attractive secretary in the main room whose job it was to answer the rare phone call and sort out the mail. I had my own cubicle, and periodically, Lillian would appear at my door or I would come out and sit on the edge of her desk and we'd gab. Eventually, we would arrive at our favorite topic of discussion: whether Special Reports was a front for something else. How could a newsletter with two hundred or so subscribers pay the rent, not to mention our two salaries?

Although I had worried at first about my ignorance, it soon became clear that I didn't have to know anything about ecology. I was to copy news releases from environmental organizations and the E.P.A., rewriting them ever so slightly so as not to plagiarize technically. In that small dark office, without the interaction and community of a classroom, I felt like Bartleby, the scrivener, Melville's disaffected clerk, who ends up responding to life by folding his arms and saying, "I would prefer not to."

I decided to apply to an M.F.A. program, not because I wanted to earn a terminal writing degree (the sound of it even scared me), but because I wanted to buy some time to do some writing. I also wanted to be part of a community of learners again. My second year in the creative writing program at Syracuse University, I held a teaching assistantship and taught several "short term" poetry courses to first-year students.

I can't say I really enjoyed this first-time teaching experience: the heavy weight of performance was on me; after all, we were the M.F.A.-ers, not the serious Ph.D.-ers, and our capability to teach academic subjects was suspect. It was as if I were back at the exam room, wanting to bolt each time I walked into my classroom. I went in with so many notes and handouts that my students could have said about my class what Peter DeVries said about writing, that he liked it well enough, but the paperwork was killing him.

As the end of graduate school rolled around, I again had to decide how it was that I was going to earn a living. I debated then, and again at several unemployed junctures in my teaching/writing life, whether to go on for a Ph.D. so that I would be taken seriously (that is, hired in a tenured position) by the academy. But every time I decided to go ahead and get my doctorate, a few days sitting in among scholarly academics convinced me that I did not belong among them. I loved living inside a book, but I much preferred creating my own to explicating already existing texts.

So when an opening came up for a poet in a poetry-in-the-schools program in Kentucky, I applied for the job. I could not believe my luck when I got it! My two-year assignment involved ten six-week residencies in different locations. Of course, I assumed these "locations" would all be in high schools, but in fact, they included grammar schools, community colleges, a convent, a correction school for girls, a state prison, an old-age home—ten vastly different communities in all.

During my time in each of these communities, in addition to my daily classes, I gave local readings, adult workshops at night in church basements or town halls, in the rectory of the church, in the nuns' dining room. For each of those six-week residencies, teaching involved total immersion in a community. Though I didn't have as much time to write as I would have liked, I can truly say that I "cut my teeth" as a teacher in Kentucky. At the end of those two years, I felt as if I could be put in front of any group of people, and I could "teach" them something about writing poetry.

In Elkton, Kentucky, one old-timer appeared in my community poetry workshop because he had heard that some lady was here with the government (Kentucky State Arts Commission) to talk about "poultry." Even after I cleared up his misunderstanding, he stayed and "dictated" his poem about growing up on a chicken farm. It turned out that he, like a few others, had never learned to read and write. And so, every evening before the poetry workshop, I taught a small group of locals how to read. I don't know if any of these students ever became fluent readers, but I certainly learned a lot from them about incorporating natural speech rhythms into what I was writing.

This was really the great discovery of why I would want to teach: I could go on learning! I didn't have to be the one who knows. How dreary! What Frost said about writing poetry ("No surprise for the writer, no surprise for the reader") also holds true for teaching. Unless a teacher is making discoveries in the classroom, rediscovering the text with the "beginner's mind" that Zen masters talk about, the class lacks the magical sense of possibility and discovery.

"To teach is to learn twice," as Joseph Joubert once said, and not only did I learn almost everything I needed to know about teaching those first two years out in the field, but I also discovered new authors and texts in my search to find works that might appeal to the different populations I was addressing. And though I learned that I could never predict how a particular class or residency would go, I did discover that the more fun I was having in the classroom, the better I was at teaching.

Sixteen years later when I came up for tenure, all joy would flow from the room the minute some observer dropped in to sit at the back and scribble notes on my performance. The old dread would fill my chest: what if I failed? This time I would not be deported from the country, but from the academy. The upshot would be the same: no place to call home. Once, I went blank with terror and had to excuse myself to use the bathroom. Really, I was headed out the door of the building. I calmed myself down, went into a stall, flushed for appearances and came back out, my heart pounding. I kept thinking of Chaucer, whose "General Prologue" I had just been teaching, of the phrase he used to describe the Parson, "First he wrought, and afterward he taught." I decided that's what I would do if I didn't get tenure. I'd go out and "wrought" for a while, and then come back on some future date and teach again. For some reason, this possibility of another option loosened the stranglehold of terror. I went back into the classroom and finished the hour. A few weeks later, the letter came, announcing that I had been awarded tenure.

I suppose of all the classes I have taught, my favorites have been the writing workshops. Generally, they are the smaller classes and, at least in my estimation, the toughest to teach. Unlike my colleagues in literature courses, writing teachers rarely get a standing ovation at the end of the semester, and evaluations are almost always mixed. After all, you have been dealing with students' creative work, and any serious critique you make, no matter how crucial and helpful it might be to them in the future, takes several years to become meaningful.

The immediate response can be defensive or dismissive. As one student wrote me in a personal letter at the end of the course, "You don't have an appreciation of different kinds of literature. You are really limited even if you are a good teacher." She had been very upset because I had suggested that she cut the endless and abstract rantings on crack of one of her characters, even if the story was "supposed to be surrealistic." Another student, whose female characters I found clichéd and a little flat, wrote in his evaluation that I was too feminine a teacher. I think he meant feminist.

Though I can joke about these critiques now, they trouble me when I receive them. One senior colleague refuses to teach workshops anymore because, as he himself admitted, if you do your job well, they're going to resent you. The final verdict is always the same: "More brilliance!" as my teacher W. D. Snodgrass used to say at the end of each workshop. The last day of the semester when I hear the applause wafting up from my colleagues' literature classrooms, I feel a pang of envy. Creative writing workshops are automatic disappointments to students who sign up, under the false impression that such "touchy-feely" courses are easy, literary therapy groups, where all you have to do is feel deeply to get a good grade.

I try to dispel this notion from the first day by emphasizing the apprenticeship aspect of the workshop. We are here to learn a craft that truly takes all of life to learn! There are models to emulate, skills to be mastered, and mostly, the habit of art to be acquired like any habit, by repetition, that is, revision, revision, revision. Craft is what I can help them with. Talent itself is unpredictable: some writers flower in their youth, like Rimbaud, with *A Season in Hell*, and some come into ripeness when they are older, like Harriet Doerr, who published *Stones for Ibarra,* her first novel, when she was in her early seventies. And talent without skills and discipline is finally useless. So I focus on the latter two "teachable" aspects of writing.

I suppose I am in the writing-teacher tradition of Theodore Roethke, who was known for his daunting assignments, including final examinations in his workshop course that included questions like: *Please write four quatrains of anapestic tetrameter on the theme of spring. Ten stanzas of terza rima with internal slant-rhymes, please.* Elizabeth Bishop, who taught poetry later at the same university, using Roethke's old classroom, found an inscription scratched out on the underside of one of the desks and signed with a student's name, "Died, June 8, 1952, in an exam of Ted Roethke's."

But though he presented himself as a stern taskmaster, what Roethke most adored about teaching was that it was "one of the few professions that permit love." No matter how rough the students' drafts are, their lives, preoccupations, worries, hopes, dreams, fears are the content. This aspect of a workshop course gives it a special charge. Meg's

villanelle is not just a villanelle whose rhyme scheme and re-
peating lines we can discuss. It also happens to be a poem
about her parents' divorce, and a discussion of the poem
will inevitably touch on the accuracy of the observations and
the rightness of the tone, which inevitably suggest issues of
emotional honesty and decorum, which, of course, have
everything to do with what is going on in Meg's life right
now. Our lives, after all, are the very matter of our art.

As a writing teacher, this is the most difficult balance to
strike: how much to focus on craft *and* how much to step
back and let students discover their own voices and concerns
without feeling they will be laughed at or penalized for
doing so. And the grade issue is always an issue in academic
teaching. Finally, you do have to stick a number on this
process that began before they ever sat down in your classroom and will continue long after they leave. My policy here
has always been to minimize the grading aspect of the course
and emphasize the lifelong process of writing. I've also told
some of my workshops what Roethke used to tell his classes,
"Those students get the highest grades who take their re-
sponsibilities of educating me the most seriously."

Needless to say, my students are constantly challenging
me to redefine old insights, to crack open my treasured
chestnuts of truth, to learn what I don't know, and to con-
front my own process of writing in order to help them. This
last is perhaps the most educational aspect of my teaching.
The best skills become almost automatic, and teaching
brings them back again to the surface to be reexamined,
sharpened, discarded, or reaffirmed. Some fellow writers
claim that this makes them self-conscious as writers, pre-
vents them from writing as spontaneously as when they are

not teaching, but I have not found this to be true. In fact, becoming momentarily aware again of what I'd forgotten reinforces that skill in my own writing.

All of this, of course, takes time, not just clock time but imaginative time. It is absorbing work—you are thinking about your students; you are reading and focusing on texts that might provide them with the examples they need to be shown at this stage of their apprenticeship; or you are trying to figure out why a student story isn't working, and then once you think you've pinpointed "the problem," you are wondering how you might help them resolve it technically. You are also reading other texts, searching for models and methods to help them master certain writing skills. Finally, you are just plain thinking about your students a lot—and all of this takes time, energy, imaginative space which you are not giving to your own work.

And so, I am back full circle to why I had to give up full-time teaching to concentrate on my writing.

NOW INSTEAD OF my usual September nightmare, in which I am walking into a classroom, having forgotten my books, or walking into a classroom in which I suddenly find I have to teach postmodern literary theory and I know nothing about it, or walking into a classroom without my clothes on, my bad dream has to do with roaming through my deserted English department building wondering where everyone is.

And then, in one of those sudden dream-state shifts, they file down the corridors, my past students, whose names come back to me like an old roll call, Mike Laba, Lauren Husted, Allan Reeder, Eliza Harding, Ann Mitsakos, Suzanne Schneider, Ofelia Barrios, Abby Manzella—a long line of them.

Goodbye, Ms. Chips

. . . Not quite Macbeth's line of kings that stretched out "to th'crack of doom," but a substantial enough crowd. Did I really teach that many young people?

It sure seems like it. These days my students are showing up not just in my dreams but in my life! I go on a book tour, and there they are in the audience. I visit a TV station, and the producer took my poetry workshop ten years ago. I call for help from a computer software company, and a former student answers. I even got a rejection slip from a magazine with a note at the bottom from a student: *Remember me?* My babies are now out there minding the world or writing their own books or teaching their own students, maybe using one of my stories or poems, maybe saying, This writer was once my teacher.

In the Name of the Novel

. . . .

I have come to Necedah to find out if I should write the novel I am thinking of writing. Necedah: the name sounds biblical, but it is actually the name given by the Winnebago Indians to the place that eventually became a small town in central Wisconsin, population 792 or 743, depending on whether you trust the sign coming into town from the east or from the south. The name means *land of the yellow waters* but the narrow Yellow River cutting through town is a dull blue-gray, the color a child might choose when all the good colors are gone from the crayon box.

I have come to be here on August 15, the feast day of the Assumption. This is the day on which Catholics celebrate the Virgin Mary's bodily "assumption" into heaven, and it is a special anniversary day at the shrine of the Queen of the

Holy Rosary, Mediatrix of Peace, just a couple of miles outside of town. Billboard signs on the highway advertise the
shrine. Perhaps it's the hype of these signs or the chipped
white entrance marker with a lackluster bed of nasturtiums
beneath it and a removable arrow hung on two steel hoops
that makes me sense that maybe I've made a bad choice, as if
I've turned off the highway into the deserted parking lot of
a landlocked Sea Shell City.

Forty-seven years ago, on August 15, 1950, Mary Ann Van
Hoof, a gaunt, big-jawed, forty-one-year-old farm woman
attracted a crowd of a hundred thousand people who came,
hoping to witness a miracle. They had heard that the Blessed
Mother had promised to appear on her big feast day. Only
once before had she officially visited this continent. In 1531,
she had appeared to Juan Diego as la Virgen de Guadalupe,
but this would be her first public appearance on United
States soil. *Life* and *Newsweek* covered the event. Special phone
lines were strung from the road so reporters could call in
their stories to newsrooms in Chicago and New York City. A
microphone and loudspeakers were set up to boom the Virgin Mary's voice as she spoke through Mary Ann out into the
sandy fields.

Mary Ann had already had seven visitations—though it
wasn't until the third one that she knew who her visitor was.
"She was about five feet tall and looked to be about eighteen
years old," Mary Ann reported. Proof had already been
given of the vision's authenticity: Blessed Mother, as Mary
Ann came to call her, requested that people of the parish
pray their rosaries every evening at eight o'clock—an evil
spirit would not have asked for that. She also mentioned
that Mary Ann was thinking of cutting her hair short, and in

fact, Mary Ann had been planning on cutting it and getting a Toni. She came up with facts and figures that manifested a mathematical bent. She showed Mary Ann a vision of "grade-school-size and high- and college-size students disobeying the sixth commandment, the fifth commandment, the second and seventh, and through these breaking the third." As for the adults, "seventy-five percent live in sin," she explained to Mary Ann, who conveyed that message to the crowds that had begun to gather at her farm. "Three-thirds of America is covered with the enemies of God," she appended. When a newspaperman scoffed that the Virgin Mary wasn't making any sense, Mary Ann made it clear that all mistakes in math and grammar were hers. The Virgin Mary had probably said two-thirds.

I read all these admissions in the compendious volumes of transcribed testimony that Mary Ann's followers have kept for the last forty-six years. Mary Ann herself died in 1984 at the age of seventy-four, toothless from knocking out most of her teeth during her "passion trances," bloated with a dropsy condition, not having lived to see the Catholic Church lift its interdict against her and her shrine. She was buried without the benefit of the Last Sacraments in unconsecrated ground just north of the shrine grounds in a small, almost-empty cemetery for "shriners." As for the shrine itself, it is still under interdict. This means that any Catholics visiting it are under chastisement by the church and cannot receive any of the sacraments without first making a public reconciliation.

I knew all this prior to coming to Necedah. But as a long-time lapsed and divorced Catholic, I am already persona non grata in any parish. As for Blessed Mother's dubious pronouncements, I have chosen to ignore them. I want to believe in Mary Ann Van Hoof. I have in mind George Eliot's words in her prelude to *Middlemarch*: "Many Theresas have been born who found for themselves no epic life wherein there was a constant unfolding of far-resonant action; perhaps only a life of mistakes, the offspring of a certain spiritual grandeur ill-matched with the meanness of opportunity." I want Mary Ann to be this failed Saint Theresa, a soul with immortal longings who fell prey to that zany American variety of the sacred that makes of Elvis Presley's birthplace a shrine and creates crazy cults where everyone drinks poisoned Kool-Aid and dies at noon. I think I might have an American spiritual tragedy to tell. And so I am joining the pilgrims at Necedah on August 15, not to witness the sun spinning or Mary Ann's presence in a ray of light, but in the name of the novel about her failed quest that I believe I want to write.

BEFORE COMING TO Necedah, I already had some doubts, but then, what novelist doesn't have doubts about her characters? You spend two, three years trying to give voice to something that does not exist anywhere but in your head. All along the way, you wonder if you are fooling yourself. This was sure to be true of Mary Ann Van Hoof, whom I first encountered in *Encountering Mary*, Sandra Zimdars-Swartz's book about Marian apparitions.

Mary Ann Van Hoof was a simple, devout farm woman of German descent who began seeing visions of the Virgin Mary in November 1949. For thirty-five years, before her death in 1984, this "victim soul," as her followers refer to her, took on all sorts of "extra suffering" for the world. Frequently, she endured the passion, writhing, and moaning as if she were being crucified—though one of her priest examiners described the "disgusting performance" as another kind of passion, "horrible to see." Several times she was marked by the stigmata, the wounds of the crucified Christ—but after the Catholic authorities hospitalized her and bandaged up her hands to see if the Virgin Mary could work through science, Mary Ann stopped getting them "externally," but suffered them internally, "where it really mattered." As time went on, her messages grew more and more paranoid. The purpose of the Virgin Mary's U.S.A. visits was to warn Americans against the Communists. There was a conspiracy afoot by the forces of Satan, who were using the Reds as a kind of front.

As her would-be novelist I wished that my budding character had had more enlightened things to say. But I had to put her patriotic paranoia in context. She was visited in the fifties, after all, and Wisconsin's favorite son, Joe McCarthy, lived just down the road in Appleton, forty miles east of Necedah. This conspiratorial view of history was part of the air that Americans were breathing at the time. And Mary Ann Van Hoof took big hungry swallows of it, which Sandra Zimdars-Swartz traced back to an unhappy childhood with a violent, abusive father who had given the young seer the sense that the world was not a safe place.

Little tendrils of interest began to bind me to this story. I was between books, hungry myself for a subject I could devour. And I had been looking for a Midwest subject, one that would plunge me into the landscape of my husband's people, German farmers from Nebraska. My husband had been such a trooper for the last three years while I worked on my second novel. Every vacation had been taken up by trips back to the Dominican Republic so I could do my research. Sometimes, lying in bed at night, my husband would ask after my characters. How was the Patria chapter going? Had I found out when it was that amapolas bloom? It was high time that I took on a subject that would allow me to immerse myself in *his* background.

So a Midwestern German farm woman with an eighth-grade education was right up my writing alley. True, my husband's people are German Lutherans—more practical, commonsensical, Protestant. But all I would have to do to imagine Mary Ann—her violent, raging father, her Spiritist mother, her own ecstatic trances and Catholic passions—was "raise the volume" on the Manns and Eichners. The way I saw it, Mary Ann Van Hoof was simply a more Latina-type German. It was natural for me to write about her.

From the bibliography in Sandra Zimdars-Swartz's book, I got the title of Mary Ann's book of testimonies and the name of her publisher. I found nothing under her name on the World Wide Web, or under the name of her publisher, or the title of her book. Resorting to old methods, I wrote a letter, addressed to her publisher, For My God and My Country, Inc., Necedah, Wisconsin. Where could I buy a copy of Mary Ann Van Hoof's book? Several weeks later, an old Russell Stover cardboard box loaded with styrofoam peanuts arrived in the mail, the kind of suspect package the Unabomber might send. I listened for a ticking bomb, but hearing nothing, I opened it. Inside I found a plethora of pamphlets and handouts about Mary Ann and the shrine, a four-page order form, a copy of *Revelations and Messages* with a bill typed out on an antique typewriter, the letters cockeyed on the paper. This whole treasure box cost me $2.50, plus $2.50 postage. Right under the $5.00 total was a note, *Thank you & God bless you!*

THROUGHOUT ITS HISTORY, the Catholic Church has not looked favorably on visitations—of the nearly eighty thousand apparitions of Mary that have been claimed since the third century A.D. only seven (about one-hundredth of one percent) have received official recognition. As one priest acquaintance pointed out, "If Mary and the saints can come down anytime with new pronouncements, then the church hierarchy and the truths of the gospel and our established tradition can just go out the window." The church's stance is usually not to approve but to say they have found nothing in their investigations to suggest that a visit to the apparition site can be harmful to someone's faith. Damning by faint praise, you might say, but it's far better than the case of Necedah, where the church has taken the extreme step of condemning the shrine and putting all those who visit and participate in shrine activities under interdict.

Hell hath no fury like church officials spurned. When the bishop's office ordered her to close down the shrine, pending approval, Mary Ann at first complied, but then, reopened her farm to pilgrims. "Who you going to listen to," she asked, "the bishop or Blessed Mother?" The bishop's emissaries countered that the Blessed Mother would not go against her own church. But Mary Ann pulled her American trump card on the Catholic hierarchy. "I am a free American citizen. This is my own property. I'll do as I wish."

"Our Lady of Necedah is none other than Mrs. Fred Van Hoof," one of the priests noted.

All of her "emotional answers . . . [in which] she reaches the tempo of a Capt. Queeg on the witness stand" had been documented in a report the investigating committee had submitted to the bishop. On the basis of this report, which included the committee's findings when Mary Ann Van Hoof had been put under observation in a Milwaukee hospital, the bishop had decided to ban the shrine. Obviously, this key report—which reporters and church officials kept alluding to—was one I should read. But it was not listed in any bibliography I could find.

My priest acquaintance suggested I contact the La Crosse diocese, which had conducted the original investigation of Mary Ann and the shrine. This report would have to be in its archives. He found me the chancellor's name and number from his priest directory, and I called numerous times and left numerous messages in which I tried to make myself sound as credible as possible. (I was a professor at Middlebury College. I was doing Marian research, and the Necedah affair had come to my attention.) Finally, one afternoon, the phone rang and I was surprised to hear the voice of a Father Doby on the other end. What did I want, he wanted to know. He sounded weary and wary, a bad combination, I decided. So I went through my prepared introduction again. I was a professor at Middlebury College. I was doing Marian research, and the Necedah affair had come to my attention.

What kind of research exactly was I doing? Father Doby wanted to know. And that's when I started to get into trouble. I was interested in writing a novel based on the experiences of Mary Ann Van Hoof. I wanted to read the report made by the investigating committee that had decided that the visions were bogus.

So was I trying to make her into some kind of heroine? Father Doby wanted to know. No, no, no, I backpedaled. The best writers don't really do that. They tell the truth of the human heart, which is complex and multifaceted. I could hear my voice going into its professor-at-Middlebury-College mode. Our job as artists was "to render the highest kind of justice to the visible universe," as Conrad had said. Surely, nothing could be wrong with that?

There was another long silence. Finally, Father Doby said that he would talk to the bishop and see what he could do and get back to me.

Of course, he never called back. I followed up with a letter to his bishop, requesting that His Excellency consider allowing Father Doby to let me review the findings of the committee. (It turned out my priest acquaintance's directory was outdated and he had given me the name of the previous bishop—so perhaps the letter never got there.) Before I left for Necedah, I called the chancery to see if either Father Doby or the bishop could meet with me. The bishop's secretary said she would give them the message, but by the time I left on August 11, I had not heard back from either official.

AS I DRIVE into Necedah, I look for signs of a novel here. I pass one of the three motels on my list, its parking lot deserted, the windows of some of the cabins boarded up. The Catholic church sports dark reddish brown cutouts of moose and reindeer climbing up the white stucco walls. (Later, I will make sense of this design. The church is called St. Francis, and these creatures are ascending towards his figure on the far right.) The Skillet Restaurant, the only eating place in town that I can see, looks closed. There's one bank, the town library, a religious bookstore, a train station, and the Yellow River, drab blue in the late afternoon light.

I take the wrong turn past the town and end up going down a flat, deserted road with a flank of fir trees on one side and train tracks backed by fir trees on the other side. Big trucks roar by with such rude velocity that my little rental car is shaken by the wind of their passing. I'm in a wilderness, tidy and endless, Midwestern—and I'm going in the wrong direction. But there's no place to turn around. I keep driving. I might end up in California.

Finally, I find a shoulder and turn back towards town. Now I start to see promising billboards, the Necedah Motel, the Queen of the Holy Rosary Shrine, the Woodbine Restaurant. The sun shines through a cloud. More good signs. For the next four days, I will keep doing this, weighing the significance of every event, as if I were back in Catholic school, my immortal soul in the balance. The stakes now are, of course, much lower. I want to write a novel, and I'm skittish and nervous with the possibility that the whole enterprise will not fly. One minute the novel seems a likely possibility, but a minute later I'm sure I'm wasting my time. What I need is what I was taught to wait and pray for back in my school days—grace. The magical and seemingly effortless coming together of all I've worked hard to put into place.

Out the other end of town, I turn right at the sign for the shrine and head down a long country road. I pass the shrine cemetery (a large white angel, wings outspread, is poised to take off from the top of a tombstone), and into a large parking lot deserted but for one R.V. with Ontario plates. A couple sits beside it on folding chairs eating supper. They wave. I wave back and walk through the gate, under the Queen of the Holy Rosary, Mediatrix of Peace, archway, past a rack of pale green wraparound skirts for pilgrims not dressed properly, to the information hut. I peer through the screen door. An old man sits with his head on the table praying the rosary. I knock softly, once, twice, until he looks up and his face breaks into a grin. "Fool ya," he says. He is laughing as he lets me in.

Why is he laughing? I wonder. "I'm just here to see the shrine." It sounds like an apology.

"You sure came to the right place," he says in such a grandfatherly, heartfelt way, that for a moment, I believe him.

THE OLD MAN turns out to be Joe, the eighty-three-year-old caretaker. While he finishes his rosary, I wander the shrine grounds. The place is spooky with its twelve "grottos" lit up, their viewing sides paneled in glass. (Later, from a former shriner, I find out that under some of these grottos are sunken, concrete storage areas for firearms and supplies in case of apocalypse.) I pass the living room of the Blessed Family's home in Nazareth, Mary at her spinning wheel, the bellows leaning against the fireplace. At the Last Supper Jesus is blessing a chalice; one apostle, no doubt Judas, looks out at me, away from the holy moment. The black-garbed Mother Cabrini points with her quill pen to a book she is holding, on which is written her promise: "To go with you if you drive fifty-five miles per hour, not over sixty." Saint Michael tries to put out a nuclear holocaust as if it were a house fire while a nuclear family (Mom, Dad, a boy and girl) kneel in their living room, praying for deliverance. "The choice is yours," the caption reads.

Some of these scenes are painted, some are "sets" with costumed mannequins posed in a tableau. The mannequins are gaudy in the genre of fifties church statuary, with stiff expressions, a superfluousness of folds on their robes, the turquoise very turquoise. At the center of this circle of shrines stands the House of Prayer, heart-shaped and still under construction. The first building had to be torn down because the pilgrim volunteers did not follow heavenly instructions as to specific measurements.)

By the time I have made the rounds and find the Sacred Spot under the four ash trees with the Blessed Mother trapped in a glass bubble, I am full of irony and disbelief. I try to make out her face through the glare of the setting sun reflecting off the glass. Her eyes follow me everywhere. (Tomorrow, a shriner will take me aside and point to this as a sign. "I've baptized her the rubberneck Madonna," she'll say, laughing.) In spite of myself, I kneel down at the kneeler. I want something. *Please, Blessed Mother,* I murmur, *please help me know if I should try to write this novel.*

AT THE NECEDAH Motel, kindness makes up for the lack of frills. The owner, Elizabeth, Catholic and from Poland ("like the pope"), takes me through three cabins before we find one where everything works, the TV, the little fridge, the air conditioner. Once she leaves and I settle in, I find three bullets on the brown-and-orange, flowered bedspread. At least they haven't been used, my husband comforts me over the phone when I call him that night. He's excited I'm in the Midwest. "So do you think it's a go?" he wants to know.

"I actually think it's a bad sign that they're here." I'm still jumpy about those bullets.

"What are you talking about?" he asks, and when I explain, he laughs.

I tell him about my explorations after I left the shrine. I drove slowly down country roads in the area known as "the shrine belt," where devotees, who left homes and jobs behind in other states and cities and towns, have settled and built their houses close to the Sacred Spot. The streets have names like Shrine Road, Queen's Way, Saint Anne's Street, Padre Pio Way, St. Joseph's Road. Night was already falling, and although there were lights on at the St. Francis of Assisi Home for Unfortunate Men and the St. Joseph Worker Hall, the big stone buildings seemed deserted. The Seven Sorrows Home for Unwanted Infants had a flag flying at half mast "in commemoration of the unborn dead." It, too, looked empty. What was going on? Had the shrine turned into a ghost town?

"This isn't a novel, this is something for *60 Minutes*," I complain to my husband.

On the grainy TV, Elizabeth Dole is giving her "spontaneous" speech on the Republican Convention floor. I've got her on mute, so I don't know what the crowd is laughing at or why, suddenly, the faces in close-up are dewy-eyed or intent. I tell Bill how at the shrine the old caretaker had told me that when a hundred thousand would gather at the farm, you could hear a pin drop once Mary Ann had come out of her farmhouse and walked the short distance to the Sacred Spot and knelt before the ash trees in seeming conversation with the air.

After we say good night, it still hangs over me, like a cloud, a sadness I hadn't anticipated. I don't want to think this, not yet anyhow, but I can't help feeling that the shrine is a sham, not the sadistic kind that *60 Minutes* would report on where someone has pulled the wool over somebody else's eyes, but the kind of sad sham where someone pulls the wool over her own eyes as well.

I pull on the bedspread, which serves as a blanket, and cover my face to block out the outdoor light that comes in through the missing slats of the venetian blinds. The spread reeks of a synthetic, flowery scent that pervades the room. The next day I tell a shriner about the strong smell in my motel room, and her face lights up. "That's the odor of sanctity!" I remember from my readings how in many reported apparitions, the appearance of Blessed Mother is signaled by a smell of roses or some other sweet scent of flowers.

"You're lucky," my shriner friend tells me. "She doesn't give everyone a sign, you know."

EARLY THE NEXT morning I drive into town to St. Francis Catholic Church for the seven-fifteen mass. One of the former shriners I spoke to yesterday on the phone advised me to go and "read what's on the door." I arrive ten minutes early but already there are a dozen or more cars in the parking lot. I am embarrassed to hang around and not go in, so I wait until the last parishioner has gone inside, then I begin to read.

There is the ban of 1955, with the heading *OFFICIAL*, signed by Bishop John P. Treacy, Bishop of La Crosse: *All claims regarding supernatural revelations and visions made by the aforemen-*

tioned Mrs. Van Hoof are false. Furthermore, all public and private religious worship connected with these false claims is prohibited at Necedah, Wisconsin. A second document, dated 1975, reiterates the ban and places the seven leaders of the shrine under interdict. Beside it, the interdict of 1985 extends the original seven-person interdict to all "those who publicly associate themselves with the shrine." Surrounding these three official documents are numerous other "admonitions" and "decrees" warning that certain so-called priests who have associated themselves with the shrine are either not priests or have been suspended by the bishop. One last document, a form titled *Request for Reconciliation with the Roman Catholic Church,* is available inside for anyone who has fallen into temptation and wants permission to come back into the fold. Red arrows on the margins of all these documents call attention to this or that name or consequence for disobedience.

The tone of these documents makes even my lapsed-Catholic stomach queasy: shades of my old nun teachers with rulers in hand ready to punish minor transgressions — but here, eternal damnation hangs in the balance, not bruised knuckles. I wonder about the wisdom of cluttering up the church door with these notices. Lost is the announcement for a church picnic, a retreat over in Appleton, a call to anyone wanting to participate in organizing the fall bazaar. But then, church doors have traditionally been the arena of church wars as Martin Luther well knew when he posted his Protestant declaration of independence on the Wittenburg church door.

Inside, the church is unbelievably full for such an early morning mass on a regular weekday. Many of the women have covered their heads, as was required during Mary Ann

Van Hoof's time—mantillas or hats or, in a pinch, a husband's handkerchief. Father James, a large man in red vestments that make him look even larger, intones the mass in what seems to me a bored, perfunctory manner. Perhaps it's all those warnings on his church door that have set me up to dislike him. But, after mass, when I step into the sacristy to see if he will talk to me, he turns out to be a calm man with a kindly manner. "Give me a moment, will ya?" Minutes later, we sit talking in the small office in the tidy, one-story house that serves as a rectory.

Father James admits that the shrine controversy has torn the town, if not his parish, in two. Even within families, some are shriners, others aren't. Kenny, for instance, Mary Ann's youngest boy, is one of the leaders at the shrine. His sister Donna fell out in 1984 and is a member of Father James's parish. What's more, it's not just a certain credulous class of people who have become associated with the place, but well-educated, upstanding members of the community, a lawyer, a school principal, a mill owner, a psychiatrist, a bookstore owner and publisher. Father James hands me a series of investigative articles written by two reporters from the *Milwaukee Journal.* According to their findings, the cult controls a solid block of five hundred votes in Juneau County—which includes Necedah—where an average of only twelve hundred voters turn out at the polls. Often, it is the shriners who decide a vote. So local politicians and officials are loath to cross them.

The series of articles is unnerving: Shrine houses stocked with arsenals of guns, waiting for an apocalyptic shoot-out. "Praise the Lord and Pass the Ammo," the article is titled. A six-hour gunfight in which one shriner killed another. A scandal at the "baby farm," as the Home for Unwanted Infants is locally known, in which the psychiatrist tried to circumcise a baby boy and cut off the tip of his penis. Another premature baby died for lack of proper care. False shrine priests with police records that include everything from telephone fraud to disorderly conduct to statutory rape; one priest even brought along his own "altar boy," a ten-year-old with whom he was having a sexual relationship.

Sitting at his desk, Father James smokes quietly as I read. Every time a stream of smoke comes my way, I lean back in my chair. When his housekeeper calls him to breakfast, I step outside, glad for the sun on my skin, the fresh air on my face, the sense of release. But the smell of Father James's cigarettes follows me everywhere, caught in my clothes, in my hair, in the files he has let me borrow. Back at the motel, in a kind of Manichean battle of smells, the evil smell of tobacco competes with the perfumey-cleanser smell.

IT IS DURING my meetings with the former shriners that I realize that my interest has shifted, away from Mary Ann Van Hoof, to them, the men and women who came to Necedah in the late sixties and early seventies—only to find themselves twenty-five years later awash on the shore of another American dream turned nightmare.

Why did they come? I put the question to each of them. In each case, they talked to me only with the understanding that I not reveal their names or identities. "These people are my neighbors," one former shriner explained. "They run things around here. They could make it very hard for me."

Why did they come? They came because they were fervent Catholics who believed that America was falling apart. The

Catholic Church was being infiltrated by progressives who were doing the work of Satan. America was about to undergo nuclear destruction. It was the sixties, though probably in this north-central area of the country, it was still the 1950s. One former shriner and her husband were living in fear of imminent disaster. They were sure that the big interstates were being built in order to send troops to hold citizens hostage in the cities. The concrete tubes and guardrails being set in place by large cranes were parts of bunkers. "We thought if we stayed in the city, we would never get out." This couple found the right visionary in Mary Ann Van Hoof.

They came because this was supposed to be a place where the real values of America would be followed. The Necedah cause is, after all, a right-wing patriotic movement as well as a religious cult, the whole enterprise run by For My God and My Country, Inc. At the center of the shrine grounds, a statue of Jesus stands below the American flag (at half mast, for the unborn dead), with George Washington on his right and Abraham Lincoln on his left. According to Mary Ann, Blessed Mother was in contact with George Washington during the founding years of this country. In fact, Blessed Mother promised to appear on top of the Washington Monument as soon as the cities were cleaned up. She came to Necedah, not just to give Americans their very own apparition, but for matters of national security. There were secret messages for the president and top officials. A constant vigil of prayer was instituted in order to save America. *Keep A Great Thing Growing: America,* reads the motto of the shrine brochure. This was God's appointed place: Necedah, Wisconsin.

"Wouldn't you have wanted to be here?" another former shriner asked me.

Once she joined, she had to swear the Total Consecration Oath—"I am Thine and all that I have is Thine to be used as You see fit." To give me an indication of how total this consecration was, she handed me the thick packet of rules shriners had to follow. Every aspect of her life was controlled: the temperature in her house, what food she put on the table, the schedule of her days and nights. "Some nights I'd get a call, Mary Ann was going into her passion and I had to be there to pray while she suffered. Maybe it'd be three in the morning, winter time. It didn't matter. Attendance was required."

Many shriners dropped out of the shrine family between 1983 and 1984, the year a series of scandals brought investigative reporters and television crews to the shrine—the shrine shoot-out Father James told me about, the phony priests, the scandals at the Infant's Home, which caused its license to be withdrawn. Finally, around the time the bishop extended the interdict, not just to the leadership, but to all who were in any way associated with the shrine, many shriners decided it was time to let go.

But after twelve years of recovery and deprogramming, these former shriners are still fearful of repercussions and, in many cases, still obsessed with the cause. One widow lives so close to the shrine that in her living room we could hear the pilgrims singing during a vigil. The shrine took over her whole life, and it will take time to get it back. Some nights when there are events, she admits, she drives by the shrine real slow just to see what is going on.

Later that Tuesday night, I attend a ceremony at the Sacred Spot, two hours of prayers in the buggy, chilly dark. About forty pilgrims—many of them shrine families—kneel or sit on benches in front of the statue of Our Lady of Necedah. On the bench beside me, two little boys in sweatshirts, hoods over their heads, mumble their prayers, rosary beads slipping through their fingers. They seem dazed with sleepiness, their lips barely moving. Soon, the smaller one slumps against the older one, dozing off. A car drives by, slowly, its headlights shining on the shrine so that someone not knowing what I now know might take the sudden beam of light as a heavenly sign.

THE MOST POIGNANT of my interviews is with Donna, Mary Ann's youngest daughter, who agrees to talk to me at the Necedah Motel. We both find the smell in my room unpleasantly strong and so we sit outside at a picnic table under some pines. With some alterations in hairstyle, weight, and fashion, Donna could be her mother. In fact, when she knocked at the door and I opened it, my heart did a quick skip, as if an apparition of Mary Ann Van Hoof were before me.

Donna dropped out of the shrine in 1984. Before the interdict, I note. The key event that allowed for her defection was her mother's death in March of that year. She already had many doubts, she admits. She was especially suspicious of all those crazy priests. But she would not have dared contradict her mother. After all, she grew up thinking her mother was a stand-in for the Blessed Mother. She blames herself . . . because maybe she should have dropped a suggestion here and there that might have led her mother to reconsider her disobedience to the church.

Before we part, I ask her the question I've been wanting to ask since we sat down, and which I've been turning over and over in my head, wondering how to ask it so that it is not insulting to her. "Do you think your mother was operating in good faith?"

Donna thinks a moment, the sadness coming back into her eyes, before she answers me. "I think Mom believed in what she was doing," and then the thought she cannot put out of her mind, "but she was misled."

Just before Donna goes, I take her picture in front of my motel door. Big-boned and blond-haired, she does look like her mother, but I would never mistake her for a shriner or even a former shriner. Unlike the others, she seems to have truly let go of the shrine business, rather than just transferred the same kind of obsessive allegiance to the Catholic Church. There is a tone about her, a sad wistfulness, as if something grand has passed out of her life. Like the rest of us, she now lives in a fallen world, various and complex and endlessly baffling. This is the world her mother was trying to cancel out with easy revelations and answers. I realize why her daughter and former followers have captured my interest. They are the ones struggling with the questions. It is in their name that a novelist must write her novels.

THE NEXT DAY, Wednesday, I drive two hours west to La Crosse, a large city on the eastern bank of the Mississippi River, where the diocesan center for this area is located. The countryside is rolling hills, golden in the late afternoon light, gentle swells as if a slow-motion wave were passing through the land and if I stopped driving and stood still, I would be borne the 160 miles to La Crosse in a hundred years. I am not going to wait that long. I drive on. Over the hills and through the dales to see Father Doby.

I no longer want to go, but I figure it's part of my job as a would-be novelist to close the records and talk to the authorities. I don't expect any surprises since, knowing what I now know, I, too, would have voted against Mary Ann's visions. And yet as I drive into the chancery grounds and glance up at the massive cathedral, its impressive dome and glinting spire backlit by the setting sun, I feel that old nagging allegiance to the underdog, the Necedah shriners with their unfinished heart-shaped House of Prayer and tacky, floor-lit grottos. The eighty-three-year-old caretaker packing off rosaries to believers in California and Iowa. (The choice of beads includes aurora borealis, pastel pearl, cocoa teardrop.) Of course, a mighty institution with the power to sanction the authenticity of a spiritual event and a spire as high as anything else in La Crosse could clobber a simple, if misguided, farm woman and her small band of believers. But I remind myself that Mary Ann and her shriners are much more complex than that. It is not so easy to turn this into a story of good and evil.

Inside his office, Father Doby points to my chair, and then, instead of choosing the chair beside mine, he sits behind his desk, as if to put an expanse of red-bound, ecclesiastical-looking tomes between us. He is a short man, so the clutter almost hides him from my view. On the wall to his left, I spot a photo of a young, slender, very pretty Father Doby, bowing his head as Pope John Paul blesses him. "From my time in Rome," he says curtly when I ask, oh, does he know His Holiness?

"I've been at the shrine for the past three days," I begin — and then, remembering the interdict, I add, "interviewing." Father Doby's face shows no response. His eyes do not look at me so much as scan me as if they were gun detectors in airports or shoplifting detectors in stores. I feel an impulse to show him my hands and say, Look, I have taken nothing.

"I also spoke to Father James," I continue. "He was very helpful, very nice." I let that compliment lie for a moment between us. Maybe it will act as a character tenderizer, parish priest peer pressure. But of course, Father Doby is not in the parish priest league; he is a lawyer, a church lawyer, which is pressure enough when you consider that his only client is God. "I thought maybe you could tell me a little about the investigation of Mary Ann Van Hoof?" We are onto the contested ground of the confidential church report he never called me back about.

Father Doby scans me. "You ask the questions, and I'll answer them if I can."

I do the internal count to ten my husband taught me to keep down that Latin temper that scares people from Nebraska. Then, I do another exercise that predates my husband and that I don't remember anyone ever teaching me to do. Since early adulthood, whenever I've caught myself on the verge of really disliking someone, I try this exercise: I imagine the hateful person as some mother's child. That is the phrase, *He is his mother's son or her mother's daughter.* I try to see the meanness or sarcasm or pushiness in the light of that understanding. The exercise doesn't always work. But if I tally up the success rate, it works about as often in controlling my temper as my husband's Nebraskan technique of counting to ten in both my languages.

I note the gray in Father Doby's hair—he is older than I thought, but younger than my forty-six years. Delicately boned, his body does not gracefully support the weight he has started putting on. In his face I see now the boy, now the grown man. I try again. Is there a certain procedure that the church follows in deciding whether an apparition is authentic or not? I know, for instance, that the church has a step-by-step process for the canonization of a saint, complete with a devil's advocate whose job is to dig up dirt on the would-be saint. But the procedure for sanctioning an apparition seems to be as vague as air.

He would not say so, Father Doby says. It's not that the apparition procedure is vague, but unlike the canonization process, which is conducted by the curia in Rome, apparitions are investigated by committees appointed by local bishops, who set up what they consider to be the important criteria. So the procedure has some flexibility.

The eyes are bright and the grin that sometimes accompanies a statement is the grin of a smart boy who can think up the right answer quicker than anyone else in his fourth-grade class.

"Well, what then is the procedure?"

"It depends on the bishop."

There is no way Father Doby is going to give me more of an answer than he needs to. I decide to appeal to his vanity. "Suppose *you* were the bishop, Father, and Mary Ann Van Hoof came to you claiming to have seen the Virgin. What would be the criteria you set up for your investigating committee?"

Amazingly, he agrees to enter this game of pretend with me. There are three simple guidelines, he explains tiredly, as if he has explained this many times before. Number one, he would tell his committee to interview as many people associated with the apparition as possible, including the Van Hoofs, the parish priest, members of her church and community, in order to ascertain the character of the seer and her family. Number two, he would have them conduct a thorough study of the said apparition's pronouncements to make sure they are all in accord with church teachings. Finally, number three, he would have them evaluate any claims of miraculous happenings.

When I finish writing the list in my journal, I do not look up. I am afraid Father Doby might stop talking if he thinks I am getting somewhere with him. "So, once you got their report back," I ask, head down, "what would you say, as bishop, would be the deciding factor in your decision not to sanction the apparitions?"

"There is no question about it," Father Doby says. "She wouldn't even get past number one—the character credibility factor." And then, as if to prove he is right, he goes on to actually tell me the highlights of the original committee's report. Many are details I had already read about in articles in journals and books. The stigmata on Mary Ann's hands had been self-inflicted in her outhouse with a fork. She also lost weight when she was put on a rigorous fast, even though she had told investigators that she had been living only on hosts and water during Lent without losing a pound. (At the hospital where she was under observation for Holy Week, she was caught trying to sneak sweets into her room.) Finally, Mary Ann's claim that she would suffer the passion on Good Friday at the strike of one—when the crucified Jesus supposedly began his agony—actually took place an hour earlier. (Her investigators had been slowing the clock in her hospital room fifteen minutes every day.)

Father Doby begins to stir behind his desk—it is time to go, I know. But I have one more question to ask him, the same question I asked Donna and keep asking myself. "Do you think Mary Ann knew what she was doing?"

"How could she not know?"

I nod, as if I accept his answer, but in my head, I still have Donna's nagging doubt. Her mother thought she was operating in good conscience. So did the hundreds of followers who came up to be near her in Necedah. But the sacred somehow got sidetracked—maybe by American commercialism or Cold War paranoia or Catholic Church repression of what lies outside its hierarchy—who knows? At any rate, Mary Ann needed to be sanctified so much that she drove a fork into the tender center of her palms. She subjected her family to the intrusion of thousands of strangers. She thrashed in a bed for hours to deliver us from our sins. In the name of what we need, we do such peculiar things.

On our way down the hall, I admit to Father Doby that I am a lapsed Catholic. "I know," he says, and when I list a few of my difficulties with the church—the ban against the ordination of women, its stance on birth control, its system of indulgences and penances—he merely remarks that I probably don't understand the actual doctrines and dogmas concerned. It is only when I go to shake hands—a habit I seem to have picked up in the Midwest—only then that I notice that his right hand is deformed, a stump with the fingers curled in on themselves. Perhaps his mother took that tranquilizer prescribed to women of my mother's generation that caused birth defects. Perhaps she heard that the Virgin was appearing to another Catholic woman just down the road. Perhaps she got too excited and needed some help keeping herself calm. I can see *her* face now in the face of her son.

• • •

AUGUST 15 DAWNS, a blustery, cloudy Thursday. My first thought, lying in bed and looking out the broken blinds of the Necedah Motel, is that this is the perfect day for signs. Big masses of clouds shift across the sky like portents or figures. Whenever the sun breaks through, rays of light beam down as they do in the Bible when God sheds his grace and a voice comes down saying, "This is my beloved son in whom I am well pleased." The wind in the trees could be that voice.

The parking lot is full—though the crowd is quite small, at most a hundred or a hundred-and-fifty pilgrims. I recall that the former shriner who showed me her packet of rules told me that each member of a family was encouraged to drive a vehicle to the shrine during anniversary days to make the lot look full. The R.V. from Ontario has been moved to the far side of the parking lot. Beside it, there is a bus from the Twin Cities. A Filipino family hurries by, small children underfoot, and old grandparents bringing up the rear. Two of the women wear long, colorful, block-print dresses and carry an arrangement of red roses—the only real flowers at the Sacred Spot today. They are followed by an African American couple—a surprise given the racist rhetoric of some of the Blessed Mother's messages. I pass another family who seem in no hurry at all. They have pulled down the back on their station wagon and are putting out napkins and sandwiches, as if this were nothing more than a college homecoming football game or a Fourth of July picnic.

At the sacred spot I watch with the rest of the crowd as the procession approaches. Flags waving, the pilgrims sing the Mary Song, the women—many of them—in light blue dresses in honor of the Virgin, the men in what would have been called, fifty years ago, their church clothes—pressed pants and a clean white shirt, a tie somebody tied too tight. Then comes the litter with a gaudy crown on a blue pillow, men in white gloves holding the handles. Behind it follow two priests, one a tall, suave, middle-aged man, whom someone in the crowd tells me is "an archbishop." He will slip out after the crowning and sit in his car in the parking lot, smoking and talking with a young, handsome guy who has been cruising the crowd, checking out the young female pilgrims. The other priest is a short, mad-looking old man in a dirty, wrinkled robe. When his tall colleague begins blessing the crown with a long rod filled with water with holes at one end like a salt shaker, a liturgical instrument known as an aspergill, the old man snatches it away and with a flourish sprinkles the crown and crowd with holy water until somebody stops him. Five or six little girls bring up the rear. They are dressed in white, first-communion outfits with tiny veils, like brides in training. When I snap their picture, a couple of the little girls look up, startled, at the sky.

Pilgrims are taking pictures, left and right, so I do not feel out of order. One shriner is videotaping the entire ceremony. I know the reason for this flurry of picture-taking is that signs are expected to show up on film, proof of miraculous happenings at Necedah. Some shriners carry photos in their pockets. One photograph I was shown was of a sun-bright dazzling sky demonstrating what the shriner called "the doorway to heaven" during a recent anniversary day.

A handful of dignitaries file into the gated area where our

Lady of Necedah waits in her glass bubble. A teenage boy carts in an old, wobbly stepladder, speckled with different color stains on all sides. Why didn't they at least paint it white, I wonder, and the next moment I'm asking myself why I would want to help these people make this shoddy enterprise look more viable.

The glass door is unlocked, and the teenage boy has to duck inside the narrow case in order to get the crown onto Mary's head. As everyone breaks out in song, the sun of course breaks through the clouds, and many heads turn up to what will later be described as a demonstration of the sun spinning. I take this opportunity to edge away and climb up a small rise so I can get a good shot of the whole crowd gathered around the four ash trees at the Van Hoof farm.

Standing on that hill, looking down at Our Blessed Mother through the lens of the camera, her Barbie-doll prettiness, her tawdry crown, I remind myself of the question I put to her the first night I was here. Should I try to write a novel about Necedah?

Today, on the feast day of her bodily assumption into heaven, I begin to understand that my prayer has been answered. I have turned into the chronicler of the survivors of a fiction, survivors of Mary Ann's fictionalizing as well as my own. The spirit-killing church bureaucrat I imagined from faraway Vermont has become, up close, an aging priest with a birth defect; the Bernadette of America has been transformed into a shrewd and histrionic farm woman with stolen sweets and a fork in her pocket. The novel I was going to write about Necedah has turned into this testament of what happens when we try to construct the fiction we need out of the facts that are out there. The word has become flesh again. As I come back down the hill to join the other pilgrims, I see that I, too, have had my vision here in Necedah, Wisconsin.

Ten of My Writing Commandments

· · · · · · · ·

I

In the beginner's mind there are many possibilities.
In the expert's mind there are few.

ZEN MASTERS

II

The obligation of the artist is not to solve the problem
but to state the problem correctly.

ANTON CHEKHOV

III

Do not be afraid!

ANGELS APPEARING TO SHEPHERDS
TENDING THEIR FLOCKS BY NIGHT

IV

If you bring forth what is inside you,
what you bring forth will save you.

If you do not bring forth what is inside you,
what is inside you will destroy you.

ST. THOMAS
GNOSTIC GOSPELS

Declarations

V

Poetry presents the thing in order to convey the feeling.
It should be precise about the thing
and reticent about the feeling.

WEI T'AI

VI

One must write a poem
the way one rules an empire,
the way one cooks a small fish.

AUTHOR UNKNOWN

VII

El papel lo aguanta todo.
(Paper holds everything.)

MAMI

VIII

You must change your life.

RAINER MARIA RILKE

IX

The function of freedom is to free someone else.

TONI MORRISON

X

If you want to be a writer, then write. Write every day!

SAMUEL JOHNSON

Grounds for Fiction

. . . .

Every once in a while after a reading, someone in the audience will come up to me. *Have I got a story for you!* They will go on to tell me the story of an aunt or sister or next-door neighbor, some moment of mystery, some serendipitous occurrence, some truly incredible story. "You should write it down," I always tell them. They look at me as if they've just offered me their family crown jewels and I've refused them. "I'm no writer," they tell me. "You're the writer."

"Oh, you never know," I reply, so as to encourage them. What I should tell them is that writing ideas can't really be traded in an open market. If they could be, writers would be multimillionaires. Who knows what mystery (or madness) it is that drives us to our computers for two, three, four years, in pursuit of some sparkling possibility that looks like dull fact to everyone else's eyes. One way to define a writer is she who is able to make what obsesses her into everyone's obsession. I am thinking of Goethe, whose *Sorrows of Young Werther*, published in 1774, caused a spate of suicides in imitation of its young hero. Young Werther's blue frock coat and yellow waistcoat became the fad. We have all been the victims of someone's too-long slide show of their white-water rafting trip or their recounting of a convoluted, boring dream. But a Mark Twain can turn that slide show into the lively backdrop of a novel, or a Jorge Luis Borges can take the twist and turn of a dream and wring the meaning of the universe from it.

But aside from talent—and granted, that is a big aside, one that comes and goes and shifts and grows and diminishes, so it is also somewhat unpredictable—how can we tell when we've got it: that seed of experience, of memory, that voice of a character or fleeting image that might just be grounds for fiction? The answer is that we can never tell. And so another way to define a writer is someone who is willing to find out. As James Dickey once explained to an audience, "I work on the process of refining low-grade ore. I get maybe a couple of nuggets of gold out of fifty tons of dirt. It is tough for me. No, I am not inspired."

"Are you all here because you want to muck around in fifty tons of dirt?" I ask my workshop of young writers the first day. Not one hand goes up unless I've told them the Dickey story first.

In fact, my students want to know ahead of time if some idea they have will make a good story. "I mean, before I spend hours and hours on it," one young man explained. I told my student what Mallarmé told his friend the painter

Degas, when Degas complained that he couldn't seem to write well although he was "full of ideas." Mallarmé's famous answer was, "My dear Degas, poems are not made out of ideas. Poems are made out of words." I told my student that if a young writer had come up to me and told me that he was going to write a story about a man who wakes up one morning and finds out that he has been turned into a cockroach, I would have told him to forget it. That story would never work. "And I would have stopped Kafka from writing his 'Metamorphosis,'" I concluded, smiling at my student, as if he might be a future Kafka.

"Well, it's just two pages," he grumbled. "And I have this other idea that might be better. About a street person who is getting Alzheimer's."

"Write both stories, and I'll read them and tell you what I think of them," I said. He looked alarmed. So I leveled with him. I told him that if he didn't want to spend hours and hours finding out if the kernel of an idea, the glimmer of an inspiration, the flash of a possibility would make a good story, he should give up the *idea* of wanting to be a writer.

As much as I can break down the process of writing stories, I would say that this is how it begins. I find a detail or image or character or incident or cluster of events. A certain luminosity surrounds them. I find myself attracted. I come forward. I pick it up, turn it around, begin to ask questions, and spend hours and weeks and months and years trying to answer them.

I KEEP A folder, a yellow folder with pockets. For a long time it had no label because I didn't know what to label it: WHATCHAMACALLITS, filed under *W,* or also under *W,*

STORY-POEM-WANNABES. Finally, I called the folder CURIOSIDADES, in Spanish so I wouldn't have to commit myself to what I was going to do in English with these random little things. I tell my students this, too, that writing begins before you ever put pen to paper or your fingers down on the keyboard. It is a way of being alive in the world. Henry James's advice to the young writer was to be someone on whom nothing is lost. And so this is my folder of the little things that have not been lost on me; news clippings, headlines, inventory lists, bits of gossip that I've already sensed have an aura about them, the beginnings of a poem or a short story, the seed of a plot that might turn into a novel or a query that might needle an essay out of me.

Periodically, when I'm between writing projects and sometimes when I'm in the middle of one and needing a break, I go through my yellow folder. Sometimes I discard a clipping or note that no longer holds my attention. But most of my curiosidades have been in my folder for years, though some have migrated to new folders, the folders of stories and poems they have inspired or found a home in.

Here's one of these curiosidades that is now in a folder that holds drafts of a story that turned into a chapter of my novel ¡YO! This chapter is in the point of view of Marie Beaudry, a landlady who, along with other narrators, gets to tell a story on Yolanda García, the writer. The little curiosity that inspired Marie's voice was a note I found in the trash of an apartment I moved into. It has nothing at all to do with what happens in my story.

Re and Mal: Here's the two keys to your father's apt. Need I say more excepting that's such a rotten thing you pulled on him. My doing favors is over as of this morning. Good luck to you two hard-hearted hannahs. I got more feeling in my little finger than the two of you got in your whole body.

Jinny

I admit that when I read this note, I wanted to move out of that apartment. I felt the place was haunted by the ghost of the last tenant against whom some violation had been perpetrated by these two hard-hearted hannahs, Re and Mal. Over the years that handwritten note stayed in my yellow folder and eventually gave me the voice of my character Marie Beaudry.

Here's another scrap from deep inside one of the pockets. It's the title of an article in one of my husband's ophthalmological journals: "Treatment of Chronic Postfiltration Hypotony by Intrableb Injection of Autologous Blood." I think I saved that choice bit of medical babble because of the delight I took in the jabberwocky phenomenon of that title.

> 'Twas brillig and the slithy toves
> Did gyre and postfiltrate the wabe;
> All hypotonious was the blood,
> And autologous the intrableb.

I have not yet used it in a story or poem, but who knows, maybe someday you will look over the shoulder of one of my characters and see that he is reading this article or writing it. I can tell you that this delight in words and how we use and misuse them is a preoccupation of mine.

Maybe because I began my writing life as a poet, the naming of things has always interested me:

> Mother, unroll the bolts and name
> the fabrics from which our clothing came,
> dress the world in vocabulary:
> broadcloth, corduroy, denim, terry.

Actually, that poem, "Naming the Fabrics," besides being inspired, of course, by the names of fabrics, was also triggered by something I picked up while reading *The 1961 Better Homes and Garden Sewing Book,* page 45: "During a question and answer period at a sewing clinic, a woman in the audience asked this question: 'I can sew beautifully; my fitting is excellent; the finished dress looks as good as that of any professional—but how do I get up enough courage to cut the fabric?'" I typed out this passage and put it away. A few months later, this fear found its way from my yellow folder to my poem, "Naming the Fabrics":

> I pay a tailor to cut his suits
> from seersucker, duck, tweed, cheviot,
> those names makes my cutting hand skittish—
> either they sound like sex or British.

Since I myself have no sewing skills to speak of, I didn't know about this fear that seamstresses experience before cutting fabric. Certainly, the year 1961, when this sewing book was published, brings other fears to mind: the Berlin Wall going up; invaders going down to the Bay of Pigs; Trujillo, our dictator of thirty-one years, being assassinated in the Dominican Republic. But this housewife in Indiana had her own metaphysical fears to work out on cloth. "How do I get up enough courage to cut the fabric?" Her preoccupation astonished me and touched me for all kinds of reasons I had to work out on paper.

You might wonder what a "serious writer" was doing reading *The 1961 Better Homes and Garden Sewing Book*. Wouldn't my time have been better spent perusing Milton or Emily Dickinson or even the *New York Review of Books* or *The Nation*. All I can say in my defense is that I believe in Henry James's advice: be someone on whom nothing is lost. Or what Deborah Kerr said in *Night of the Iguana,* "Nothing human disgusts me." I once heard a writer on *Fresh Air* tell Terry Gross that one of the most important things he had ever learned in his life was that you could learn a lot from people who were dumber than you. You can also learn a lot from publications that are below your literary standards: housekeeping books, cookbooks, manuals, cereal boxes, and the local newspapers of your small town.

These last are the best. Even if some of this "news" is really glorified gossip—so what? Most of our classics are glorified gossip. Think of the Wife of Bath's inventory of husbands or the debutante's hair-rape in "The Rape of the Lock." How about Madame Bovary's seamy affair? Is what happened to Abelard over his Héloïse or to Jason for pissing off Medea any less infamous than the John and Lorena Bobbit story of several years ago? The wonderful Canadian writer Alice Munro admits that she likes reading *People* magazine, and "not just at the checkout stand. I sometimes buy it." She goes on to say that gossip is "a central part of my life. I'm interested in small-town gossip. Gossip has that feeling in it, that one wants to know about life."

I've gotten wonderful stories from the *Addison Independent,* the

Valley Voice, even the *Burlington Free Press* that would never be reported in the *Wall Street Journal* or the *New York Times:*

11-YEAR-OLD GIRLS TAKE CAR
ON TWO-STATE JOYRIDE

Two 11-year-old girls determined to see a newborn niece secretly borrowed their grandfather's car, piled clothes on the front seat so they could see over the steering wheel and drove more than 10 hours.
Neither one of them had ever driven a car before, said Michael Ray, Mercer County's juvenile case worker. The youngsters packed the Dodge Aries with soda, snacks, and an atlas for their trek from West Virginia to the central Kentucky town of Harrodsburg. "They were determined to see that baby," said caseworker Ray.

You could write a whole novel about that. In fact, in Mona Simpson's latest novel, *A Regular Guy,* eleven-year-old Jane di Natali is taught by her mother to drive their pickup with wood blocks strapped to the pedals so her short legs can reach them. Little Jane takes off on her own to see her estranged father hundreds of miles away. I wonder if Mona Simpson got her idea for Jane's odyssey from reading about these two eleven-year-olds.

Here's another article I've saved in my yellow folder:

MISDIAGNOSED PATIENT FREED AFTER 2 YEARS

A Mexican migrant worker misdiagnosed and kept sedated in an Oregon mental hospital for two years because doctors couldn't understand his Indian dialect is going home.

Adolfo Gonzales, a frail 5-foot-4-inch grape picker who doesn't speak English or Spanish, had been trying to communicate in his native Indian dialect of Trique.

Gonzales, believed to be in his 20s, was born in a village in Oaxaca, Mexico. He was committed in June 1990 after being arrested for indecent exposure at a laundromat. Charges later were dropped.

I couldn't get this story out of my head. First, I was—and am —intensely interested in the whole Scheherazade issue of how important it is to be able to tell our stories to those who have power over us. Second, and more mundanely, I was intensely curious about those charges that were later dropped: indecent exposure at a laundromat. What was Adolfo Gonzales doing taking his clothes off in a laundromat? Why was he in town after a hard day of grape picking? I had to find answers to these questions, and so I started writing a poem. "It's a myth that writers write what they know," the writer Marcie Hershman has written. "We write what it is that we need to know."

> The next payday you went to town
> to buy your girl and to wash your one
> set of working clothes.
>
> In the laundromat, you took them off
> to wring out the earth you wanted
> to leave behind you.
>> from "Two Years Too Late"

Of course, you don't even have to go to your local paper. Just take a walk downtown, especially if you live in a small town, as I do. All I have to do is have a cup of coffee at Steve's

Diner or at Jimmy's Weybridge Garage and listen to my
neighbors talking. Flannery O'Connor claimed that most
beginners' stories don't work because "they don't go very far
inside a character, don't reveal very much of the character.
And this problem is in large part due to the fact that these
characters have no distinctive speech to reveal themselves
with." Here are some examples of my fellow Vermonters
talking their very distinctive and revealing speech.

> He's so lazy he married a pregnant woman.
> I'm so hungry I could eat the north end out of a south-
> bound skunk.
> The snow's butt-high to a tall cow.
> More nervous than a long-tailed cat in a room full of
> rocking chairs.
> I'm so sick that I'd have to get well to die.

Of course if, like Whitman, you do nothing but listen, you
will also hear all kinds of bogus voices these days, speaking
the new doublespeak. In our litigious, politically overcor-
rected, dizzily spin-doctored age, politicians and public
figures have to use language so that it doesn't say anything
that might upset anyone. Here's a list of nonterms and what
they really stand for:

Sufferer of fictitious disorder syndrome:	Liar
Suboptimal:	Failed
Temporarily displaced inventory:	Stolen
Negative gain in test scores:	Lower test scores
Substantive negative outcome:	Death

We're back to "Treatment of Chronic Postfiltration Hypotony
by Intrableb Injection of Autologous Blood," what Ken Mac-

rorie in his wonderful book about expository writing, *Telling Writing*, calls "Engfish"—homogenized, doctored-up, approximate language that can't be traced to a human being.

I tend to agree with what Dickinson once said about poetry, "There are no approximate words in a poem." Auden even went so far as to say that he could pick out a potential poet by a student's answer to the question, "Why do you want to write poetry?" If the student answered, "I have important things to say," then he was not a poet. If he answered, "I like hanging around words listening to what they say," then maybe he was going to be a poet.

I got enmeshed in one such string of words when I visited the United Nations to hear my mother give a speech on violation of human rights. At the door an aide handed me the list of voting member countries and the names caught my eye: Dem Kampuchea, Dem Yemen, Denmark, Djibouti, Dominica, Dominican Republic, Ecuador, Egypt. . . . When I got home, I started writing a poem, ostensibly about hearing my mother give that speech, but really because I wanted to use the names of those countries:

> I scan the room for reactions,
> picking out those countries
> guilty of her sad facts.
> Kampuchea is absent,
> absent, too, the South African delegate.
> I cannot find the United States.
> Nervous countries predominate,
> Nicaragua and Haiti,
> Iraq, Israel, Egypt.
> > from "Between Dominica and Ecuador"

But of course, it's not just words that intrigue writers, but the stories, the possibilities of human character that cluster around a bit of history, trivia, gossip.

For instance, Anne Macdonald's book, *Feminine Ingenuity*, inspired a character trait of the mother in *How the García Girls Lost Their Accents*. According to Macdonald, at the beginning of the twentieth century, 5,535 American women were granted patents for inventions, including a straw-weaving device, an open-eye needle for sewing hot-air balloons, and special planking designed to discourage barnacles from attaching themselves to warships. These intriguing facts gave me a side of the mother's character I would never have thought up on my own. Inspired by the gadgetry of her new country, Laura García sets out to make her mark: soap sprayed from the nozzle head of a shower when you turn the knob a certain way; instant coffee with creamer already mixed in; time-released water capsules for your potted plants when you were away; a key chain with a timer that would go off when your parking meter was about to expire. (And the ticking would help you find your keys easily if you mislaid them.)

Sometimes the inspiration is history. History . . . that subject I hated in school because it was so dry and all about dead people. I wish now my teachers had made me read novels to make the past spring alive in my imagination. For years, I wanted to write about the Mirabal sisters, but I admit I was put off by these grand historical abstractions. It wasn't until I began to accumulate several yellow folders' worth of vivid little details about them that these godlike women became accessible to me. One of my first entries came from my father, who had just returned from a trip to the Dominican Republic: "I met the man who sold the girls pocketbooks at El Gallo before they set off over the mountain. He told me he warned them not to go. He said he took them out back to the stockroom supposedly to show them inventory and explained they were going to be killed. But they did not believe him." I still get goosebumps reading my father's letter dated June 5, 1985. It went in my yellow folder. That pocketbook-buying scene is at the end of the novel I published nine years later.

So what are you to conclude from this tour of my yellow folder? That this essay is just an excuse to take you through my folder and share my little treasures with you? Well, one thing I don't want you to conclude is that this preliminary woolgathering is a substitute for the real research that starts once you have a poem or story going. In "Naming the Fabrics," for instance, though I was inspired by the plaintive question asked at a sewing clinic, I still had to go down to the fabric store and spend an afternoon with a very kind and patient saleslady who taught me all about gingham and calico, crepe and gauze. I spent days reading fabric books, and weeks working on the poem, and years going back to it, revising it, tinkering with it. For my story, "The Tent," I had to call up the National Guard base near Champaign, Illinois, and get permission from the base commander to go observe his men setting up a tent. ("What exactly do you need this for?" he asked at least half a dozen times.) Sometimes I think the best reason for a writer to have a reputable job like being a professor at a university or a vice president of Hartford Insurance Company is so you can call up those base commanders or bother those salesladies in fabric stores as if you do have a real job. Otherwise, they might think you are crazy and lock you up like poor Adolfo Gonzales.

On the whole, I have found people to be kind and generous with their time, especially when you ask them to talk about something they know and care about. Many people have actually gone beyond kindness in helping me out. I remember calling up the local Catholic priest, bless his heart, who really deserves, I don't know, a plenary indulgence for tolerance in the face of surprise. Imagine getting an early-morning call (my writing day starts at 6:30, but I really don't do this kind of phone calling till about 7:30 since I do want my sources to be lucid). Anyhow, imagine an early-morning call at your rectory from a woman you don't know who asks you what is the name of that long rod priests have with a hole on one end to sprinkle people with holy water? I'd be lying if I tried to make drama out of the phone call and say there was a long pause. Nope. Father John spoke right up, "Ah yes, my aspergill."

One thing I should add—the bad news part of all this fun, but something writers do have to think about in this litigious age—what is grounds for fiction can also be, alas, grounds for suing. All three of my novels have been read by my publisher's lawyer for what might be libelous. Thank goodness Algonquin's lawyer is also a reader who refuses to vacuum all the value out of a book in order to play it safe. Still, I have had to take drinks out of characters' hands and make abused ladies disabused and make so many changes in hair coloring and hairstyle that I could start a literary beauty parlor.

But even if your fictional ground is cleared of litigious material, there might still be grounds for heartache. Your family and friends might feel wounded when they can detect—even if no one else can—the shape of the real behind the form of your fiction. And who would want to hurt those very people you write for, those very people who share with you the world you are struggling to understand in your fiction for their sake as well as your own?

I don't know how to get around this and I certainly haven't figured out what the parameters of my responsibility are to the real people in my life. One of my theories, which might sound defensive and self-serving, is that there is no such thing as straight-up fiction. There are just levels of distance from our own life experience, the thing that drives us to write in the first place. In spite of our caution and precaution, bits of our lives will get into what we write. I have a friend whose mother finds herself in all his novels, even historical novels set in nineteenth-century Russia or islands in the Caribbean where his mother has never been. A novelist writing about Napoleon might convey his greedy character by describing him spooning gruel into his mouth, only to realize that her image of how a greedy man eats comes from watching her fat Tío Jorge stuff his face with sweet habichuelas.

I think that if you start censoring yourself as a novelist—*this is out of bounds, that is sacrosanct*—you will never write anything. My advice is to write it out, and then decide, by whatever process seems fair to you—three-o'clock-in-the-morning insomniac angst sessions with your soul, or a phone call with your best friend, or a long talk with your sister—what you are going to do about it. More often than not, an upset reaction has more to do with people's wounded vanity or their own unresolved issues with *you* rather than what you've written. I'm not speaking now of meanness or revenge thinly masquerading as fiction, but of a writer's serious attempts to render justice to the world she lives in, which includes, whether she wants it to or not, the people she loves or has tried to love, the people who have been a part of the memories, details, life experiences that form the whole cloth of her reality—out of which, with fear and a trembling hand, she must perforce cut her fiction.

But truly, this is a worry to put out of your head while you are writing. You'll need your energy for the hard work ahead: tons and tons of good *ideas* to process in order to get those nuggets of pure prose. What Yeats once said in his poem, "Dialogue of Self and Soul," could well be the writer's pledge of allegiance:

> I am content to follow to its source,
> every event in action or in thought.

And remember, no one is probably going to pay you a whole lot of money to do this. You also probably won't save anyone's life with anything you write. But so much does depend on seeing a world in a grain of sand and a heaven in a wildflower. Maybe we are here only to say: house, bridge, aspergill, gingham, calico, gauze. "But to say them," as Rilke said, "remember oh, to say them in a way that the things themselves never dreamed of existing so intensely."

But this is too much of an orchestral close for the lowly little ditty that starts with a newspaper clipping or the feel of a bolt of gingham or a cup of coffee at the Weybridge Garage. The best advice I can give writers is something so dull and simple you'd never save it in your yellow folder. But go ahead and engrave it in your writer's heart. If you want to be a writer, anything in this world is grounds for fiction.

Writing Matters

· · · · · · · ·

One of the questions that always comes up during question-and-answer periods after readings is about the writing life. The more sophisticated, practiced questioners usually ask me, "Can you tell us something about your process as a writer?" Younger, less self-conscious questioners tend to be more straightforward, "What do you write with? Is it a special kind of pen? What time do you start? How many hours do you spend at the computer? Do you keep a journal?"

In part, this is the curiosity we all have about each other's "processes," to use the terminology of my experienced questioner. Just recently, an acquaintance lost her husband, and during a small supper with friends at our house, she recounted the story of the night of his death. How she was at the hospital, how her husband was in good form (the husband was British, so I could hear his language surviving in her description), how she thought to ask him was he in any pain, how he had said no, how she had driven home, how she had just finished her supper when the call came, how she had hung up and gone to sit in his chair—

At this point, some question came up about the name of her husband's doctor, and when our friend returned to her story, it was to speak in generalities about grief and the future. I waited for her to finish, and then I surprised myself by blurting out, "You were saying that you were sitting in his chair. . . ?"

"Oh that's right," she said, "I was sitting in his chair. I had gotten myself a glass of milk. . . ."

Perhaps it was unkind of me to return her to that intense and intimate moment of getting the news, but our friend seemed almost relieved to be taking us with her through that dark night of her grief. The telling of the story decreases our sense of isolation. My sister, a therapist, whose clientele is primarily Latino, has worked with refugees who have survived incredible trauma—villages burnt, relatives tortured or shot before their eyes. They are numb and silent with grief. My sister says she knows they are going to make it when they can tell her the story of exactly what happened to them.

We need to tell, and we also want to know (don't we?) the secret heart of each other's lives. Why are we so ashamed of this? Perhaps that is why we love good novels and poems— because we can enter, without shame or without encountering defensiveness or embarrassment, the intimate lives of other people.

But the other part of my questioner's curiosity about the

writing life has to do with a sense we all have that if we can only get a hold of the secret ingredients of the writing process, we will become better writers. We will have an easier time of it if we only find that magic pencil or know at which hour to start and at which hour to quit and what to sip that might help us come up with the next word in a sentence.

I always tell my questioners the truth: listen, there are no magic solutions to the hard work of writing. There is no place to put the writing desk that will draw more words out of you. In grad school, I had a friend who claimed that an east-west alignment was the best one for writing. The writing would flow and be more in tune with the positive energies. The north-south alignment would cause blocks as well as bad dreams if your bed was also thus aligned. "Not to mention," she mentioned, "it'll be harder to reach orgasm."

See, I tell my questioners, isn't this silly?

But even as I say so, I know I am talking out of both sides of my mouth. I admit that after getting my friend's tip, I lined up my writing desk (and my bed) in the east-west configuration. It wasn't that I thought my writing or my love life would improve, but I am so impressionable that I was afraid that I'd be thinking and worrying about my alignment instead of my line breaks. And such fretting would affect my writing adversely. (My love life was pretty tame already.) Even as recently as this very day, I walk into my study first thing in the morning, and I fill up my bowl of clear water and place it on my desk. And though no one told me to do this, I somehow feel this is the right way to start a writing day.

Of course, that fresh bowl of water sits on my desk on

good *and* bad writing days. I know these little ceremonies will not change the kind of day before me any more than a funeral service will bring back the dead or a meditation retreat will keep trouble out of my life. The function of ritual is not to control this baffling universe but to render homage to it, to bow to the mystery. Similarly, my daily writing rituals are small ways in which I contain my dread and affirm my joy and celebrate the mystery and excitement of the calling to be a writer.

I use the word *calling* in the old religious sense: a commitment to a life connected to deeper, more profound forces (or so I hope) than the marketplace, or the academy, or the hectic blur of activity, which is what my daily life is often all about. But precisely because it is a way of life, not just a job, the writing life can be difficult to combine with other lives that require that same kind of passion and commitment—the teaching life, the family life, the parenting life, and so on. And since we writers tend to be intense people, whatever other lives we combine with our writing life, we will want to live them intensely, too. Some of us are better at this kind of juggling than others.

After twenty-five years of clumsy juggling—marriages, friendships, teaching, writing, community work, political work, caring for young people, one or the other suddenly crashing to the floor because I just couldn't sustain the increased intensity of trying to do them all—I think I've finally figured out what the proper balance is for me. Let me emphasize that this is not a prescription for anyone else. My friend, the novelist, critic, poet, teacher Jay Parini, can juggle six or seven lives successfully at once (write, teach, review, cook, edit, and be a good father, husband, friend), but alas, I'm of the Gerald Ford school of writers who can't chew gum and write iambic pentameter at the same time. (Spondaic chewing throws me off!) I can do two, maybe three intense lives at once: writing and being in a family; writing and teaching and being in a family; writing and teaching and doing political work; but if I try to add a fourth or fifth: writing and being in love and teaching and maintaining a tight friendship and doing political work and taking in the local waif—I fall apart; that is, the writing stops, which for me, is the same thing as saying I fall apart.

But still, I'm glad I haven't let such potential breakdowns stop me. I keep juggling, picking up one life and another and another, putting aside the writing from time to time. We only have one life, after all, and we have got to live so many lives with it. (Another reason why the writing life appeals so much is that you can be, at least on paper, all those selves whose lives you can't possibly live out in the one life you've got.) My advice is, if you are sorely tempted to try out a new adventure, go for it! Just don't forget where you are headed, and knowing this will imbue that adventure with even more resonance and richness. (Like going to a party with a lover you know you are going to spend the night with.)

Living other lives enriches our writing life. The tension between them can sometimes exhaust us, this is true—but the struggle also makes the hard-won hours at the writing desk all the more precious. And if we are committed to our writing, even if there are what seem impossibly long periods in which we have to put the writing aside in a concerted, focused way while we get our moneymaking careers started or while we raise our very young children, the way we lead our lives can make them lives-in-waiting to be writing lives.

What do I mean by the writing life? For me, the writing life doesn't just happen when I sit at the writing desk. I mean a life lived with a centering principle, and mine is this, that I will pay close attention to this world I find myself in. "O taste and see that the Lord is good," says one of my favorite psalms. I've always trusted this psalm precisely because it does not say, "O think and meditate that the Lord is good." Instead we are encouraged to know the sacred by living our lives with all our senses fully engaged.

Another way to put it is that writing life is a life lived with all the windows and doors opened. "My heart keeps open house," was the way the poet Theodore Roethke put it in a poem. And rendering what one sees through those opened windows and doors in language is a way of bearing witness to the mystery of what it is to be alive in this world.

THIS IS ALL very high-minded and inspirational, my questioner puts in, fine talk for a reading when we are sitting in a room with other aficionados of the craft. But what about when we are alone at our writing desks, feeling wretchedly anxious, wondering if there is anything in us worth putting down? How about some advice we can take home with us to carry us through the mundane and hard parts of a writing day?

Just as my friend took us through the night of losing her husband, as her telling the story helped her survive the experience and helped the rest of us by reminding us of the full journey of our lives, let me take you through the trials and tribulations of a typical writing day. It might help as you also set out onto that blank page, encounter one adventure or mishap after another and wonder—do other writers go through this?

The answer is probably yes.

NOT MUCH HAS happened at six-twenty or so in the morning when I enter my writing room above the garage. I like it this way. The mind is free of little household details, worries, commitments, voices, problems to solve. In fact, it's probably still rising up from the bottom of a dream. In the summer, the locust trees on the south side make me feel as if I've climbed into a tree house and pulled up the ladder after me. It helps, of course, that I have no children to wake up and feed and pack off to school or drive to day care. I also have a husband who knows how to put his own cereal in his own bowl and who, like me, enjoys having some solitary time in the early morning to read and reflect or putter in his garden before going off to work.

My mood entering the room depends on what happened with my writing the day before. If the previous day was a good one, I look forward to the new writing day. If I was stuck or uninspired, I feel apprehensive. Today might be the day when the writing life comes crashing to the floor, and I am shown up for the sham I am. In short, I can't agree more with Hemingway's advice that a writer should always end his writing day knowing where he is headed next. It makes it easier to come back to work.

Now I am going to leap way ahead of myself to about two-thirty or three in the afternoon: the end of my writing day. I leave the room over the garage. I put on my running clothes, and I go for a run. Before I married Bill, I wasn't a person into exercise. I mean, if I could take the escalator one flight, I took the escalator one flight. Running was what I did to get away from people or dogs who were chasing me. When I turned forty, Bill presented me with the *The Thirty-Five-Plus Good Health Guide for Women*. I read through the first few chapters, and the same advice was repeated over and over: "Hey, girl, start exercising! Your body is no longer for free!" The nerve, I thought. But I did start walking, and then, because I tend towards impatience, I started running.

Now, I can't stand not running a little bit every day. In part it's that this exercise does make me feel better. But one of the best perks of running has been that it allows me to follow Hemingway's advice. I don't always know where I am headed in my writing at the end of the workday, but after I run, I usually have one or two good ideas. Running helps me work out glitches in my writing and gives me all kinds of unexpected insights. While I run down past the Fields's house, through Tucker Development, down to the route that goes into town, and then back, I've understood what a character is feeling or how I'm going to organize an essay or what I will title my novel. I've also had a zillion conversations with dozens of worrisome people, which is much better than trying to have these conversations with them while I am trying to write. Also, since I am not near a phone, I am not tempted to call them up and actually have it out with them. I've saved a lot of friendships and relationships and spared myself plenty of heartaches this way.

As an addendum, I want to add that about a year ago, my husband and I gave each other a running machine for Christmas. We are both well over thirty-five, and we live in Vermont, where for at least four out of twelve months, every outdoor running surface is covered with snow or ice or both. Having the machine has made running in the dead of winter so much more pleasant and safer. But the loss when I run indoors has been that my mind does not fall into the same kind of musing as when I jog outdoors. Part of the problem is that indoor running is so boring that I am tempted to turn on the TV to make the time pass, and of course—my old juggling problem—I can't run, watch TV, and resolve a question in plot at the same time. On the other hand, I now know the Barney song, how to cook Swedish meatballs as the Galloping Gourmet does, and how to avoid all kinds of scams from watching the talk shows.

THAT FIRST ENTRY into the writing room in the early morning is just a brief visit. I fill my writing bowl and say hello to my two old cemíes (stone and wooden Taino deities from the Dominican Republic) and make sure my Virgencita has fresh flowers, if it is summer, or a lit candle, in the winter. Then I head downstairs to the kitchen and my own ministration, a cup of strong Dominican coffee, which Bill and I bring back by the suitcase. Sometimes I think we plan our trips "home" according to our coffee supply in the deep freeze in the basement.

I drink my coffee in the study, reading poetry (Jane Kenyon, George Herbert, Rita Dove, Robert Frost, Elizabeth Bishop, Rhina Espaiuat, Jane Shore, Emily Dickinson . . .). I like to start the day with a poem or two or three or four. This is the first music I hear, the most essential. Interestingly, I like to follow the reading of poetry with some prose, as if, having been to the heights I need to come back down to earth. (I'm reminded of Frost's wonderful lines about climbing a birch tree, "Earth's the right place for love: / I don't know where it's likely to go better.")

I consider this early-morning reading time a combination of pleasure-reading time, when I read the works and authors I most love, and finger-exercise reading time, when I am tuning my own voice to the music of the English language as played by its best writers. That is why I avoid spending my early-morning reading time on magazines and fast-read books and how-to books and newspapers, all of which I enjoy, but all of which use language to provide information, titillation, help, gossip, and in many cases in our consumer culture, to sell something. That's not the chorus I want to hear. I also try never to use this reading time for reading that I must do for teaching or for professional reasons (possible blurbing, book reviewing).

Finally, I use this time for reading only in English. I made a discovery one summer when I was reading poetry in Spanish in the early morning. I'd move on to my writing and find myself encountering difficulties, drawing blanks left and right as I tried to express a thought or capture an image or strike the right tone in a passage. I finally figured it out: the whole rhythm of my thinking and writing had switched to my first, native tongue. I was translating into, not writing in, English. I could hear the ropes and pulleys and levers and switches in what I was writing, as if I were unloading the words off a boat that had just come in from another language, far away.

Reading for pleasure — I love the phrase, may all my readers read me in this way! — is for me a wonderful way to prepare for doing my own writing. Not all writers feel this way. In fact, some of my writer friends confess that they can't read other writers when they are in the middle of their own novels. They feel they will lose their own voices and start to imitate someone else. But I know that I am stuck with my own voice. I can't write like Michael Ondaatje or Stephen Dixon or Annie Proulx or Toni Morisson any more than I can have their fingerprints. That's not why I invite these writers to say a few words to me in the early morning before I set out on my own journey.

There's an old Yiddish story about a rabbi who walks out in a rich neighborhood and meets a watchman walking up and down. "For whom are you working?" the rabbi asks. The watchman tells him, and then in his turn, he asks the rabbi, "And whom are you working for, rabbi?" The words strike the rabbi like a shaft. "I am not working for anybody just yet," he barely manages to reply. Then he walks up and down beside the man for a long time and finally asks him, "Will you be my servant?" The watchman says, "I should like to, but what would be my duties?"

"To remind me," the rabbi says.

I read my favorite writers to remind me of the quality of writing I am aiming for.

NOW, IT'S TIME to set out: pencil poised, I read through the hard copy that I ran off at the end of yesterday's writing day. I used to write everything out by longhand, and when I was reasonably sure I had a final draft, I'd type it up on my old Selectric. But now, I usually write all my prose drafts right out on the computer, though, for the same reason that I read poetry for its linguistic focus first thing in the morning, I need to write out my poems in longhand, to make each word by hand.

This is also true of certain passages of prose and certainly true for times when I am stuck in a novel or story. Writing by hand relieves some of the pressure of seeing something tentative flashed before me on the screen with that authority that print gives to writing. "This is just for me," I tell myself, as I scratch out a draft in pencil. Often, these scribblings turn into little bridges, tendrils, gossamer webs and nets that take me safely to the other side of silence. When I'm finally on my way, I head back to the computer.

But even my hard copies look like they've been written by hand. I once visited a sixth-grade class to talk to them about my writing process. The teacher had asked me to please emphasize revision, as her students were always resisting working on their writing. No problem, I said. I brought in several boxes of folders with ten or twenty drafts of certain stories. The hard copies were heavily marked with my revising pencil. The teacher told me that the day after my visit, she was going over my presentation with her class, and she asked them, "So, what does Julia write with?"

"With a pencil!" they all shouted. Obviously, what they remembered were not the hard copies but all the scribblings, jottings, arrows, crossings-out, lists in the margins.

With all those emendations, my drafts are almost unreadable. In fact, if I wait several days before transferring these revisions to my computer copy, I can't read them myself. As I revise, I begin to hear the way I want a passage to sound. About the third or fourth draft, if I'm lucky, I start to see the shape of what I am writing, the way an essay will go, a character will react, a poem unfold.

Sometimes if Bill and I go on a long car trip, I'll read him what I am working on. This is a wonderful opportunity to "hear" what I've written. I always end up slashing out whole paragraphs and long passages. It reminds me of how my students describe having their writing workshopped as having it "torn apart." I always imagine a pack of hungry, evil-looking wild dogs when my students use this phrase. Actually, I've found that even if a listener doesn't respond in a negative way, the process of reading my work to someone else does tear apart that beauteous coating of self-love in which my own creation comes enveloped. I start to hear what I've written as it would sound to somebody else. This is not a bad thing if we want to be writers who write not just for ourselves and a few indulgent friends.

When I'm done with proofing the hard copy of the story or chapter or poem, I take a little break. This is one of the pleasures of working at home. I can take these refreshing breathers from the intensity of the writing: go iron a shirt or clean out a drawer or wrap up my sister's birthday present. Not so good as "breathers" for me are activities like answering the phone or making phone calls or engaging with other people in a way that is anything other than brief. Otherwise, I am lured into their lives or into musing on a problem they have presented me with or worrying over some tension between us. And there goes the writing day, down the telephone cable.

Admittedly, this makes it hard to have people around when I'm working, and this is where having a home writing-room is not such a great idea. I finally caved in and bought one of those machines therapists use that makes white noise. (Now there are fancier models that deliver oceans and rainfalls and cocks crowing in the morning.) Even so, I'm acutely sensitive to the presence of guests and family in the house and the writing day is just not the same as when I have the house to myself. If I had to do it over, I would build a writing space apart from my living space. Of course, it would have to be big enough for an ironing board, shopping bags of wrapping supplies, a small stove for cooking, and all the bureaus I would want to organize.

After I've taken a break, I take a deep breath and turn on my computer. What I now do is transcribe all my handwritten revisions on to my computer, before I launch out into the empty space of the next section of the story or essay or the chapter in a novel. This is probably the most intense time of the writing day. I am on my way, and even with the help of the insights from yesterday's run, which I jotted down in my journal, I don't know exactly where it is I am going. But that's why I'm writing, to find out.

ON THE GOOD days, an excitement builds up as I push off into the language, and sentence seems to follow sentence. I catch myself smiling or laughing out loud or sometimes even weeping as I move through a scene or a stanza. "Poetry is a way of thinking with one's feelings," Elizabeth Bishop wrote in a letter to May Swenson, and certainly writing seems to integrate parts of me that are usually at odds. As I write, I feel unaccountably whole; I disappear! That is the irony of this self-absorbed profession: the goal finally is to vanish. "To disappear," the young poet Nicole Cooley says in a poem in the voice of Frida Kahlo, "I paint my portrait again and again."

That is why if there is a sudden interruption—a neighbor appears at the door with a petition he wants me to sign, or the UPS man pulls up and honks his horn—they are met with a baffled, startled look. "What's wrong?" the delivery guy with clipboard wants to know. "Aren't you Julia Alvarez?" Honestly, I could say, no, I'm not. She'll be home after two. Why don't you come back then if you want to talk to *her?*

In fact, my family is now used to this daily disappearance—though not without occasional resentment. Many a time, a call from one of my sisters begins, "It's so hard to get in touch with you, because of course, I can't call before two." I admit that the comment makes me a little defensive. What if I had "a normal job," what if I were a road worker, jackhammering a hole in the earth, or a surgeon doing fine embroidery stitches on someone's heart? I wouldn't be available at all during the workday. What grates, I think, is the idea that I am home and choosing to ignore them. My mother has joked that she better not die before two in the afternoon. I've learned to tease back, "No, Mami, please feel free to die any time you want. But have them notify me after two, if you don't mind."

Okay, okay, if I heard on the message machine that my mother was dying or that my sister was upset about not getting a certain job or that Bill just heard some sad news about the health of a friend of ours, I'd take the call. But the truth is that when I'm having a good writing day, I "disappear" into the writing. I don't come downstairs to listen to my messages. Many times, especially if the noise machine is on, I don't even hear the phone ring.

On bad days, on the other hand, I race downstairs and answer the phone with such a desperate, cheery HELLO! that callers wonder if they've dialed one of those 900 numbers where operators are standing by to render some dubious service. Afterwards, I wander out onto the deck and look longingly south towards the little spire of the Congregational church and wish another life for myself. Maybe I should join some clubs, be a community organizer, have lunch with a friend? I look again and see the peaked roofs of the handsome college on the hill. Maybe I shouldn't have given up tenure? Oh dear, what have I done with my life?

I have chosen it, that's what I've done. So I take a deep breath and go back upstairs and sit myself down and work over the passage that will not come. As Flannery O'Connor attested: "Every morning between 9 and 12, I go to my room and sit before a piece of paper. Many times, I just sit for three hours with no ideas coming to me. But I know one thing: if an idea does come between 9 and 12, I am there ready for it." The amazing thing for me is that years later, reading the story or novel or poem, I can't tell the passages that were easy to write, the ones that came forth like "greased lightning" (James Dickey's phrase), from those other passages that made me want to give up writing and take up another life.

On occasion, when all else fails, I take the rest of the day "off." I finish reading the poet or novelist with whom I began the day, or I complain to my journal, or I look through a picture book of shoes one of my characters might wear. But all the while I am feeling profound self-doubt—as if I were one of those cartoon characters who runs off a cliff, and suddenly looks down only to discover, there's no ground beneath her feet! Those are the days Bill comes home, and I'm at the door saying things like, "I want to go to nursing school, or let's sell everything and move to the D.R., or what would you think if I cut off all my hair or started the first merengue school in Middlebury?"

I'VE ALREADY TAKEN you to what happens at the end of the writing day, a good run that clears the head and heart and resolves some of those glitches that no amount of waiting out in the writing chair will resolve. After the run, the rest of the workday is taken up by what I call the writing biz part of being a writer. What this involves, in large part, is responding to the publicity machine that now seems to be a necessary component of being a published writer. Answering mail, returning phone calls, responding to unsolicited mansucripts from strangers or to galleys from editors who would so appreciate my putting in a good word for this young writer or translation or series. Ironically, all this attention can sometimes amount to distraction that keeps me from doing the work that brought these requests to my door in the first place.

Recently, a writer friend sent me a copy of the infamous, cantankerous postcard that Edmund Wilson used to send out in answer to the many requests that came his way. The heading reads, *Edmund Wilson regrets that it is impossible for him to:* then comes a list of twenty-one things Edmund Wilson will not do, including judging literary contests, giving interviews, autographing books for strangers, supplying photographs of himself, making statements for publicity purposes, and answering questionnaires.

I admit that I don't want to be that inaccessible. All along the way, I found helpers who did read my manuscript, did give me a little of their busy day. These are favors I can never pay back, I can only pass on. And so I do try to answer my own mail and read as many galleys by new writers as I possibly can and return phone calls to those who need advice I might be able to give. But finally, I do think that my primary responsibility is to deliver the goods in book form, not to be the Miss Florence Nightingale of the Literary World.

The part of the writing biz I find the hardest is the traveling. As a writer, you live a solitary, sedentary life—most writers I know are homebodies, maybe even mildly agoraphobic. Suddenly, you are shuttling from city to city, pretending you know where you are. You are not writing, and yet you are talking about writing constantly, so you feel like a dancer tied to a chair while her favorite music is playing. You also get weary, moving from hotel to hotel, even if they are very nice hotels that you should be grateful your publisher put you in because it shows that your publisher values you. Still, you feel cranky when you call down for an ironing board and the hotel is too fancy to have "guest ironing boards," though they do have laundry service. I WANT TO DO MY OWN IRONING! you want to yell at the front-desk people. But you can't do that, because the next morning your picture's going to be in the local paper, and these people are going to post it in the lobby with a sign that says, Don't buy this book, as it was written by an unpleasant woman who has to have an ironing board at eleven o'clock at night. So you let them iron your blouse for seven dollars, or you decide you'll wear your blouse wrinkled, what the hell, no one's looking at your blouse anyway. They want to know what your writing process is. They want to know where you get your ideas. They want to know what you do on a bad writing day besides tear out your hair and iron *all* your blouses.

Even as I complain, I also have to say that there is one wonderful aspect of touring—meeting my readers face to face. Nothing is sweeter than to hear the affirmation of strangers who don't owe you a thing and who have spent good hard cash buying your book. Their comments, smiles, tears, uh-hums as you read, little gifts, love notes are gasoline in the tank, and the memory of them fuels your courage on bad, and on good, writing days.

Back at home, when I'm finally finished with my writing biz or I've put it aside in the growing pile for tomorrow, I head to town to run errands or see a friend or attend a talk at the college. As the fields and farms give way to houses and lawns, I feel as if I'm reentering the world. After having been so intensely a part of a fictional world, I love this daily chance to connect with the small town I live in, to find out how everybody else is doing. Ann at Kinneys wants to know how it's going. Alisa at the College Store fills me in on her dad, the writer. At the post office, the two lovely ladies oblige me by going through their stamp folders to find me a batch of Virgencitas (old Christmas stamps) or butterflies or love swans.

How's it going? everyone asks me, as if they really want to know all about my writing day.

IT IS THE end of the reading. I've said everything I can say about my writing process, and then some, but the audience doesn't want to leave. I remember how it was in childhood when you just wanted to linger at your parents' party; you wept unconsolably when some aunt or nursemaid picked you up and told you to say good night.

It is late: the uncles who are heavy drinkers are getting into their cups; the women are bunching into groups and talking about their lives now that they are sure everyone is fed and happy. There is nothing for you to do at the party, for heaven's sake. You are four years old, five years old. You can't have a martini or dance the tango with a plastic rose in your mouth like your sexy aunt Marisol. But the idea that you are close to the exciting energy of a grown-up party makes you want to fight sleep and stay right there on the couch, eyelids drooping as you keel over, protesting, "I am *not* sleepy!"

The same phenomenon takes place at a reading, I've noticed. A good one, I mean. A not-so-good one, people are excusing themselves long before it's over and from the middle of the long rows, making everyone stand up to let them squeeze by. You can't help but notice when a whole phalanx of the audience stands up. You tell yourself they are going to the bathroom, that's all. But they don't come back. You tell yourself they have kids in day care who have to be picked up—you don't want those kids to grow up needing therapy, now do you? But the glimpse you caught of "them" was of an elderly woman in a pink cardigan, a boy with a Grateful Dead T-shirt, people with disposable time. Oh well, it's probably good for your character to have a bad reading every once in a while. Just as long as it's not the same week as a bad review or news from your dentist that you are going to need that root canal after all.

So it is the end of a good reading, the audience lingers. It's late in Salt Lake City or Portland or Iowa City. Outside the bookstore windows, the sky is dark and star-studded. It's that literary time of day you find in Hemingway's novels and in short stories like "A Clean Well-Lighted Place," when "it was late and everyone had left," and the bookstore people are already mentally pushing the movable bookshelves back in place and trying to remember who is supposed to be on tomorrow night when the next writer on tour rolls into town. Then, that last hand goes up, and someone in the back row wants to know, "So, does writing really matter?"

This once really happened to me on a book tour. I felt as if I'd just gotten hit "upside the head," an expression I like so much because it sounds like the blow was so hard, the preposition got jerked around, too. Does writing matter? I sure hope so, I wanted to say. I've "done" sixteen cities. I've published six books. I've spent most of my thinking life, which is now over thirty years, writing. Does writing really matter? It is the hardest, and the best, question I've been asked anywhere.

Let's take out the *really,* I said. It makes me nervous. I don't *really* know much of anything, which is why I write, to find things out. Does writing matter?

In my darker moods, I want to say, probably not. Has a book ever saved a person's life? Has a novel ever fed the hungry? It is, no doubt, a meaningless human activity to while the time away before our turn comes to join the great blank page. But that is my three-o'clock-in-the-morning insomniac response, which, when I was an adolescent and then in some of my unhappy thirties, I thought was the "right" time of day when "real" answers came to me. I'm older now. I don't expect "real" answers, and the time of day I prefer for figuring out the meaning of the universe is early morning, after a strong cup of that Dominican coffee. Before dinner with a tall glass of cold white wine is also a good time.

It matters, of course, it matters. But it matters in such a small, almost invisible way that it doesn't seem very important. In fact, that's why I trust it, the tiny rearrangements and insights in our hearts that art accomplishes. It's how I, anyhow, learned to see with vision and perplexity and honesty and continue to learn to see. How I keep the windows and doors open instead of shutting myself up inside the things I "believe" and have personally experienced. How I move out beyond the safe, small version of my life to live other lives. "Not only to be one self," the poet Robert Desnos wrote about the power of the imagination, "but to become each one."

And this happens not because I'm a writer or, as some questioners put it, "a creative person." I'll bet that even those who aren't writers, those who are concerned with making some sense of this ongoing journey would admit this: that it's by what people have written and continue to write, our stories and creations, that we understand who we are. In a world without any books, we would not be the same kind of critter. "At the moment we are drawn into language, we are as intensely alive as we can be; we create and are created," N. Scott Momaday, the Native American author, claims in his book *The Man Made of Words*. "That existence in a maze of words is our human condition."

But one of the characters in Robert Hellenga's *The Sixteen Pleasures* argues the opposite, "Books were my life. But what did I ever learn that I didn't already know in my heart." I admit that this also has the ring of truth for me, but the truth is, that I wouldn't have been conscious of this truth unless I had first read it in Hellenga's book. I don't know what I know in my heart unless somebody—myself included—has put it into words. "Art is not the world," Muriel Rukeyser reminds us, "but a knowing of the world. It prepares us."

Prepares us for what? my questioner in the back row wants to know. And again I have to admit that I don't really know what it prepares us for. For our work in the world, I suppose. Prepares us to live our lives more intentionally, ethically, richly. At this point, a whole phalanx of people stands up to go. A hand shoots up. "You mean to say that if Hitler had read Tolstoy he would have been a better person?"

That is a hard one, I admit. Let's say that it would have been worth a try. Let's say that if little Hitler had been caught up in reading Shakespeare or Tolstoy and was moved to the extent that the best books move us, he might not have become who he became. But maybe, Tolstoy or no Tolstoy, Hitler would still have been Hitler. We live, after all, in a flawed world of flawed beings. In fact, some very fine writers who have written some lovely things are not very nice people. I won't mention any names.

But I still insist that while writing or entering into the writing of another, they were better people. If for no other reason than they were not out there, causing trouble. Writing is a form of vision, and I agree with that proverb that says, "Where there is no vision, the people perish." The artist keeps that vision alive, cleared of the muck and refuse and junk and little dishonesties that always collect and begin to cloud our view of the world around us.

Some time ago, I had a wonderful friend, Carole, who had a way of stringing together a bunch of words that made the lights come on in my head. I'd go on and on about some problem, and Carole would toss out one of her gems. "Hey, babe," she'd say, "put your check mark on the side of light." Or, "You've got too big a soul in too small a personality." Or,

"You've got to stop pulling up the little shoots to see if the roots have grown." This last was her take on my habit of second-guessing decisions.

Carole spoke, and suddenly I'd feel a tremendous sense of clarity. I could *see* myself. I could *see* other people. See them "in the light of love," another Carolism. It was as if she had turned the switch yet once more on a three-way light, and the world brightened, ever so slightly, but very definitely.

This is the way in which I feel writing matters. It clarifies and intensifies, it deepens and connects me to others. "We are," as Jim Harrison says in *Legends of the Fall,* "so largely unimaginable to one another." But writing allows us inside those others and knits us together as a human species. And because writing matters in this way to me, it does something else. It challenges me, not just to read and have that private enjoyment of clarity, but to pass it on.

By now a whole phalanx of my audience has fallen asleep on the couches that the bookstore people dragged over from the alcove to give the reading a cozy feel. My questioner in the back of the room has to go home to relieve her baby-sitter. My readers, who for this brief evening have become real people, come forward to have their books signed and offer some new insight or ask a further question. That they care matters. That they are living fuller versions of themselves and of each one because they have read books matters. The world goes from bright to brilliant to luminous, so that for brief seconds, we see clearly everything that matters.

BILL EICHNER

Julia Alvarez left the Dominican Republic for the United States in 1960 at the age of ten. She is the author of six novels, two books of nonfiction, three collections of poetry, and eight books for children and young adults. Her work has garnered wide recognition, including the 2013 National Medal of Arts, a Latina Leader Award in Literature in 2007 from the Congressional Hispanic Caucus Institute, the 2002 Hispanic Heritage Award in Literature, the 2000 Woman of the Year by *Latina* magazine, and inclusion in the New York Public Library's 1996 program "The Hand of the Poet: Original Manuscripts by 100 Masters, from John Donne to Julia Alvarez."

A writer-in-residence at Middlebury College, Alvarez and her husband, Bill Eichner, established Alta Gracia, an organic coffee farm—literacy arts center, in her homeland, the Dominican Republic.

Recommended Reading

IN THE TIME OF THE BUTTERFLIES,
a novel by Julia Alvarez

When the bodies of three beautiful sisters—leading opponents of Gen. Rafael Leonidas Trujillo's dictatorship—are found near their wrecked Jeep at the bottom of a 150-foot cliff on the north coast of the Dominican Republic, the official state newspaper reports their deaths as accidental. In this extraordinary novel, the voices of Las Mariposas (The Butterflies)—Minerva, Patria, María Teresa, and the survivor, Dedé— speak across the decades to tell their own stories, from hair ribbons and secret crushes to gunrunning and prison torture, and to describe the everyday horrors of life under Trujillo's rule. Through the art and magic of Julia Alvarez's imagination, the martyred Butterflies live again in this novel of courage and love and the human cost of political oppression.

"A fascinating and powerful picture of a family and a nation's history." —*The Dallas Morning News*

FINALIST FOR THE NATIONAL BOOK CRITICS CIRCLE AWARD

A NATIONAL ENDOWMENT FOR THE ARTS BIG READ SELECTION

AN ALGONQUIN READERS ROUND TABLE EDITION WITH READING GROUP GUIDE AND OTHER SPECIAL FEATURES · FICTION · ISBN 978-1-56512-976-4 E-BOOK ISBN 978-1-61620-099-2

HOW THE GARCÍA GIRLS LOST THEIR ACCENTS,
a novel by Julia Alvarez

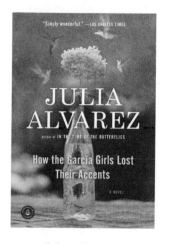

When their father's role in an attempt to overthrow a tyrannical dictator is discovered, the García sisters—Carla, Sandra, Yolanda, and Sofía—and their family must flee their home in the Dominican Republic.

They arrive in New York City in 1960 to a life far removed from their dangerous, if genteel, existence in the Caribbean, where a maid can serve lemonades on a silver tray and an uncle can be disappeared by the dictator's secret police. In the wild and wondrous and not always welcoming U.S.A., their parents try to hold on to their old ways, but the girls try to lose themselves and find new lives: by forgetting their Spanish, by straightening their hair and wearing fringed bell bottoms. For them it is at once liberating and excruciating to be caught between the old world and the new. Acclaimed writer Julia Alvarez's brilliant and buoyant first novel sets the García girls free to tell their most intimate stories about how they came to be at home—and not at home—in America.

"A joy to read."
—*The Cleveland Plain Dealer*

"Subtle . . . Powerful . . . Reveals the intricacies of family, the impact of culture and place, and the profound power of language."
—*The San Diego Tribune*

AN ALGONQUIN READERS ROUND TABLE EDITION WITH READING GROUP GUIDE AND OTHER SPECIAL FEATURES • FICTION • ISBN 978-1-56512-975-7
E-BOOK ISBN 978-1-61620-098-5